"Brandon Smith has written a bold, brilliant, and beautiful theological interpretation of John's Apocalypse. Smith reads with a mixture of attention to the text and the various pressures that the text exerts upon the reader to think of God in triune terms. Smith's reading of the Apocalypse is historically sensitive and theologically attuned to John's story of God Almighty, the Lamb, and the Spirit who speaks to the churches. This book sets a new bar in the theological interpretation of Scripture."

Michael F. Bird, academic dean and lecturer in theology at Ridley College in Melbourne, Australia, and author of *Introducing Paul: The Man, His Mission and His Message*

"An exciting new chapter of the history of biblical exegesis is unfolding in real time. Exegetes like Brandon Smith are leading us, with theological sophistication and evangelical zeal, beyond the tired (not to mention unchurchly) polarities of 'high' vs. 'low' Christology and 'scientific' vs. 'confessional' hermeneutics into a robustly and unapologetically *trinitarian* reading of the Christian Bible. A landmark study."

Wesley Hill, associate professor of New Testament at Western Theological Seminary

"Remarkably, no significant work on the Trinity in the Apocalypse had been written, but Brandon Smith has remedied that deficiency in this astute book. Smith's study represents theological interpretation of Scripture at its best as he investigates the trinitarian contours in the Apocalypse. Still, we don't have an example of an author imposing his construct onto the biblical text; instead, Smith demonstrates persuasively that the Trinity informs and pervades the Apocalypse. Biblical exegesis and theological retrieval in this instance are illuminating dialogical partners, and we can be grateful to Smith both for providing a model for theological and exegetical work and for deepening our understanding of the Apocalypse."

Thomas R. Schreiner, James Buchanan Harrison Professor of New Testament Interpretation at the Southern Baptist Theological Seminary

"Brandon Smith's excellent book takes one of our most mystifying doctrines—the Trinity—and one of our most mystifying early Christian texts—Revelation—and illumines them both through his distillation of research on pro-Nicene theology. In this, he demonstrates how the tools and readings of early Christian authors can help us to approach Scripture better."

Madison N. Pierce, associate professor of New Testament at Western Theological Seminary

"Amid the twenty-first century 'trinitarian retrieval' currently underway, Brandon Smith's book stands out as the kind of project desperately needed—firmly grounded in exegetical rigor, clearly shaped by the narratival structure of the biblical canon, keenly aware of the unique literary features of John's Apocalypse, and uniquely capable of drawing out the theological implications of those textual realities. This is a model for constructive theological reflection on Holy Scripture."

Matthew Emerson, dean of theology, arts, and humanities at Oklahoma Baptist University

"The old insult *obscurum per obscurius* means trying to explain one obscure thing by way of something even more obscure. Surely a study of the Trinity in the book of Revelation runs this risk, we might fear. But instead, Brandon Smith surprises us with clarity and calmness, a firm grasp of the main lines of biblical truth, and a compelling vision of the big picture of Christian doctrine. Highly recommended as an exercise in reading Scripture with classic doctrinal categories for the purpose of knowing God."

Fred Sanders, Torrey Honors College, Biola University

"Brandon Smith's important work furthers the recent movement to reassert the intellectual integrity of viewing the New Testament as foundational to the church's orthodox doctrinal tradition. With sophistication and care, he engages the interplay between the text of Revelation and its early interpreters as an entry into the text's divinely revealed meaning. *Trinity* and *trinitarian*, rather than being conceptual impositions on the text, are convincingly shown to be a dynamic framework for truthfully confessing God's self-offering to the church in his Scriptures. In the process the book of Revelation's historically fraught role in Christian self-understanding is wonderfully focused, enlivened, and empowered. Deploying wide scholarship and lucid writing, Smith provides readers with a rich exegetical and theological feast, on a table set by one of the Bible's most fruitful books."

Ephraim Radner, professor of historical theology at Wycliffe College, University of Toronto

The Trinity in the Book of Revelation

Seeing Father, Son, and Holy Spirit in John's Apocalypse

◆◆◆◆◆◆◆◆◆◆◆◆◆◆◆◆◆◆◆◆◆◆◆◆

Brandon D. Smith

Foreword by Lewis Ayres

An imprint of InterVarsity Press
Downers Grove, Illinois

InterVarsity Press
P.O. Box 1400 | Downers Grove, IL 60515-1426
ivpress.com | email@ivpress.com

©2022 by Brandon Dean Smith

All rights reserved. No part of this book may be reproduced in any form without written permission from InterVarsity Press.

InterVarsity Press® is the publishing division of InterVarsity Christian Fellowship/USA®.
For more information, visit intervarsity.org.

Scripture quotations have been taken from the Christian Standard Bible®, Copyright © 2017 by Holman Bible Publishers. Used by permission. Christian Standard Bible® and CSB® are federally registered trademarks of Holman Bible Publishers.

The publisher cannot verify the accuracy or functionality of website URLs used in this book beyond the date of publication.

Cover design and image composite: Kate Irwin
Interior design: Daniel van Loon

ISBN 978-1-5140-0418-0 (print) | ISBN 978-1-5140-0419-7 (digital)

Printed in the United States of America ∞

Library of Congress Cataloging-in-Publication Data
Names: Smith, Brandon D., author.
Title: The Trinity in the Book of Revelation : seeing Father, Son, and Holy Spirit in John's Apocalypse / Brandon D. Smith ; foreword by Lewis Ayres.
Description: Downers Grove, IL : IVP Academic, [2022] | Includes bibliographical references and index.
Identifiers: LCCN 2022035741 (print) | LCCN 2022035742 (ebook) | ISBN 9781514004180 (priint) | ISBN 9781514004197 (digital)
Subjects: LCSH: Bible. Revelation–Criticism, interpretation, etc. | Trinity–Biblical teaching.
Classification: LCC BS2825.52 .S59 2022 (print) | LCC BS2825.52 (ebook) | DDC 228/.06–dc23/eng/20220906
LC record available at https://lccn.loc.gov/2022035741
LC ebook record available at https://lccn.loc.gov/2022035742

30 29 28 27 26 25 24 23 | 13 12 11 10 9 8 7 6 5 4 3 2

To Christa, Harper, Emma, and Amelia.
May your vision always be fixed on our triune God.

Contents

Foreword by Lewis Ayres	ix
Acknowledgments	xiii
Series Introduction: Studies in Christian Doctrine and Scripture	xv
Abbreviations	xxi
Author's Note on Sources	xxv
Introduction: Doing Theology with the Trinity	1
1. Toward a Trinitarian Reading of Revelation	7
2. Father: The One Seated on the Throne	37
3. Son: The Slain Lamb and Risen King	69
4. Holy Spirit: The Revealer to John and Speaker to the Churches	138
5. A Constructive Account of the Trinity in Revelation	173
Bibliography	195
Name Index	213
Subject Index	216
Scripture Index	218

Foreword

by Lewis Ayres

It is a commonplace that theologians today—especially younger theologians—work in a more ecumenical mode than did previous generations. Theologians who are deeply embedded in their tradition—as Brandon Smith is in his, and I am in mine!—nevertheless find dialogue partners far beyond what might seem their natural community. Those who manage to keep this balance offer great hope for the future. That future is, of course, in God's providential, benevolent, and mysterious hands—not in ours. All that those of us who attempt to argue faithfully can do is to seek to enter the truth more deeply and attempt to share it respectfully and lovingly with others.

Perhaps the most significant feature of this new ecumenical outlook is that, despite our significant and currently unresolvable doctrinal differences, many from widely divergent traditions have come to recognize that the deep Christian tradition offers us the resources needed to think through the mighty theological mysteries that confront and dazzle the student of Christian theology. By "the deep Christian tradition" I mean the history of responses of men and women to God's call over the long centuries since the resurrection and ascension of our Lord, and since the sending of the Spirit at Pentecost. We will necessarily view this tradition from a variety of perspectives and with different understandings of its authority in view. But for many now, it is in turning to that tradition that we best find resources for describing God's action among us and resources for reading the Scriptures. And from this long tradition, it is the early, vibrant centuries of the Christian church that have drawn the attention of perhaps the widest group of theologians.

Further, perhaps nowhere is this new interest more apparent than in work on trinitarian theology and scriptural exegesis. It should surprise no one that Orthodox and Catholic theologians turn to this deep tradition as they seek to articulate classical trinitarian theology, but it is noteworthy that a host of theologians in (for example) the Baptist and Presbyterian traditions have also begun to turn toward early Christian theology as a key resource for explaining and exploring God's revelation to us of the triune life. In some ways this is no new development—there is a number of Baptist church-historians who have made important contributions over the past few decades to our understanding of early Christian theology. What does seem to be new is the rise of a new generation of younger Baptist theologians who wish to use the resources of the early church to present a fully scriptural account of the divine being and economy.

Many of these figures have been caught by the sheer power and beauty of the expositions of Scripture that they have found from this period. Many have come to recognize that older narratives—in which this period sees the overcoming of true Christian faith by "Greek philosophy"—hold little water, and that early Christian theology is *both* deeply exegetical *and* philosophically engaged (rather as is Paul's own engagement with Jewish Scripture!). As we seek to avoid the perennial danger of reinventing the wheel in every generation, it is only right that we turn again to the figures who played such an elemental and foundational part in drawing from Scripture one of its most central themes—the inseparable unity and yet irreducibility of Father, Son, and Spirit.

It is within these contexts that Smith writes. In the first place his theology is deeply informed by attention to the heritage of early Christian thought. In the second place his goal is to read Scripture, in this case the book of Revelation, in aid of a compelling presentation of God's self-revelation. The book unfolds as a dialogue between careful engagement with modern scholarship on Revelation and the manner in which pro-Nicene trinitarian patterns of scriptural reading may lead us to understand the possibilities of this complex and mysterious text more fully. As the book proceeds, Smith draws us deep into the text of Revelation by careful study of key passages. At the end we are left with an important challenge: to read this text anew as an integral part of Scripture's revelation of the simple and undivided life of Father, Son, and Spirit. His work should be welcomed by all interested in the constant renewal of Christian thought.

Acknowledgments

THIS BOOK IS A SOMEWHAT condensed version of my PhD dissertation for Ridley College. That dissertation took three years to write and probably nine years off my life. I imagine I could write an entire book of acknowledgments to all the people who played roles in helping me finish this book, but I can only mention a few here.

First, perhaps the greatest outcome of writing this book was the ways in which the triune God encouraged, challenged, and molded me. I love him and his Word more deeply and experientially after writing this book than I would have otherwise.

Thank you to Christa, my wife and best friend. I promised at the outset of the dissertation phase that I would not have to apologize to you in my acknowledgements because I would not let it affect our family. I am sure apologies are in order nonetheless, because there is no doubt you sacrificed more than anyone as I wrote. You are my hero and more like Christ than anyone I know. I love you.

To my girls, Harper, Emma, and Amelia, your joy, enthusiasm, and simple, unwavering love has humbled and softened me in ways I am not sure I can even comprehend. I am a better man because of you. Just hearing your voices lights up the darkest of days.

Dad, your consistency, resolve, and wisdom inspire me to be a better husband, father, and follower of Jesus. Seeing you confess Christ and be baptized is one of the great joys of my life. Thank you for always telling me I was smarter and more talented than I really am—it helped me persevere in the countless times when I felt like a complete failure and fraud.

Mike Bird, my Doktorvater, mentor, and friend, thank you for modeling how to be a rigorous yet unpretentious scholar. Your supervision of the dissertation was always pointed and direct yet laced with grace and compassion (and, of course, plenty of humor). It has been a privilege to study under your tutelage. Special thanks also to my secondary supervisor, Scott Harrower, for your feedback, resource recommendations, and encouragement. Also, I would have never written my dissertation in the first place without the early encouragement of Alan Thompson.

A special thanks also to Lewis Ayres, who was one of my PhD examiners. You went above and beyond the call of duty by meeting with me, offering additional feedback on this manuscript, and ultimately writing the foreword.

In terms of this project turning from dissertation to academic monograph, I could not be more grateful for Daniel Treier, Kevin Vanhoozer, and David McNutt's enthusiasm for the project and for bringing this book into the wonderful SCDS series.

Finally, the final version of this book would not be possible without the feedback and insights of many people, including Cody Barnhart, John Behr, Glenn Butner, Stephen Carlson, Matt Emerson, J. R. Gilhooly, Wesley Hill, Winston Hottman, Jason Lee, Peter Leithart, Darian Lockett, Billy Marsh, Russell Meek, Madison Pierce, Stephen Presley, Fred Sanders, Patrick Schreiner, Tom Schreiner, David Starling, Ched Spellman, Scott Swain, Brian Tabb, Adonis Vidu, Robyn Whitaker, Shawn Wilhite, Tyler Wittman, and the guy on my Southwest flight from Nashville to Chicago who said Revelation should not be in the canon.

Series Introduction
Studies in Christian Doctrine and Scripture (SCDS)

DANIEL J. TREIER AND KEVIN J. VANHOOZER

THE STUDIES IN CHRISTIAN DOCTRINE and Scripture (SCDS) series attempts to reconcile two disciplines that should never have been divided: the study of Christian Scripture and the study of Christian doctrine. Old walls of disciplinary hostility are beginning to come down, a development that we hope will better serve the church. To that end, books in this series affirm the supreme authority of Scripture, seeking to read it faithfully and creatively as they develop fresh articulations of Christian doctrine. This agenda can be spelled out further in five claims.

1. We aim to publish constructive **contributions to systematic theology** rather than merely descriptive rehearsals of biblical theology, historical retrievals of classic or contemporary theologians, or hermeneutical reflections on theological method—volumes that are plentifully and expertly published elsewhere.

The initial impetus for the SCDS series came from supervising evangelical graduate students and seeking to encourage their pursuit of constructive theological projects shaped by the supremacy of Scripture. Existing publication venues demonstrate how rarely biblical scholars and systematic theologians trespass into each other's fields. Synthetic treatments of biblical theology garner publication in monograph series for biblical studies or evangelical biblical theology. A notable example is a companion series from IVP Academic, New Studies in Biblical Theology. Many of its volumes have theological significance, yet most are written by biblical scholars. Meanwhile, historical retrievals of theological figures garner publication in monograph series for historical and systematic theology. For instance, there have been entire series devoted to figures such as Karl Barth or the patristic era, and even series named for systematic theology tend to contain figure-oriented monographs.

The reason for providing an alternative publication venue is not to denigrate these valuable enterprises. Instead, the rationale for encouraging constructively evangelical projects is twofold and practical: the church needs such projects, and they form the theologians undertaking them. The church needs such projects, both addressing new challenges for her life in the world (such as contemporary political theology) and retrieving neglected concepts (such as the classic doctrine of God) in fresh ways. The church also needs her theologians not merely to develop detailed intellectual skills but also ultimately to wrestle with the whole counsel of God in the Scriptures.

2. We aim to promote **evangelical** contributions, neither retreating from broader dialogue into a narrow version of this identity on the one hand, nor running away from the biblical preoccupation of our heritage on the other hand.

In our initial volume, *Theology and the Mirror of Scripture*, we articulate this pursuit of evangelical renewal. We take up the well-known metaphor of mere Christianity as a hallway, with particular church traditions as the rooms in a house. Many people believe that the evangelical hallway is crumbling, an impression that current events only exacerbate. Our inspection highlights a few fragmenting factors such as more robust academic engagement, increased awareness of the Great Christian Tradition and the variety of evangelical subtraditions, interest in global Christianity, and interfaces with emergent Christianity and culture. Looking more deeply, we find historical-theological debates about the very definition of *evangelical* and whether it reflects—still, or ever—a shared gospel, a shared doctrine of God, and a theological method that can operationalize our shared commitment to Scripture's authority.

In response, prompted by James 1:22-25, our proposal develops the metaphor of a mirror for clarifying evangelical theology's relation to Scripture.

The reality behind the mirror is the gospel of God and the God of the gospel: what is revealed in Christ. In disputes about whether to focus on a center or boundaries, it may seem as if evangelicalism has no doctrinal core. But we propose treating what is revealed in Christ—the triune God and the cross of Christ, viewed in the mirror of Scripture—as an evangelical anchor, a center with a certain range of motion. Still, it may seem as if evangelicalism has no hermeneutical coherence, as if interpretive anarchy nullifies biblical authority. But we propose treating Scripture as *canonical testimony*, a God-given mirror of truth that enables the church to reflect the wisdom that is in Christ. The holistic and contextual character of such wisdom gives theology a dialogic character, which requires an evangelical account of the church's catholicity. We need the wisdom to know the difference between church-destroying heresy, church-dividing disagreements that still permit evangelical fellowship, and intrachurch differences that require mutual admonition as well as forbearance.

Volumes in the SCDS series will not necessarily reflect the views of any particular editor, advisory board member, or the publisher—not even concerning "evangelical" boundaries. Volumes may approach perceived boundaries if their excellent engagement with Scripture deserves a hearing. But we are not seeking reform for reform's sake; we are more likely to publish volumes containing new explorations or presentations of traditional positions than radically revisionist proposals. Valuing the historic evangelical commitment to a deeply scriptural theology, we often find that perceived boundaries are appropriate—reflecting positions' biblical plausibility or lack thereof.

3. We seek fresh understanding of Christian doctrine **through creatively faithful engagement with Scripture.** To some fellow evangelicals and interested others today, we commend the classic evangelical commitment of *engaging Scripture*. To other fellow evangelicals today, we commend a contemporary aim to engage Scripture with *creative fidelity*. The church is to be always reforming—but always reforming according to the Word of God.

It is possible to acknowledge *sola Scriptura* in principle—Scripture as the final authority, the norming norm—without treating Scripture as theology's primary source. It is also possible to approach Scripture as theology's primary source in practice without doing that well.

The classic evangelical aspiration has been to mirror the form, not just the content, of Scripture as closely as possible in our theology. That aspiration has potential drawbacks: it can foster naive prooftexting, flatten biblical diversity, and stifle creative cultural engagement with a biblicist idiom. But we should not overreact to these drawbacks, falling prey to the temptation of paying mere lip service to *sola Scriptura* and replacing the Bible's primacy with the secondary idiom of the theologians' guild.

Thus in *Theology and the Mirror of Scripture* we propose a rubric for applying biblical theology to doctrinal judgments in a way that preserves evangelical freedom yet promotes the primacy of Scripture. At the ends of the spectrum, biblical theology can (1) rule out theological proposals that contradict scriptural judgments or cohere poorly with other concepts, and it can (5) require proposals that appeal to what is clear and central in Scripture. In between, it can (2) permit proposals that do not contradict Scripture, (3) support proposals that appeal creatively although indirectly or implicitly to Scripture, and (4) relate theological teaching to church life by using familiar scriptural language as much as possible. This spectrum offers considerable freedom for evangelical theology to mirror the biblical wisdom found in Christ with contextual creativity. Yet it simultaneously encourages evangelical theologians to reflect biblical wisdom not just in their judgments but also in the very idioms of their teaching.

4. We seek **fresh understanding of Christian doctrine**. We do not promote a singular method; we welcome proposals appealing to biblical theology, the history of interpretation, theological interpretation of Scripture, or still other approaches. We welcome projects that engage in detailed exegesis as well as those that appropriate broader biblical themes and patterns. Ultimately, we hope to promote relating Scripture to doctrinal understanding in material, not just formal, ways.

As noted above, the fresh understanding we seek may not involve altogether novel claims—which might well land in heresy! Again, in *Theology and the Mirror of Scripture* we offer an illustrative, nonexhaustive rubric for encouraging various forms of evangelical theological scholarship: projects shaped primarily by (1) hermeneutics, (2) integrative biblical theology, (3) stewardship of the Great Tradition, (4) church dogmatics, (5) intellectual history, (6) analytic theism, (7) living witness, and (8) healing resistance. While some of these scholarly shapes probably fit the present series better than others, all of them reflect practices that can help evangelical theologians to make more faithfully biblical judgments and to generate more creatively constructive scholarship.

The volumes in the SCDS series will therefore reflect quite varied approaches. They will be similar in engaging one or more biblical texts as a key aspect of their contributions while going beyond exegetical recital or descriptive biblical theology, yet those biblical contributions themselves will be manifold.

5. We promote scriptural engagement in **dialogue with catholic tradition(s)**. A periodic evangelical weakness is relative lack of interest in the church's shared creedal heritage, in the churches' particular confessions, and more generally in the history of dogmatic reflection. Beyond existing efforts to enhance understanding of themes and corpora in biblical theology, then, we hope to foster engagement with Scripture that bears on and learns from loci, themes, or crucial questions in classic dogmatics and contemporary systematic theology.

Series authors and editors will reflect several church affiliations and doctrinal backgrounds. Our goal is that such commitments would play a productive but not decisive hermeneutical role. Series volumes may focus on more generically evangelical approaches, or they may operate from within a particular tradition while engaging internal challenges or external objections.

We hope that both the diversity of our contributor list and the catholic engagement of our projects will continually expand. As important as those contextual factors are, though, these are most fundamentally studies in Christian *doctrine* and *Scripture*. Our goal is to promote and to publish constructive evangelical projects that study Scripture with creative fidelity and thereby offer fresh understanding of Christian doctrine. Various contexts and perspectives can help us to study Scripture in that lively way, but they must remain secondary to theology's primary source and soul.

We do not study the mirror of Scripture for its own sake. Finding all the treasures of wisdom in Christ to be reflected there with the help of Christian doctrine, we come to know God and ourselves more truly. Thus encountering God's perfect instruction, we find the true freedom that is ours in the gospel, and we joyfully commend it to others through our own ministry of Scripture's teaching.

Abbreviations

1 Apol.	Justin, *Apologia i*
1-2 Clem	1-2 Clement
1-3 En.	1-3 Enoch
1QM	War Scroll
1QS	Community Rule Scrolls
2 Apol.	Justin, *Apologia ii*
2 Bar.	2 Baruch
AB	Anchor Bible
A.J.	Josephus, *Antiquitates judaicae*
Antichr.	Hippolytus, *De antichristo*
AugStud	*Augustinian Studies*
AUSS	*Andrews University Seminary Studies*
Barn.	Barnabas
BBR	*Bulletin for Biblical Research*
BECNT	Baker Exegetical Commentary on the New Testament
BTCB	Brazos Theological Commentary on the Bible
C. Ar.	Athanasius, *Orationes contra Arianos*
CBR	*Currents in Biblical Research*
CIT	Current Issues in Theology
Comm. Jo.	Origen, *Commentarii in evangelium Joannis*
CTR	*Criswell Theological Review*
Decr.	Athanasius, *De decretis*
Det.	Philo, *Quod deterius potiori insidari soleat*
Diogn.	Diognetus

Dion.	Athanasius, *De sententia Dionysii*
D.S.S.	Basil the Great, *De Spiritu Sancto*
Ep. Afr.	Athanasius, *Epistula ad Afros episcopos*
Ep. Serap.	Athanasius, *Epistulae ad Serapionem*
Epid.	Irenaeus, *Epideixis tou apostolikou kērygmatos*
ERT	*Evangelical Review of Theology*
Exp. Ps.	Augustine, *Expositions on the Psalms*
ExAud	*Ex Auditu*
FAT	*Forschungen zum Alten Testament*
GBS	*Gorgias Biblical Studies*
Gig.	Philo, *De gigantibus*
Gos. Phil.	Gospel of Philip
Haer.	Irenaeus, *Against Heresies*
Herm.	Tertullian, *Adversus Hermogenem*
HBT	*Horizons in Biblical Theology*
Her.	Philo, *Quis rerum divinarum heres sit*
Hom. Jer.	Origen, *Homilies on Jeremiah*
Hom. Lev.	Origen, *Homilies on Leviticus*
HTR	*Harvard Theological Review*
Ign. *Eph.*	Ignatius, *To the Ephesians*
Ign. *Magn.*	Ignatius, *To the Magnesians*
Ign. *Pol.*	Ignatius, *To Polycarp*
Ign. *Rom.*	Ignatius, *To the Romans*
Ign. *Smyrn.*	Ignatius, *To the Smyrnaeans*
Ign. *Trall.*	Ignatius, *To the Trallians*
IJST	*International Journal of Systematic Theology*
ITQ	*Irish Theological Quarterly*
JBL	*Journal of Biblical Literature*
JECS	*Journal of Early Christian Studies*
JETS	*Journal of the Evangelical Theological Society*
JTI	*Journal of Theological Interpretation*
JTS	*Journal of Theological Studies*
LNTS	Library of New Testament Studies
Mart. Ascen. Isa.	Martyrdom and Ascension of Isaiah
Metaph.	Aristotle, *Metaphysica*

NIGTC	New International Greek Commentary
NIVAC	NIV Application Commentary
NSD	New Studies in Dogmatics
Odes Sol.	Odes of Solomon
OECS	Oxford Early Christian Studies
OECT	Oxford Early Christian Texts
Or.	Gregory of Nazianzus, *Orationes*
Pel.	Plutarch, *Pelopidas*
Phileb.	Plato, *Philebus*
Prax.	Tertullian, *Against Praxeas*
Princ.	Origen, *De principiis*
ProEccl	*Pro Ecclesia*
Pss. Sol.	Psalms of Solomon
RFP	*Reformed Faith & Practice*
SBJT	*The Southern Baptist Journal of Theology*
SCDS	Studies in Christian Doctrine and Scripture
Schol. Apoc.	Origen, *Scholia in Apocalypsem*
SJT	*Scottish Journal of Theology*
SNTS	Society for New Testament Studies Monograph Series
SP	Sacra Pagina
Spec.	Philo, *De specialibus legibus*
Strom.	Clement of Alexandria, *Stromateis*
Syn.	Athanasius, *De synodis*
Tg. Isa.	Targum Isaiah
Th. Oec.	Maximus the Confessor, *Capita theologica et oeconomica*
THNTC	Two Horizons New Testament Commentary
Theog.	Hesiod, *Theogonia*
ThTo	*Theology Today*
TMSJ	*The Master's Seminary Journal*
TNTC	Tyndale New Testament Commentaries
Tom.	Athanasius, *Tomus ad Antiochenos*
TS	*Theological Studies*
VC	*Vigiliae Christianae*
VCS	Vigiliae Christianae Supplements
Virt.	Philo, *De virtutibus*

WBC	Word Biblical Commentary
Wis	The Wisdom of Solomon or the Book of Wisdom
WTJ	*Westminster Theological Journal*
WUNT	Wissenschaftliche Untersuchungen zum Neuen Testament
ZAC	*Zeitschrift für Antikes Christentum*

Author's Note on Sources

STYLE AND ABBREVIATIONS GENERALLY follow the *SBL Handbook of Style* (2nd ed.), though one should always consult this book's abbreviations page where applicable. English Bible citations generally follow the Christian Standard Bible (CSB), and Old and New Testament references follow their English chapter and verse numbers. The source for translations of non-English and ancient sources are cited in footnotes on the first instance, whether my own translation or drawn from other published or critical editions. The Greek text used for Revelation is drawn from Nestle-Aland (28th ed.).

Introduction
Doing Theology with the Trinity

Doing theology is a holy act that should not be undertaken by the proud or belligerent. Or, as Gregory of Nazianzus warns, theology is "a serious undertaking, not just a subject like any other."[1] When it comes to trinitarian theology in particular, Gilles Emery highlights where our motivations should lie: "Trinitarian theology is an exercise of contemplative wisdom and a work of purification of understanding based upon receiving the revelation of God in faith (it is 'faith seeking understanding')."[2] That is the goal of this study: to contemplate and grow in our understanding of the triune God, whom we worship and stake our lives on.

Maximus the Confessor's opening words in his *Chapters on Theology* reveal much about his theological presuppositions: "God is one, without first principle, incomprehensible, throughout being the total potentiality of being; he excludes absolutely the concept of temporal or qualified existence."[3]

In his introduction, we see Maximus's priority in discussing the foundation for Scripture and theology: the triune God. This God is one, uncreated, eternal, incomprehensible, self-sufficient, and unchanging. If one

---

[1] *Or.* 27.3. Unless otherwise noted, English translations are from St. Gregory of Nazianzus, *On God and Christ: The Five Theological Orations and Two Letters to Cledonius*, trans. Frederick Williams and Lionel Wickham (Crestwood, NY: St Vladimir's Seminary Press, 2002).

[2] Gilles Emery, *The Trinity: An Introduction to Catholic Doctrine on the Triune God*, trans. Matthew Levering (Washington, DC: The Catholic University of America Press, 2011), xiii.

[3] *Th. Oec.* 1.1. English translation from St Maximus the Confessor, *Two Hundred Chapters on Theology*, trans. Luis Joshua Salés (Yonkers, NY: St Vladimir's Seminary Press, 2015).

wants to read Scripture rightly, then, one must recognize and confess that this God who inspired the Scriptures is supreme, authoritative, and perfect. Maximus and his theological forebears, based on their reading of Scripture, affirmed this truth about God and Scripture, and this became their core presupposition any time they engaged with the biblical text.

Indeed, we cannot deny that we all have theological presuppositions that influence how we read the text based on myriad contextual factors. For example, people raised in different socioeconomic environments in different parts of the world in different centuries may emphasize texts differently based on their own lived experiences or based on practical application in evangelistic environments. Denominationally, a Baptist and a Presbyterian will read certain passages about baptism or church polity differently based on their own presuppositions or based on judgments they have made about a network of related passages. Presuppositions are unavoidable, but we should not automatically assume that our presuppositions are *bad*. Instead, we should be aware of our presuppositions and ask if our presuppositions hinder our faithfulness to the text.[4] So, I have come to believe through studying Scripture that confessing God as triune is faithful to the presentation of the text itself; thus, I make no apology that as a Christian, I confess that God is triune and expect him to present himself in Scripture as such. Reading Scripture, then, is a worshipful endeavor. Put succinctly: if our reading of Scripture is explicitly trinitarian as we recognize God's providence and self-revelation, then "the doctrine of God becomes itself an exegetical tool."[5]

For me, then, a trinitarian reading of Revelation is a reciprocal endeavor that comes from a presupposition about who God is, but that presupposition has been influenced and shaped by the text itself. Simply put, one should not promote a trinitarian reading of Revelation unless it is a faithful reading of Revelation in particular and Scripture in general. Hopefully, the following

---

[4]In laying out a vision for a distinctly African hermeneutic, for example, Elizabeth Mburu notes the required balance: "We need an African hermeneutic, one that raises questions that a hermeneutic from a different environment would not" yet "to understand the text, the reader must endeavor to step into the world of the biblical text and allow the text to speak for itself so that no faulty assumptions interfere with the interpretive process"; cf. Elizabeth Mburu, *African Hermeneutics* (Carlisle, UK: Langham, 2019), 6-9.
[5]R. B. Jamieson and Tyler R. Wittman, *Biblical Reasoning: Christological and Trinitarian Rules for Exegesis* (Grand Rapids, MI: Baker Academic, 2022), 64.

chapters will show that a trinitarian reading of Revelation is, indeed, a faithful reading.

Now, we can all admit that reading Revelation is difficult. It seems that every commentary, monograph, article, or sermon on the book of Revelation starts with this same lament. And while interpretations of Revelation vary wildly, this shared sense of confusion and wonder unites all of us who seek to understand it. And then we have decided to add on the doctrine of the Trinity, which hardly anyone would describe as an easy doctrine to grasp. I feel the weight of G. K. Chesterton's famous quip: "Though St. John the Evangelist saw many strange monsters in his vision, he saw no creature so wild as one of his own commentators."[6] When you are done reading this book, you may very well be tempted to say the same of me.

Common interpretations of Revelation—from the pew to the pulpit to the podium—are located somewhere between two poles: Revelation is either a first-century political document or a book of eschatological predictions.[7] But apocalyptic works are much more than political tracts or stories predicting the world's end. Most often, apocalyptic works are written to an audience in times of suffering. The seer pulls back the veil for his audience to show them a glimpse into divine purposes, revealing to them that God has not abandoned and will one day vindicate them.[8] And Revelation, beyond all its interpretive quandaries, is rife with rich language and imagery about the words and deeds of the triune God who is bringing all of history to its culmination. So, while Christians might be tempted to *overlook* the Trinity in Revelation rather than *look for* the Trinity first, we must remember that God most clearly reveals himself in his words and deeds.

John's trinitarian theology can be summed up this way: the Holy Spirit has shown him the purposes of the eternal Father, who has sent his divine

---

[6]G. K. Chesterton, *Orthodoxy* (New York: John Lane, 1909), 29.
[7]I think it contains elements of both an "anti-imperial" political document undercutting first-century Rome *and* a book about the future eschaton.
[8]The definition of "apocalyptic literature" has been a source of debate for years, but the general definition proposed here should be relatively uncontroversial. Frank J. Matera, *New Testament Theology* (Louisville: Westminster John Knox, 2007), 402, argues that Revelation is more than simply an apocalyptic work. It is an apocalypse in that it points to events that will soon take place; a prophecy in that it testifies to the Word of God and Jesus Christ; and a letter in that it addresses seven specific churches. This leads him to define Revelation as "an apocalypse prophecy communicated in the form of a letter, intended to be read aloud in the assemblies of the churches in Asia Minor."

Son—slain as the Lamb and exalted as King—in order to inaugurate and then finally to complete the triune God's plan of making all things new. Thus, any meaningful interpretation of Revelation must be undergirded by and subservient to its portrayal of the Father, Son, and Spirit's identity and activity. So, a trinitarian reading of Revelation brings clarity and coherence to a book full of diverse and disparate language, symbols, and scenes. For John, the Father sits on the throne and in some sense is the source of divine activity, and his purposes are not only concentrated upon but also consummated in Christ.[9] Moreover, John depicts the Holy Spirit as a powerful divine agent with "an intensely personal quality"[10] who drives the book's major points and moments. The Spirit is active in both obvious and surprising ways in John's Apocalypse, elevated above a mere angelic or impersonal agent of God. This stark theocentric character of Revelation simultaneously highlights the identity and mission of Jesus as well as the Spirit within the divine nature and plan.

This book will offer a trinitarian reading of Revelation by rigorous interaction with the text, engagement with modern scholarship, and drawing on the early church's classic trinitarian reading strategies and conceptual categories. Rather than merely adopting the answers to orthodoxy's doctrinal test, we will see that their methods for arriving at such conclusions enhance our theological reading. In short, I will argue that a trinitarian reading of Revelation is not an imposition on the text but rather is drawn from a close reading of the text.

In chapter one, we will discuss the context and methodology for this study. In particular, we will survey various debates related to theological readings of Scripture and the church's classical formulations of trinitarian theology, followed by an approach for a trinitarian reading of Revelation. In chapters two through four, we will apply our approach to select passages in the book of Revelation related to the Father, Son, and Holy Spirit that highlight their

---

[9]Oscar Cullman, *The New Testament: An Introduction for the General Reader*, trans. Dennis Pardee (Philadelphia: Westminster, 1968), 120-21, noted that Revelation's distinctive Christian flavor separates it from other Jewish apocalypses because it sees the future in an already/not yet framework wherein divine history has already culminated in Jesus Christ, with only a few future events left to take place.

[10]Larry W. Hurtado, "Observations on the 'Monotheism' Affirmed in the New Testament," in *The Bible and Early Trinitarian Theology*, ed. Christopher A. Beeley and Mark E. Weedman (Washington, DC: The Catholic University of America Press, 2018), 62.

nature and relationships to one another, noting the ways in which our trinitarian reading brings clarity and coherence to these important passages. Finally, chapter five will address ways this approach contributes to modern conversations on trinitarian theology and exegesis, as well as church life and practice.

We should all be seeking understanding by faith, including when we participate in the task of theology. As John Webster wonderfully said, "Theology is thus most properly an invitation to read and reread Scripture, to hear and be caught up by Scripture's challenge to a repentant, nonmanipulative heeding of God's Word."[11] As someone who has been redeemed and transformed by the triune God, his Scriptures, and the living Christian tradition, I pray that this book will also encourage you to seek his face not only in Revelation but in the entirety of the biblical canon.

---

[11] John Webster, *The Culture of Theology*, ed. Ivor J. Davidson and Alden C. McCray (Grand Rapids, MI: Baker Academic, 2019), 77.

ONE

Toward a Trinitarian Reading of Revelation

REVELATION IS A CONFUSING BOOK. Did I mention that already? For two millennia of Christian biblical interpretation, most people have recognized that one single methodology, approach, or exegetical tool cannot support the weight of this confusion. Indeed, a brief glance at Revelation's history of interpretation shows a range of conclusions regarding genre, narrative, prophecy, and theological themes.[1] Anyone who reads Revelation understands intuitively that it might take a whole range of tools to build a useful framework. Add to this the complexities of the doctrine of the Trinity, and the problems multiply. So, as we move toward a trinitarian reading of Revelation, it will be helpful to survey some of the tools that have been used in both trinitarian theology and biblical interpretation that we might put in our toolbelts as we seek to bring coherence and clarity to Revelation's trinitarian theology.

High/Low Christology and Binitarianism

Much of the mid- to late twentieth-century debates about the Christology of early Christians once centered on the distinction between "high" and "low" Christologies.[2] High Christology indicated that Jesus was in some

---

[1] Timothy Beal, *The Book of Revelation: A Biography* (Princeton, NJ: Princeton University Press, 2018) is a good introduction to the history of interpretation.
[2] Portions of this section are drawn from Brandon D. Smith, "What Christ Does, God Does: Surveying Recent Scholarship on Christological Monotheism," *CBR* 17, no. 2 (2019): 184-208.

sense divine, exalted, and/or worthy of worship alongside Israel's God. Low Christology, on the other hand, indicated that Jesus was a mere man, subordinated agent, and/or a vicegerent of Israel's God. Andrew Chester lays out the various possibilities of how Christology developed among the earliest Christians: (1) it is "utterly alien" to the Jewish context; (2) it gradually developed within Jewish categories; (3) it rapidly developed within the Jewish context and categories, most likely in the pre-Pauline or Pauline traditions; and (4) it was inherent from the beginning and therefore required no development.[3] In the early days of the high/low debate, Martin Hengel asserted that "with regard to the development of *all* the early Church's christology . . . more happened in the first twenty years than in the entire later, centuries-long development of dogma."[4] The discussion around this development has led to ongoing debates regarding Jesus' person and agency, as noted above. We will engage this debate at length in chapter three, but we will survey below a few representative examples with respect to Revelation.

Though the high/low bifurcation has dominated much of the last fifty years of scholarly debate, this distinction is not as common today; instead, modern scholars spend their efforts more directly focusing on Jesus' relationship to intermediary figures, divine identity, the nature of monotheism, and the devotional practices of the early church. These modern discussions can be divided into two major camps with respect to Revelation. On the one hand, scholars such as James McGrath and Adela Yarbro Collins have noticed varying levels of subordination and divine agency in Revelation. For example, when discussing Revelation in particular, McGrath concedes that worship of Christ is a key theme in Revelation, but "were Revelation intended to make a Christological point by applying worship language to Jesus that is normally reserved only for God . . . it misses many opportunities to make this point in a clear and unambiguous manner."[5] For McGrath, Jesus does not share an ontological identity with God but instead "the divine

---

[3]Andrew Chester, "High Christology—Whence, When and Why?" *Early Christianity* 2 (2011): 22-50.
[4]Martin Hengel, *Studies in Early Christology* (New York: T&T Clark, 1995), 383, is quoted here for succinctness, but a similar quote and discussion was introduced in *Son of God: The Origin of Early Christology and the Jewish-Hellenistic Religion* (Philadelphia: Fortress, 1976), 2.
[5]James F. McGrath, *The Only True God: Early Christian Monotheism in Its Jewish Context* (Urbana, IL: University of Illinois Press, 2009), 72.

throne and titles."⁶ In his view, Jesus is an anointed figure in Revelation, but he is clearly subordinate to God. For Collins, John in Revelation "seems to portray the risen Jesus as an angel or at least in angelomorphic terms" rather than the "high" Christology associated with other books of the New Testament.⁷ We must also consider similar arguments from scholars such as Loren Stuckenbruck and Charles Gieschen, who discuss the possibility that early Christians, including John, affirmed some sort of angel Christology or angelomorphic Christology in which Christ was either an angel or at times appeared in the form of an angel.⁸

On the other side, scholars such as Richard Bauckham, Larry Hurtado, and Ian Paul argue for a Christology in Revelation that highlights Jesus' divinity.⁹ For them, John folds Jesus into the identity of YHWH and/or includes him in devotional patterns historically reserved for YHWH.¹⁰ As I mentioned above and will discuss in further detail later, Hengel was a prominent figure in the "early high Christology" conversation for his insistence that Jesus was recognized in divine terms quite early in the Christian movement, greatly influencing Bauckham, Hurtado, and others we will discuss in chapter three. Bauckham, focusing on Jesus' identification with YHWH of the Old Testament (OT), stresses that John has an "extraordinarily high Christology," placing Jesus on the "Creator side" of a sharp Creator-creature divide, leaving no doubt that "what Christ does, God

---

⁶McGrath, *Only True God*, 74. We will interact with his work more later, but McGrath's basic point is that transferring names and titles was common in Jewish agency tradition, wherein a unique person might have the authority to act on God's behalf (e.g., Enoch-Metatron in *3 Enoch*).

⁷Adela Yarbro Collins and John J. Collins, *King and Messiah as Son of God: Divine, Human, and Angelic Messianic Figures in Biblical and Related Literature* (Grand Rapids, MI: Eerdmans, 2008), 189. Yarbro Collins wrote the latter four chapters of the volume.

⁸See, for instance, Loren T. Stuckenbruck, *Angel Veneration and Christology: A Study in Early Judaism and in the Christology of the Apocalypse of John*, WUNT 2, no. 70 (Tübingen: Mohr Siebeck, 1995); and Charles A. Gieschen, *Angelomorphic Christology: Antecedents and Early Evidence*, AGJU 42 (Leiden: Brill), 1998.

⁹As we will see in later chapters, they do not always agree on every detail or nuance but agree generally on the early Christian belief in the identical divinity of the Father and Jesus within the bounds of Jewish monotheism.

¹⁰These authors deal with Revelation in places, as we will see as the book progresses, but also raise important questions and concerns within the broader discussion about the earliest Christology. See, for instance, Richard Bauckham, *Jesus and the God of Israel: God Crucified and Other Studies on the New Testament's Christology of Divine Identity* (Grand Rapids, MI: Eerdmans, 2008); Larry W. Hurtado, *Lord Jesus Christ: Devotion to Jesus in Earliest Christianity* (Grand Rapids, MI: Eerdmans, 2003); and Ian Paul, *Revelation* (Downers Grove, IL: IVP Academic, 2018).

does."[11] Hurtado, for instance, noted that McGrath exaggerates the ongoing development of christological beliefs in the Christian community and in turn misses the radicalness of the New Testament (NT) authors' devotional practices[12] and further argues that Christ is clearly worshiped next to God in Revelation 4–5.[13] Ian Paul is more strident, saying that Revelation is "the most developed *trinitarian* theology of any New Testament book."[14] Though James Dunn raises issues with confessional readings of the text, he nonetheless notes that "unlike the other main writings in the New Testament [Revelation's] affirmation of the deity of Christ is unqualified" and "should not be played down."[15]

However, not everyone agrees with these two camps. For instance, Udo Schnelle detects a blurrier Christology in Revelation: "On the one hand, in Revelation Christ or the Lamb is clearly subordinate to God.... On the other hand, this clear primacy of theology in Revelation has its counterpart in the comprehensive participation of Jesus in the work of God, yielding a Christology with a theocentric profile.... The tension cannot be resolved in one direction or the other."[16]

Schnelle's point signifies the reason why these two camps exist. Indeed, precisely because the presentation of Christ's agency in Revelation can be complicated, we will discuss further details concerning these debates and their relevance for understanding Revelation's Christology in chapter three.

In addition to christological debates, the person and agency of the Holy Spirit adds another wrinkle to this discussion, as many scholars debate over

---

[11]Richard Bauckham, *The Theology of the Book of Revelation* (Cambridge: Cambridge University Press, 1993), 63. Bauckham, *Jesus and the God of Israel*, 58-59, has raised concerns about patristic theology's "divine nature" logic, a logic that I have mentioned above as important to our argument in this book. I will address these concerns briefly in chap. 5.

[12]Larry W. Hurtado, "Early Christian Monotheism," *Expository Times* 122, no. 8 (2011): 383-86. This article is a review of McGrath's *The Only True God*, which is quoted above.

[13]Larry W. Hurtado, "Revelation 4–5 in the Light of Jewish Apocalyptic Analogies," *JSNT* 25 (1985): 105-24.

[14]Paul, *Revelation*, 4; emphasis added.

[15]James D. G. Dunn, *Did the First Christians Worship Jesus?: The New Testament Evidence* (Louisville: Westminster John Knox, 2010), 130-32. Dunn hedges his bets slightly, however, noting the rebuttal that the highly symbolic nature of Revelation might skew whether John still belongs to the "low" Christology club. He asks, "Is the imagery perhaps better described as surreal than as real metaphysics?"

[16]Udo Schnelle, *Theology of the New Testament*, trans. M. Eugene Boring (Grand Rapids, MI: Baker Academic, 2009), 755. I discovered after concluding this chapter that Malcolm B. Yarnell III also employs this quote to make a similar point in *God the Trinity* (Nashville: B&H Academic, 2016), 211.

the Spirit's apparent divinity in Revelation or the assertion that the Spirit (or "spirit") is likely an angel or some other type of divine agent. For some, like Hurtado, the Spirit is portrayed in the biblical text as a divine agent, but ultimately early Christian worship patterns reflected "binitarian exclusivist monotheism, able to accommodate Jesus, but disdainful of any other god or lord as rightful recipient of devotion."[17] As we will see in chapter four, a Father-Son binitarianism that subordinates the Spirit is a debate that continues today.

This brief survey makes clear that the theology, Christology, and pneumatology of Revelation prompts a range of views when attempting to understand how God, Jesus, and the Spirit relate to one another. Yet this debate proceeds from what is largely undebatable: John the seer has a theological commitment, an intense messianic devotion, and a pneumatic experience. Indeed, Revelation prompts the reader to consider the trinitarian dynamics of the book, so that even those above who disagree with a trinitarian reading ultimately feel pressured to respond to the narrative presence of the Father, Son, and Spirit.

In chapters two through four, we will address these concerns and demonstrate the benefits of our trinitarian reading through theological interpretation and patristic retrieval; in chapter five, we will discuss the ongoing benefit and potential shortcomings of these high/low and binitarian conversations. The rest of this present chapter will begin to move in that direction by turning to specific terms, tools, and reading strategies—both ancient and modern—that will help us engage in a trinitarian reading of Revelation.

Theological Interpretation and Biblical Pressures

In recent years, scholars have taken up the task of bridging the gap between canonical interpretation, biblical theology, the history of interpretation, and theological exegesis and/or theological interpretation of Scripture (TIS) vis-à-vis the doctrine of the Trinity.[18] This study will draw on and (hopefully)

---

[17]Larry W. Hurtado, "The Binitarian Shape of Early Christian Worship," in *The Jewish Roots of Christological Monotheism: Papers from the St. Andrews Conference on the Historical Origins of the Worship of Jesus*, ed. Casey C. Newman, James R. Davila, and Gladys S. Lewis (Waco, TX: Baylor University Press, 2017), 212.

[18]Though the definition of TIS is somewhat elusive, I resonate with Daniel Treier and Uche Anizor's self-aware and confessional definition: "The reading of biblical texts that consciously seeks to do justice to their nature as the Word of God, embracing the influence of theology on the interpreter's enquiry, context, and methods, not just results"; cf. Daniel J. Treier and Uche

contribute to this discussion. Though some of the following scholars' presuppositions and conclusions may vary from my own—for instance, this book will contain a more distinctly confessional and patristic or premodern bent than some of their works—many of us who are engaged in the TIS conversation are indebted to them and their paradigms. The following brief overview illustrates a set of recent contributions to this discussion that have influenced this study's methodology and will help clarify some of this book's interpretive assumptions.

David Yeago's "The New Testament and the Nicene Dogma" has been perhaps the most influential single article on this topic.[19] In this article, he lays out a "concept-judgment paradigm," which states that a creedal doctrine can be biblical even if the creeds use different words than the biblical text does. So, one can use a conceptual word like "Trinity" to render the same judgment about God as the biblical text. Highlighting Philippians 2:6-11 as an example, Yeago contends that Paul's description of Jesus as "equal to God" and having a "name above every name" renders the same judgment as creedal language "of one substance." Yeago locates this confession within the ecclesial context of the early church, noting that they must have considered Jesus to be divine: "This remarkable identification reflects the inner logic of the worship of the church in the Spirit. Whether the text from Philippians is an actual fragment of early Christian liturgy, or a free composition of Paul, its background is clearly the liturgical acclamation of Jesus."[20] So, though ὁμοούσιος (*homoousios*) is not technically a biblical word, Athanasius and others used this term to explain what they understood the Bible to be teaching about Jesus' relationship to God. While we must be sensitive to the complexities of patristic interpretation and theologies, Yeago's paradigm helps us see generally that a trinitarian reading is not foreign to the

---

Anizor, "Theological Interpretation of Scripture and Evangelical Systematic Theology: Iron Sharpening Iron?" *SBJT* 14, no. 2 (2010): 4-17; emphasis original. See also Daniel J. Treier, "Biblical Theology and/or Theological Interpretation of Scripture?: Defining the Relationship," *SJT* 61, no. 1 (2008): 16-31. Jeremy M. Kimble and Ched Spellman, *Invitation to Biblical Theology: Exploring the Shape, Storyline, and Themes of Scripture* (Grand Rapids, MI: Kregel Academic, 2020), 15-118, offers a useful introduction to some of these issues. See also, Hank Voss, "From 'Grammatical-historical Exegesis' to 'Theological Exegesis': Five Essential Practices," *ERT* 37, no. 2 (2013): 140-52.

[19] David S. Yeago, "The New Testament and the Nicene Dogma: A Contribution to the Recovery of Theological Exegesis," *ProEccl* 3, no. 2 (1994): 152-64.

[20] Yeago, "New Testament and the Nicene Dogma," 155.

NT, though later writers may use different terminology and make particular hermeneutical or rhetorical moves on their own terms and in the constellation of other biblical passages and imagery.

Brevard Childs lauded Yeago's work, saying:

> The decisive contribution of Yeago lies in correctly insisting that traditional Christian exegesis understood its theological reflection to be responding to the coercion or pressure of the biblical text itself. It was not merely an exercise in seeking self-identity, or in bending an inherited authority to support a sectarian theological agenda. His illustration is fully persuasive that the church's struggle with the testimony to God, found in both Testaments, finally forced a triune formulation of the identity of the one God, even though neither Testament made explicit reference to the Trinity.[21]

Childs used this idea of "the coercion of the biblical text" in numerous works to highlight the way the text "coerces" or "pressures" the reader into a theological reading.[22] He deftly wrote between two worlds, as a critic of historical-critical scholarship from the perspective of a theologian, while also maximizing its best elements from the perspective of a biblical scholar. Moreover, Childs notes that a "reader response" element is inherent to theological reflection; however, he is quick to warn against a subjective reader response that does not attend to the canonical and textual witness of Scripture.[23] I join Childs in his aversion toward a non-textual, reader-response reading, but as I noted above, a close reading of the text highlights the trinitarian dynamic of Revelation in a way that pressures us into considering its theological implications.

Kavin Rowe's discussion on the use of κύριος ("Lord") in the Gospel of Luke also assists our work here. Consciously drawing on Childs's idea of "coercion" with his notion of "biblical pressures"[24]—that biblical writers were "pressured" by Israel's Scriptures into making theological claims about Jesus'

---

[21]Brevard S. Childs, "Toward Recovering Theological Exegesis," *ProEccl* 6, no. 1 (1997): 17.

[22]See, for example, Brevard Childs, *Biblical Theology of the Old and New Testaments: Theological Reflection on the Christian Bible* (Minneapolis: Fortress, 1992), 12, and "Interpreting the Bible Amid Cultural Change," *ThTo* 54 (1997): 203. This study will use "pressure" instead of "coercion" to avoid confusion and potential negative connotations.

[23]Childs, *Biblical Theology of the Old and New Testaments*, 335-36.

[24]C. Kavin Rowe, "Biblical Pressure and Trinitarian Hermeneutics," *ProEccl* 11, no. 3 (2002): 295-312.

oneness with YHWH—he says, "Luke chose a different way to express the identity of Jesus, one much more like Mark and Matthew, but he shares with Paul and John a remarkably similar—if not the same—underlying judgment about the identity of Jesus."[25]

Rowe's argument is that Luke designates Jesus as "Lord" as a way to conceptualize for his readers the identity of Jesus alongside YHWH, who is called "Lord" throughout the OT. Drawing on Childs, Rowe rightly notes that the early church asked the same question we should still be asking: "Who is the God of *the whole Bible*? and How do we read the Bible in light of this God?" given the two-Testament witness of the biblical canon.[26] One can argue from this juncture, then, that patristic interpreters followed the lead of biblical writers like Luke, heeding biblical pressures as they contemplated the roles, relationships, and identities of the respective divine persons. We will see that John's language at times pressures readers to make certain judgments about the nature and relationships between the persons, and these pressures help us rule out certain alternate readings. These pressures help us see along with Rowe that "there is (or can be) a profound continuity, grounded in the subject matter itself, between the biblical text and traditional Christian exegesis and theological formulation."[27] Childs and Rowe, then, remind us that a close reading of the text requires theological reflection. We could expand on this claim slightly, and further assert that rightly *understanding* the theological content as retrospective readers is a type of divine pressure via divine illumination (Lk 24:36-49; Jn 14:26; 1 Cor 2).

Hill, in his discussion on the trinitarianism of Paul, says that the high and low Christology debates threaten to "obscure the way in which, for Paul, the identities of God, Jesus, and the Spirit are constituted by their relations with one another."[28] Rather than placing Jesus and the Spirit at various points on a vertical axis below God, Hill contends that a "reciprocal web of relations" is a better representation of "the patterns of New Testament speech

---

[25]C. Kavin Rowe, *Early Narrative Christology: The Lord in the Gospel of Luke* (Grand Rapids, MI: Baker Academic, 2009), 29.
[26]Rowe, "Biblical Pressure and Trinitarian Hermeneutics," 295; emphasis added. Cf. Childs, *Biblical Theology of the Old and New Testaments*, 376.
[27]Rowe, "Biblical Pressure and Trinitarian Hermeneutics," 308.
[28]Wesley Hill, *Paul and the Trinity: Persons, Relations, and the Pauline Letters* (Grand Rapids, MI: Eerdmans, 2015), 25.

about God, Christ, and the Spirit."[29] Further, Hill does not find fruitful the bifurcation between biblical exegesis and theological constructions; rather, he makes the basic claim, "If trinitarian theology can assist in the task of interpreting Paul," then "interpreting Paul is of benefit to trinitarian theology."[30] We will see in the following chapters how Hill's model serves as a viable and helpful methodological aid. For example, understanding the "web of relations" over and against a type of hierarchical "vertical axis" will help us see that the persons' economic missions presented in Revelation need not indicate a type of subordination, ontological or otherwise.

These hermeneutical aids and reading strategies will serve as methodological guardrails as we engage in a trinitarian reading of Revelation in two ways. First, they function as fruitful tools for mitigating against anachronism because their paradigms in different ways attempt to read the biblical text in light of its own present and native theological dynamic. Though anachronism is a danger, ultimately all historical inquiry requires certain tools and labels if one wants to avoid mere nominalism that is unable to speak generally or holistically. The true judgment regarding anachronism is not whether a tool is alien to the historical situation but rather whether the tool highlights the judgments of the text itself. So theological readings in general and patristic readings in particular focus on the text and thus find their own foundations rooted in trying to understand the text itself through the eyes of the human author and divine providence. They further help us avoid eisegesis because they are attuned to the text itself, paying attention to the biblical author's grammatical choices, use of intertextuality, and theological judgments.

Second, then, they allow us to consider more specifically in each chapter how pro-Nicene tools help elucidate John's native theology with respect to the unity and distinction of our triune God.[31] The pro-Nicenes used tools to aid their understanding of God's nature and activity, and their conceptual tools can in turn enable us to work through some of the interpretive difficulties in Revelation related to God's nature and activity. I will address

---

[29]Wesley Hill, *Paul and the Trinity: Persons, Relations, and the Pauline Letters* (Grand Rapids, MI: Eerdmans), 167.
[30]Hill, *Paul and the Trinity*, 47.
[31]We will further define various words and concepts in later chapters as they are specifically applicable.

these concepts directly in the following chapters through brief historical surveys and throughout our exegesis of passages. For now, we will consider this book's approach in light of these interpretive issues and models.

Toward a Trinitarian Reading of Revelation

In what follows, I will first define the two primary terms used throughout this book—trinitarian reading and close reading. Then, an explanation of some methodological points of emphasis will clarify this study's interdisciplinary approach to theology, exegesis, and history.

1. What is a trinitarian reading? This phrase does not suggest that John used the same terminology as those who affirmed the Councils of Nicaea (AD 325) or Constantinople (AD 381), nor am I saying that we need the creeds in order to see trinitarian theology in Revelation.[32] Rather, a trinitarian reading observes the way in which the Father, Son, and Holy Spirit are of the same divine nature (e.g., a singular will, power, and authority) and yet are also distinct persons in Revelation. So, I will argue in this book that John's understanding of the identities and relationships between the Father, Son, and Spirit is not terminologically identical to the later Christian creeds but is nonetheless *trinitarian* because he makes strong claims for the divine nature of the Son and the Spirit combined with their inseparable activity with the Father. The church fathers and those who formed the orthodox trinitarian creeds sought to be faithful to the biblical text as they articulated their theology, so reading alongside them—as the church has done for most of its history—can prove useful for us as well.

Of course, trinitarian language was articulated differently throughout the later centuries, and this trajectory was by no means linear or tidy;[33]

---

[32]Of course, the word "Trinity" is not used in Revelation nor anywhere else in the Bible, so I acknowledge that using this term is itself technically anachronistic. We could also use the phrase a "triadic reading" with respect to Revelation itself to point out the same dynamics. However, for our purposes, I will note below a level of reciprocity between a trinitarian reading of Revelation and later patristic theology.

[33]Several scholars have rightly noted that it is a mistake to divide up early theological controversies into "trinitarian" or "christological," as though they can be easily excluded from one another or neatly defined; see Lewis Ayres, *Nicaea and Its Legacy: An Approach to Fourth-Century Trinitarian Theology* (Oxford: Oxford University Press, 2004), 3; John Behr, *The Nicene Faith*, part 1 (Crestwood, NY: St Vladimir's Seminary Press, 2004), 33; R. P. C. Hanson, *The Search for the Christian Doctrine of God: The Arian Controversy, 318–381* (Grand Rapids, MI: Baker Academic, 2005), xx. However, I will use the term *trinitarian* as a catchall term, not to downplay the

indeed, from Jesus' resurrection through the patristic era, trinitarian language was certainly not systematized because it was used by different figures in light of various contextual, missional, and cultural concerns and situations, particularly in response to dissident and varying theologies.[34] So, trinitarian language and thought cannot be described in terms of mere development, as though it improved (or devolved) over time. So, instead of a value judgment about which era or particular theologian is "best," it is better to acknowledge certain *trajectories* of thought in the first few centuries of Christian history, as early Christians intentionally built on those who came before them. We will see these trajectories more clearly in subsequent chapters, but a general overview will be helpful at this stage. To start, the trinitarian language for the Father, Son, and Spirit contained in the biblical texts—what we might call *incipient* trinitarianism[35]— contributed to a unified scriptural portrayal of trinitarian theology in distinct ways, based on the book's particular genre, audience, or argumentation. This canonical coherence allowed later theologians to interpret these texts and begin to distill them into well-defined biblical-theological judgments across various scriptural books. For example, the Gospel of Matthew's "I have come" statements; the Gospel of John's "in the beginning," "I and the Father are one," and "I will send a Counselor" statements; and Paul's reworking of the *Shema* in 1 Corinthians 8:6 do not compete with one another, but instead make related judgments about the Son's preexistence, the Spirit's distinct divine prerogatives, and the divine personal relations between them.

---

complexities related to the development of the doctrine and term, but to acknowledge for retrieval purposes the basic trinitarian tenets that were developed or debated, as summarized by Khaled Anatolios, *Retrieving Nicaea: The Development and Meaning of Trinitarian Doctrine* (Grand Rapids, MI: Baker Academic, 2011), 36-38.

[34]I am ultimately unconvinced by John Henry Newman's classic attempt to chart a trajectory of continuity in the early development of doctrine; see John Henry Newman, *An Essay on the Development of Christian Doctrine* (London: Pickering, 1878). On the one hand, the patristic theologians we will note in this book have in common a general attempt to explain the transcendent and heavenly nature of Christ and, at times, the Spirit. On the other hand, any attempt to flatten out the development of doctrine in the patristic period is always found wanting. At best, we are able to note the sometimes similar and other times disparate trajectories and influences from one author or century to the next.

[35]I use "incipient" to simply acknowledge that the biblical canon does not contain a systematic approach to the doctrine of the Trinity, at least not in the modern sense of the term, but nonetheless offers a coherent doctrine of the Trinity.

In the second and third centuries, trinitarian terminology took different forms, sometimes in relation to Jewish or Greek philosophical questions about the divine nature and activity, some of which set a trajectory for later theological controversies around and after the Council of Nicaea.[36] We see this, for instance, in the "*Logos* Christology" and "two hands" theology of Irenaeus regarding the Son and Spirit[37] and in Origen's work on the eternal generation of the Son and its implications for the divine nature and activity.[38] These ideas prefigure fourth-century theology, but there is nonetheless a notable stabilizing of theological definitions and terminology after this period.[39]

In the latter part of the fourth century, pro-Nicene trinitarianism emerged. Lewis Ayres employs the term "pro-Nicene" to describe the "culture" of theologies in the latter fourth century that were "recognized as orthodox by the Council of Constantinople (381) and by subsequent imperial decrees."[40] Though not a neat-and-clean consensus, the term "pro-Nicene" indicates a type of *habitus* among fourth-century theologians in language, logic, and practice that animates historic Christian orthodoxy.[41] As the book unfolds,

---

[36]As Ayres notes: "The fourth-century debates were themselves dependent on modes of arguing philosophically about scriptural texts that Christians had been shaping since the early second century"; Lewis Ayres, "Scripture in Trinitarian Controversies," in *The Oxford Handbook of Early Christian Biblical Interpretation*, ed. Paul M. Blowers and Peter W. Martens (Oxford: Oxford University Press, 2019), 439. As we will see, it is possible that this subversion of Greco-Roman philosophies is already evident in the biblical texts themselves.

[37]See, for instance, *Haer.* 3.16.4 and 4.5.2. John Behr, *The Way to Nicaea* (Crestwood, NY: St Vladimir's Seminary Press, 2001), 126, notes that "Irenaeus clearly anticipates the key point which emerged centuries later in the christological controversies surrounding Chalcedon: the one and same Jesus Christ is what it is to be both God and man." For a fuller treatment, see Eric Osborn, *Irenaeus of Lyons* (Cambridge: Cambridge University Press, 2001). We also see something similar in Tertullian's polemics on the "economy" of God, arguing for distinctions among the Father, Son, and Spirit against modalistic teachings that collapse the persons into one identical person or being; cf. *Prax.* 1.1, 5.

[38]See, for instance, *Princ.* 1.2.1-3.

[39]Again, I do not use the word "stable" as a value judgment; rather, it is an acknowledgement that orthodox trinitarian language did not change as drastically after the pro-Nicene "consensus."

[40]Ayres, *Nicaea and Its Legacy*, 239. The complexities and developments between Nicaea and Constantinople will be addressed in various places in subsequent chapters, but we should note that Constantinople sought to reaffirm and expand on Nicaea, while the burgeoning pro-Nicenes were seeking a consensus against other dissident and varying theologies. For a helpful survey of the "idea of Nicaea" as a polemic in the fifth-century conciliar context, see Mark S. Smith, *The Idea of Nicaea in the Early Church and Councils, AD 431-451*, OECS (Oxford: Oxford University Press, 2018).

[41]Ayres, *Nicaea and Its Legacy*, 236-40, notes that there must be some "flexibility" given to this term because of the nuances among theologians but generally identifies three "central principles" of pro-Nicene theology: "1. a clear version of the person and nature distinction, entailing

we will more directly interact with pro-Nicene theology and some important trajectories that led to it, as they pertain to our present study.

In later chapters, when engaging key patristic theologians, there is no assertion that the historical-cultural situatedness, choice of terminology, or rhetorical style of any individual theologian is monolithic, either with respect to John or each other. Again, the trajectories of trinitarian theology are complex, and theological reflection on scriptural texts did not happen in a vacuum; so, while I will be sensitive to the contextual factors of a theologian's intellectual life and thought, it is beyond the scope of this book to fully engage every historical-cultural nuance. Instead, interaction with these theologians in subsequent chapters will offer avenues of basic theological retrieval—showing that the church's reception of biblical texts, including Revelation, produced trinitarian theological language, logic, and rhetoric that is still beneficial to current issues in theology and exegesis. As Wesley Hill has argued,

> Approaching the task of theological interpretation of the Bible armed with a particular doctrinal framework is not—or should not be—to find oneself shoehorning the Bible into an alien conceptual apparatus but is rather to find oneself searching out (1) how that framework may have arisen from exegesis itself and (2) how it may best be understood as an effort to enable ongoing exegesis in turn.[42]

This reciprocal relationship between theological confession and rigorous exegesis will be practiced throughout this book.

As we work through select passages, I will utilize a "pro-Nicene toolkit"[43] of trinitarian conceptual categories to help build a theological-exegetical scaffolding for the divinity of the persons and their relations, including but

---

the principle that whatever is predicated of the divine nature is predicated of the three persons equally and understood to be one (this distinction may or may not be articulated via a consistent terminology); 2. clear expression that the eternal generation of the Son occurs within the unitary and incomprehensible divine nature; 3. clear expression of the doctrine that the persons work inseparably."

[42]Wesley Hill, "In Defense of 'Doctrinal Exegesis': A Proposal, with Reference to Trinitarian Theology and the Fourth Gospel," *JTI* 14, no. 1 (2020): 22.

[43]I owe this terminology to Fred Sanders in personal correspondence (April 10, 2021). Sanders has drawn out similar types of retrieval categories in many of his works, such as "Chalcedonian categories" for Christology in "Introduction to Christology: Chalcedonian Categories for the Gospel Narrative," in *Jesus in Trinitarian Perspective: An Intermediate Christology*, ed. Fred Sanders and Klaus Issler (Nashville: B&H Academic, 2007), 1-41, and "conciliar Christology" as a

not limited to (1) eternal relations of origin—the "ordered" (taxis; τάξις) relations among the Father, Son, and Holy Spirit in the divine life; and (2) inseparable operations—that the three persons of the Trinity always act with one singular will, power, and authority as the one God. In discussing this unity and distinction between the persons, some scholars have used the term *redoublement*—the patristic idea that we must talk about God "twice over" in biblical texts, noting what the Father, Son, and Spirit have in common (divine nature) and what distinguishes them from one another (processions or missions).[44] For our purposes, then, *redoublement* enables us to speak about the unity and distinction among the persons in John's theology without unnecessarily emphasizing one aspect over another. These types of tools allow for a trinitarian reading that acknowledges (1) there is one divine nature and thus one divine power and will, so the divine persons do not act unilaterally or confusedly; (2) persons act, not natures, so each divine person carries out distinct economic operations or missions in creation and salvation (e.g., the Son becomes incarnate, not the Spirit) as one person subsisting in the singular divine nature, with a distinct mode of operation within the unified, inseparable divine action; and (3) this unity and distinction are not at odds with one another, but are rather a way to speak about the unity of the divine power and will, and then "double back" to talk about their relations and operations or missions as divine persons carrying out divine acts on the basis of the one divine nature. As Adonis Vidu has rightly argued, "The unity and distinction between the persons [are] equally basic," and so we should be careful to uphold both.[45]

"framework" for theological readings in "Biblical Grounding for the Christology of the Councils," *CTR* 13, no. 1 (2015): 93-104.

[44] This term is owed to Ghislain Lafont, *Peut-on Connaître Dieu en Jésus-Christ?* (Paris: Cerf, 1969). See its use also in Gilles Emery, *The Trinity: An Introduction to Catholic Doctrine on the Triune God*, trans. Matthew Levering (Washington, DC: The Catholic University of America Press, 2011), 86-94; and Hill, *Paul and the Trinity*, 99-103. I should note here that I am using the term in a constructive and methodological way as I define it in this paragraph, while acknowledging along with Ayres "that there are in fact many forms of 'redoublement' to be found in the Trinitarian tradition"; cf. Lewis Ayres, *Augustine and the Trinity* (Cambridge: Cambridge University Press, 2010), 260.

[45] Adonis Vidu, *The Same God Who Works All Things: Inseparable Operations in Trinitarian Theology* (Grand Rapids, MI: Eerdmans, 2021), xv-xvi. In relation to *redoublement*, Vidu helpfully draws on Aquinas's idea of "equiprimordialism" (that two things exist together as equally fundamental): "the nature of God and his tripersonality . . . are, in fact, one and the same thing, in reality, though regarded from different perspectives, respectively substantial and relational" (147).

Moreover, along with the pro-Nicenes, we must be precise and careful when discussing who God is ontologically in his divine nature (θεολογία; theology) and how he has revealed himself in creation, redemption, and so on (οἰκονομία; economy).[46] When we affirm that the Father, Son, and Spirit are of the same divine nature or substance and act inseparably as distinct persons, we should avoid two issues: (1) a division in the singular divine will such that we claim three divine "centers of consciousness" working together as a coordinated "team"; or (2) a collapsing of the distinction of the persons such that we become functional modalists claiming the three persons are just "modes" or "masks" of the same singular divine person.[47] The doctrine of the Trinity is not built on a mere confusing mathematical equation—e.g., 1+1+1=3—but rather on a biblical idiom that speaks of the oneness and threeness of the triune God, taking into account the richness and depth of the one God's self-revelation as Father, Son, and Holy Spirit. Where one is tempted to highlight unity to the point of modalism, Scripture highlights the distinction of persons; where one is tempted to separate the persons into a tritheistic model, Scripture equally highlights their irreducible unity.

Now, if the triune God who has providentially inspired Revelation and the rest of Scripture seeks to reveal himself—and it seems clear that he has—then we should expect to pick up on these trinitarian dynamics when we read and interpret the text. As we will see, a pro-Nicene impulse will allow us to talk about each divine person as truly and fully God with the same singular divine nature and its entailments, showing that there is no need to assume an ontological subordination with respect to Jesus or the Spirit simply because there are ordered processions or missions, as we will see in

---

[46]I use "theology" and "economy" here because it is the more classical distinction—most notably introduced to Christian theology by Origen of Alexandria and picked up by the Cappadocians and others—but I recognize that the usage is less common today. So, when referring to the divine nature of the divine persons, I will primarily use the language of "ontology" or "ontological" rather than "theology" since "theology" can have broader and more general definitions that might confuse the reader in subsequent discussions. A similarly worded but clear version of this appears in Origen, *Hom. Jer.* 18.6.3, in which he speaks about the distinction between God "in relation to himself" (καθ' ἑαυτόν) and "his plan" (οἰκονομία).

[47]This is precisely why "mode of operation" is specifically used above in relation to the personal distinctions of divine persons. The persons are not modes of one person, but rather three distinct persons subsisting in and as the one divine nature and acting within the one divine will.

some of our interlocuters' arguments in subsequent chapters.[48] These categories are, then, not merely doctrinal formulation, nor am I concerned with recovering pro-Nicene categories because it is fashionably retro; rather, they serve as helpful guides to understand God's revelation of himself, which is our ultimate aim as readers of Scripture. Though this pro-Nicene toolkit is heuristic in a sense, nonetheless I see a substantial agreement between Revelation's trinitarian dynamic and pro-Nicene trinitarianism.

2. What is "a close reading of the text"? This phrase suggests paying attention to textual clues—grammatical and narrative choices—native to John's writing that illuminate his theological commitments.[49] Moreover, John uses native language and concepts familiar to his audience—particularly the christological interpretation of the OT, patterns of devotion, and religious experience—to describe the apparent distinction of persons within the nature and identity of Israel's one God. As Ian Paul observes:

> The task of describing the trinitarian dynamic in the book of Revelation is fascinating for two main reasons. First, there is an extraordinary diversity of terms, actions, and ideas deployed in relation to the understanding of God (the Father), Jesus, and the Spirit and their inter-relationship, far in excess of any other text of comparable length in the rest of the New Testament, and there is some real diversity and discontinuity with and between these ideas. Secondly, the complexity and internal self-references within the book create a sophisticated intratextual web which needs careful exploration if we are to discern the theological picture that the text is painting.[50]

---

[48] In other words, *redoublement* provides a healthy reciprocity between the unity and distinction and/or between ontology and economy. It also mitigates against the concern Chris Tilling has rightly shown: oftentimes scholars assert the unity of the divine nature or identity by virtue of the persons' divine actions or "roles," but then at other times inconsistently talk about or emphasize the strict distinction between nature and action; Chris Tilling, *Paul's Divine Christology* (Grand Rapids, MI: Eerdmans, 2015), 35-62. Andrew Ter Ern Loke, *The Origin of Divine Christology* (Cambridge: Cambridge University Press, 2017), 82-83, reflects on Tilling's concern and offers other helpful ways to determine valid and invalid ways of discussing the relationship between ontology and action.

[49] This phrase is at risk of overuse in academia, but it nonetheless highlights the posture of the interpreter. It is not a given that one insists upon reading with the flow of the biblical text. We might think here of phrasing by John Webster, *Holy Scripture: A Dogmatic Sketch*, CIT (Cambridge: Cambridge University Press, 2003), 129: "The concepts and language of Christian dogmatics 'follow through' the act of reading Scripture; they are the transposition into reflective terms what is learned from *attentive reading*" (emphasis mine).

[50] Ian Paul, "The Trinitarian Dynamic in the Book of Revelation," in *Trinity Without Hierarchy: Reclaiming Nicene Orthodoxy in Evangelical Theology*, ed. Michael F. Bird and Scott Harrower (Grand Rapids, MI: Kregel Academic, 2019), 86.

Simply put, if one investigates the roles and descriptions of the Christ or the Lamb and the Spirit in Revelation, a trinitarian dynamic is clear and thus must be engaged. The aids and reading strategies below will assist our trinitarian reading, not by helping us impose trinitarianism onto the text, but rather enabling a close reading of the text by alleviating many of the theological-exegetical difficulties that we will encounter. Ultimately, then, these aids help us read Revelation better.

It is also important to note that a close reading of Revelation does not entail a historical-critical or stunted historical-grammatical approach that finds the sole meaning of the text within a modernistic notion of the *sensus literalis*—the literal sense—which seeks to psychoanalyze the human author by recreating his mindset through observing literary clues and historical context.[51] This approach breaks away from much of the Christian tradition's general (but certainly not monolithic) understanding of the literal sense: the historical and literary context of Scripture as the grounding for the spiritual or theological sense(s).[52] A modern response to this posture is *sensus plenior*—an attempt to recover a concern for the "fuller sense" or deeper theological meaning that the divine author intended through canonical reflection and the Spirit's illumination.[53] While these categories can

---

[51] Historical-critical and historical-grammatical approaches are not synonymous. Generally speaking, historical-critical approaches view Scripture as "any other book," whereas proponents of historical-grammatical approaches tend to view Scripture as an authoritative text. However, both approaches are similar in their emphasis on the historical and literary environment of each individual author and their audience. An important essay at the genesis of this discussion is Benjamin Jowett, "On the Interpretation of Scripture," *Essays and Reviews*, 7th ed. (London: Longman, Green, Longman, and Roberts, 1861), 330-443. Jowett argues here that Scripture has a single meaning, which rests in the mind of the human author and his immediate audience. This edition of *Essays and Reviews*, a collection of essays from a handful of English churchmen, was explicitly written to challenge "traditional" theological views—in this case the theological or spiritual sense of Scripture's meaning.

[52] For a discussion of the issues, see Brevard Childs, "The 'Sensus Literalis' of Scripture: An Ancient and Modern Problem," in *Beiträge zur Alttestamentlichen Theologie: Festschrift für Walter Zimmerli*, ed. Herbert Donner (Göttingen: Vandenhoeck and Ruprecht, 1977), 80-94. Also see William M. Marsh, *Martin Luther on Reading the Bible as Christian Scripture: The Messiah in Luther's Biblical Hermeneutic and Theology* (Eugene, OR: Pickwick, 2017) for a survey of Luther's view on the literal sense and, by extension, ways some reformers retrieved patristic exegesis.

[53] Don C. Collett, *Figural Reading and the Old Testament: Theology and Practice* (Grand Rapids, MI: Baker Academic, 2020), especially 41-57 and 139-45. Collett makes the compelling case that this divide is a modernistic construction based on an overwrought concern about authorial intent. I am not arguing that "authorial intent" is necessarily problematic—I will refer to John's intent extensively in this book—but we should take care to explain what we mean by "authorial intent," how many "authors" there are, the distinction between and unity of God and the biblical authors, and so forth.

be useful in certain contexts, we are ultimately not required to choose between the literal and fuller sense, or to spend our time trying to separate the intentions of two authors—one human, the other divine. Instead, we can acknowledge that the meaning of the text is wrapped up in the inseparable relationship between the human author and the Holy Spirit who providentially inspired him. For millennia, Christians have viewed the meaning of the text as rooted in God's self-revelation in history, recorded by human authors according to his providence and inspiration (Ex 7:14; Jer 1:5, 30:2; 2 Tim 3:16-17; 2 Pet 1:21, 3:15-16; Rev 1:11).[54] This underlying assumption requires an attentiveness to the nature of Scripture as divine revelation, as well as a concern for "the way the words go"[55] in the various genres, themes, intertextual connections, and other textual features that make up the biblical witness.[56]

This does not mean, then, that we shun all facets of historical inquiry when it comes to exegesis; however, we cannot visit John on Patmos and ask him questions about his thought process in writing Revelation—we can only read and seek to interpret the witness he has left us. So, we must acknowledge that we cannot and need not read John's mind in order to understand all of his intentions and presuppositions, so the historical-grammatical method only gets us so far; that said, the historical-grammatical method's emphasis on textual and historical prudence can help us probe Revelation's text in order to ascertain judgments about his theology. For example, John clearly constructs Revelation as a combination of apocalypse and epistle, with a prologue and epilogue (Rev 1:4-6; 22:21), and his method for applying concepts and allusions varies but is not haphazard.[57] As Ched Spellman

---

[54] As Stephen E. Fowl, *Theological Interpretation of Scripture* (Eugene, OR: Cascade, 2009), ix, notes, the recent explosion in scholarly work on TIS reflects something Christians have been doing "from the very beginning."

[55] This phrase is drawn from Aquinas's "*salva circumstantia litterae*" in, for example, *De Potentia Dei* 4.1c. and used effectively in modern works such as Kevin J. Vanhoozer, *The Drama of Doctrine: A Canonical Linguistic Approach to Christian Doctrine* (Louisville, KY: Westminster John Knox Press, 2005), 167.

[56] For a seminal essay on premodern exegesis and the "senses" in contrast with modern critical scholarship, see David C. Steinmetz, "The Superiority of Pre-Critical Exegesis," *ThTo* 37, no. 1 (1980): 27-38. Steinmetz rightly contends that though the premodern treatment of the senses of Scripture had its defects, modern critical scholarship does not always adequately grapple with the nature of the text, namely its divine inspiration and canonical unity.

[57] So I disagree with R. H. Charles's assertion that the Apocalypse's author was "unintelligent" and "ignorant"; see R. H. Charles, *A Critical and Exegetical Commentary on the Revelation of St. John*,

reminds us, "The overall framework of the book of Revelation contains textual clues that help guide readers in their understanding of its literary meaning, its theological message, and its expectations for those reading this 'book.'"[58] These textual clues are crucial and are situated under the providence of God's revelation and ordering of Scripture as a unified canon.

A close reading of Revelation thus prompts the reader to consider the trinitarian dynamics of the book, not as a subjective reader response where anything goes, but as a response to the theological pressures arising from the text. We will see that God's address through the text of Revelation places pressure on its audience to wrestle with certain theological issues (e.g., Jesus' and Spirit's nature and activity), which has yielded a variety of responses in Christian theological reflection. Ultimately, John's discourse about God is complex and contested, and yet one of its historical effects was to contribute to the trinitarian arguments of later theologians. The questions now before us are: how did Revelation contribute, and is it appropriate to retrieve their formulations if one is concerned with making sense of the contextual and phenomenal features of John's Apocalypse? With respect to these features, this book endeavors to demonstrate that (1) John's grammatical and narratival choices highlight the nature and agency of God (the Father), Christ, and Holy Spirit; and (2) the hermeneutical tools described in the following section and pro-Nicene tools and trajectories covered in subsequent chapters have the capacity, when applied to the book of Revelation, to help frame and develop trinitarian doctrine.

It is worth noting that many scholars today tend to see any type of theological or confessional reading as anachronistic or eisegetical. Indeed, it is a veritable nonstarter in certain pockets of scholarship to propose that a trinitarian reading could be a "close reading of the text" in the first place.

---

vol. 1 (Edinburgh: T&T Clark, 1920), xxii. I also disagree with Rudolf Bultmann, *Theology of the New Testament*, trans. Kendrick Grobel (Waco, TX: Baylor University Press, 2007), 175, who says that John "does not reflect about the past which in Christ has been brought to its end and out of which believers have been transplanted into a new beginning. Hence the present is understood in a way not basically different from the understanding of it in the Jewish apocalypses: namely as a time of temporariness, of waiting. The clear symptom of this understanding is the fact that *pistis* is essentially conceived as 'endurance,' as in Judaism."

[58] Ched Spellman, *Toward a Canon-Conscious Reading of the Bible: Exploring the History and Hermeneutics of the Canon* (Sheffield, UK: Sheffield Phoenix Press, 2014), 207. Spellman further asserts that John writes in this way "to exhort [his readers] to become certain types of readers."

As Ulrich Mauser wrote: "The historically trained New Testament scholar will today proceed with the task of interpretation without wasting a minute on the suspicion that the trinitarian confessions of later centuries might be rooted in the New Testament itself, and that the trinitarian creeds might continue to function as valuable hermeneutical signposts for modern understanding."[59]

It is impossible to answer every critic or charge of bad hermeneutics, but it is nonetheless important to heed this warning. I will conclude this chapter, then, with an explanation of an approach to interpretation that takes the Bible seriously on its own terms and in light of the Christian tradition, with the aim of showing that a trinitarian reading is, indeed, drawn from a close reading of the text.

A Theological-Canonical Approach

Kevin Vanhoozer rightly said that "God must not be an 'afterthought' in biblical interpretation . . . instead, God is prior to both the community and the biblical texts themselves."[60] In light of this truth, this study will employ what I (uncreatively) call a *theological-canonical* approach to interpretation.[61]

---

[59] Ulrich Mauser, "One God and Trinitarian Language in the Letters of Paul," *HBT* 20, no. 2 (1998): 100. Adela Yarbro Collins, "The Use of Scripture in the Book of Revelation," in *New Perspectives on the Book of Revelation*, ed. Adela Yarbro Collins (Bristol, CT: Peeters, 2017), 32, has warned similarly: theological readings have "distracted an interpreter from paying attention to the features in the text that do not fit that model."

[60] Kevin J. Vanhoozer, "Introduction: What Is Theological Interpretation of the Bible?," in *Dictionary for Theological Interpretation of the Bible*, ed. Kevin J. Vanhoozer (Grand Rapids, MI: Baker Academic, 2005), 22.

[61] Aside from those cited above, recent works that have shaped my thinking on this topic include: Matthew W. Bates, *The Birth of the Trinity: Jesus, God, and Spirit in the New Testament and Early Christian Interpretations of the Old Testament* (Oxford: Oxford University Press, 2015); Matthew Y. Emerson, *Christ and the New Creation: A Canonical Approach to the Theology of the New Testament* (Eugene, OR: Wipf & Stock, 2013); Mark S. Gignilliat, *Reading Scripture Canonically* (Grand Rapids, MI: Baker Academic, 2019); Matthew Levering, *Participatory Biblical Exegesis: A Theology of Biblical Interpretation* (Notre Dame, IN: University of Notre Dame Press, 2008); Madison N. Pierce, *Divine Discourse in the Epistle to the Hebrews: The Recontextualization of Spoken Quotations of Scripture*, SNTS 178 (Cambridge: Cambridge University Press, 2020); Darrin Sarisky, *Reading the Bible Theologically*, CIT (Cambridge: Cambridge University Press, 2019); Ephraim Radner, *Time and the Word: Figural Reading of the Christian Scriptures* (Grand Rapids, MI: Eerdmans, 2016); Spellman, *Toward a Canon-Conscious Reading of the Bible*; Scott R. Swain, *Trinity, Reading, and Revelation: A Theological Introduction to the Bible and Its Interpretation* (London: T&T Clark, 2011) and *The Trinity and the Bible: On Theological Interpretation* (Bellingham, WA: Lexham, 2021); Daniel J. Treier, *Introducing Theological Interpretation of Scripture: Recovering a Christian Practice* (Grand Rapids, MI: Baker Academic, 2008); Vanhoozer, *Drama of Doctrine*; Francis

This approach will be applied in the exegetical sections in the following chapters and offers some guardrails to show that a trinitarian reading of Revelation is drawn from a close reading of the text.

Theological. The Bible is a *theological* book in the plainest sense—it is a *logos* (word) about *theos* (God). Rhyne Putman is right, however, in warning us that theology is "categorically different" from any other "-ology," such as biology.[62] The Bible is a collection of books written by human authors under the inspiration of the Holy Spirit as a testimony to God's self-revelation in history, so its content is therefore determined by and rooted in God himself. Indeed, since its primary subject matter is God, we cannot read Scripture apart from taking theology into account. So while historical-grammatical tools help us understand some of the issues "behind" the text, they are just that: tools. Therefore, my method is aided by historical-grammatical tools, but not completely bound by them. As mentioned above, to insist solely on the modernistic version of *sensus literalis* can at times flatten out the biblical text's rich canonical depth, minimize the truth of divine inspiration, and treat Scripture as an historical document to be described rather than a divine book through which we encounter the triune God. This divine inspiration and spotlighting of the triune God's words and deeds pressures us to make sense of his portrayal. And as we also saw above, a theological reading of Scripture built on trinitarian foundations was essential to premodern exegesis—and rightly so. We cannot read Revelation rightly without a *theological* approach.

Canonical. The Bible is a two-Testament book, which means that we cannot isolate Revelation as a mere historical piece of data, or even as an isolated book among other biblical friends and/or rivals. This is not to deny Revelation's distinct contribution to the canon—I will emphasize this point in the final chapter—but we must also recognize that it is one piece of a larger canon of sixty-six books that is partially, if not primarily, understood in light of its intertextuality with and witness to the OT. Christopher Seitz is right:

Watson, *Text and Truth: Redefining Biblical Theology* (Grand Rapids, MI: Eerdmans, 1997); and Webster, *Holy Scripture*.

[62]Rhyne R. Putman, *The Method of Christian Theology: A Basic Introduction* (Nashville: B&H Academic, 2021), 10.

The NT declares the authority of the Old, and the apostolic witness to Christ is authoritative precisely because it is "in accordance with the [OT] Scriptures." The authority of both the NT and the Christian Scripture as a twofold witness is derived from the claims of the OT—claims presupposed in the NT and asserting themselves in the milieu from which its own composition, as the "apostles" half of the "prophets and apostles," is coming about.[63]

As we will see, John's extensive use of the OT highlights the obvious benefit of and reason for a canonical approach.

We cannot read Revelation rightly without a *canonical* approach. This approach does not ignore John as a real person who wrote a real piece of literature rife with OT intertextuality to a real first-century audience; however, it also highlights how divine providence and inspiration shaped the biblical witness in such a way that "YHWH" and "the Trinity" are inescapably synonymous. For instance, in God's unfolding revelation in human history, the incarnation of the Son—the λόγος ἔνσαρκος—is the economic unveiling of the triune life. Likewise, the Spirit's relationship to and inseparable work with the Father and Son highlights the same canonical continuity. Both the OT and NT contain this data, for we would not know that the Son and Spirit are truly divine persons without the OT's witness to the nature and activity of YHWH. So, we are concerned here not primarily with debates about canon formation or variant canon lists but rather with the theological claim that God has providentially inspired a unified, lasting witness about himself through the writings of human authors, which we now have in the form of the biblical canon.[64] In the triune God's self-revelation and ordering of all of creation (and by extension, Scripture), we do not merely affirm the Trinity based on retrospective readings of the OT, as though YHWH somehow *became* triune in light of the incarnation and Pentecost.

---

[63]Christopher R. Seitz, *The Character of Christian Scripture: The Significance of a Two-Testament Bible* (Grand Rapids, MI: Baker Academic, 2011), 75.

[64]It is notoriously difficult to define the unity of the biblical canon. Some may call it a "story," others may call it a "two-part history," and still others may call it "progressive revelation." These ways of describing biblical unity can have heuristic value; however, we must caveat this language with the recognition that Scripture is a different "thing" as the revelation of God than a typical story that moves from point A to B. I will speak more consistently of Scripture as a unified "witness" to highlight the revelation of God's providence and ordering of creation. This is not to deny the distinct contributions of the OT and NT to the unified witness but rather to acknowledge that its content and character are not merely bound to the time-and-space historical experiences of his creatures. More on this below.

Instead, we see that the subject matter of the biblical canon has always been a unified and providentially ordered witness to the perfect and unchanging nature and activity of the triune God.[65] So, in the case of John, it is not merely that he and the NT authors were self-consciously inventing a new form of monotheism as an experiential reader response; rather, their writings were divinely inspired revelation in continuity with the divinely inspired revelation of the OT (2 Pet 1:21; 3:16). Put another way, though the OT and NT are a unified witness to the triune God in different historical or economic moments, they are complementary and interconnected: the OT gives the NT much of its logic and grammar, as well as a basis for its authority; the NT provides a culmination to God's promises in the OT and makes plain things which were once hidden.[66] To speak of Scripture as God's revelation is to make a theological, even metaphysical, claim. As Seitz has said plainly, "Canon functions in an explicitly theological context."[67] In sum: this theological-canonical approach affirms that the unity of God's nature and activity (three in one) implies the unity of his revelation in the biblical witness (sixty-six in one).[68]

Conclusion

The following chapters on the Father, Son, and Holy Spirit will be organized in two main ways. First, I will discuss patristic conceptions of each person, with a survey of major figures and key ideas that helped shape pro-Nicene trinitarianism. This will orient us to the types of theological moves we will make as we work our way through specific passages in Revelation. Second,

---

[65]Don Collett, "Reading Forward: The Old Testament and Retrospective Stance," *ProEccl* 24, no. 2 (2015): 178-96, draws out this distinction well, noting that some modern "Christotelic" models treat the relationship between the OT and NT as a matter of mere experiential consciousness, such that the OT only points to Christ in a retrospective manner or as a deficient testimony when compared to Christ and the new covenant. However, he rightly points out that the "traditional" reading, which highlights God's a priori providential ordering of Scripture, offers a better avenue for understanding "the inexhaustible richness and scope of the OT as *Christian* Scripture" (196); emphasis original.
[66]This draws on Collett, "Reading Forward," 188, and his interaction with Christopher R. Seitz, *Figured Out: Typology and Providence in Christian Scripture* (Louisville, KY: Westminster John Knox, 2001), 113.
[67]Christopher R. Seitz, *The Elder Testament: Canon, Theology, Trinity* (Waco, TX: Baylor University Press, 2018), 26.
[68]This "66-in-1" language assumes my own Protestant tradition regarding the canon, though this book's argument certainly does not rise or fall with this delineation.

we will interpret specific passages in Revelation, chosen because of their clear triadic framing, in which one or more of the persons are shown in terms of their divine nature and activity, as well as their relationship to one another. Through these passages, we can see the trinitarian dynamic most clearly.

By surveying the patristic sources on trinitarianism and showing Revelation's place in the development of doctrine, I will show that John's theology was used in later trinitarian discourse and that reading Revelation is also aided by similar theological concepts used by patristic theologians. In turn, we will see that some patristic language can be a helpful conceptual guide for understanding John's theology but, at the same time, that we need not anachronistically force later trinitarian language into the text of Revelation in order to engage in a trinitarian reading.[69]

When we consider the text of Revelation in the exegetical sections of each chapter, we will see the legitimacy of our claim that a trinitarian reading is not an imposition on the text but rather is drawn from a close reading of the text. Notably, it will be argued that John hinges his doctrine of the Father, Son, and Spirit on the OT and Christian tradition[70] as a theo-logical trajectory or fulfillment of Jewish monotheism in God's providential, two-Testament witness, oftentimes using concepts and language that bear a family resemblance to other sources.[71] So, the passages we cover are not a

---

[69]Though, as Loke, *Origin of Divine Christology*, 16, has pointed out, historians often must use so-called anachronistic language as an explanatory function for past events, so it should not be considered entirely odd to use later terminologies to refer to Jesus' divinity. That said, I will attempt to avoid anachronism as much as possible.

[70]By this I mean that at the very least John was a recipient of Israel's Scripture and the oral Jesus tradition, which is why his writings mirror contemporary Christian writings. Whether he had access to other Christian writings is beyond the scope of this book, and we cannot fully know the answer anyway, as I have already noted.

[71]John's source material and criteria by which he employs allusions has been debated for years. Given that John appears to have a strong grasp on multiple languages and makes use of whichever version best underscores his point, one can consult Beale's conclusion that John consciously and subconsciously borrows from both the MT and the LXX, considering that he seemingly "draws from both Semitic and Greek biblical sources and often modifies both." See G. K. Beale, *The Book of Revelation*, NIGTC (Grand Rapids, MI: Eerdmans, 1999), 78. Garrick V. Allen, *The Book of Revelation and Early Jewish Textual Culture*, SNTS 168 (Cambridge: Cambridge University Press, 2017), 5, asserts that "John read, interpreted, and reused scripture in a manner commensurate with the practices of scriptural reuse operative in Second Temple Judaism." For a helpful discussion on the debate especially between Beale and Steve Moyise, see Jon Paulien, "Criteria and Assessment of Allusions to the Old Testament in the Book of Revelation," in *Studies in the Book of Revelation*, ed. Steve Moyise (New York: T&T Clark, 2001), 113-29; and "Dreading

piecemeal attempt to show some trinitarian highlights but rather to show a consistent trinitarian discourse throughout Revelation that is also in accordance with the unified biblical witness. Regarding Revelation's scriptural rootedness, Peter Leithart asserts,

> Revelation is a book of the Bible, and it operates within the world and history described in the OT and NT. Creation, fall, flood, Babel, Abraham, Sodom, Egypt, plagues, exodus, conquest, temple, tabernacle, kingdom, exile, Elijah, Isaiah, Ezekiel, Daniel, return, rebuilding: These books, people, and events provided the coordinates of John's imagination, long before he was swept up by the Spirit to see visions of God. He *did* have an ecstatic visionary experience, but what he saw reflected the events and institutions of the Bible, and when he recorded them he naturally recorded them in the vernacular he knew, the vernacular of the Scriptures.[72]

As Leithart says elsewhere, the New Testament authors' christological and ecclesiological readings of the OT are not "some bizarre form of sacred hermeneutics" but rather "are giving us pointers to the nature of reading itself: clues to the meaning of meaning, the functions of language, and the proper modes of interpretation."[73]

It is clear from the text that John grappled with the implications of Jesus' and the Holy Spirit's relationship to YHWH, and in the end he does not hesitate to apply divine titles and characteristics of YHWH to the Son and Spirit, nor does he downplay clear worship of the persons even as they stand next to God. As Michael Bird has described regarding "the birth of Christology":

> At the risk of simplification I would suggest that early Christologies emerged as the attempt to express, in belief and devotion, what the earliest Christ-believers thought God had revealed in the life, passion, resurrection, and exaltation of Jesus of Nazareth. In addition, there was a palpable need to make

---

the Whirlwind Intertextuality and the Use of the Old Testament in Revelation," *AUSS* 39, no. 1 (2001): 5-22. Further, as J. Julius Scott Jr., *Customs and Controversies: Intertestamental Backgrounds of the New Testament* (Grand Rapids, MI: Baker Books, 1995), 371, reminds us: "Although historical study provides much necessary and helpful information, we can never know and feel all that the writer and his original readers experienced."

[72]Peter J. Leithart, *Revelation 1-11*, The International Theological Commentary on the Holy Scripture of the Old and New Testaments (New York: Bloomsbury T&T Clark, 2018), 4; emphasis original.

[73]Peter J. Leithart, *Deep Exegesis: The Mystery of Reading Scripture* (Waco, TX: Baylor University Press, 2009), viii.

sense of what they had experienced of Jesus in their own communal and interior religious life.[74]

John joins this line of early Christian writers attempting to explain the roles and relationships of Jesus and the Spirit proximate to God the Father in light of Jewish monotheism, Christian worship of Jesus, experience of the Spirit, and prophetic and interpretive traditions. While John uses these elements historically and literarily in his writing, we also must acknowledge that the revelation he received confirms not a new thing per se, but rather a continuation of God's providential promise-keeping throughout history.

Further, John's descriptions of Father, Son, and Spirit resonate with common early Christian discourse about God. For example, in 1:1 he shows that the Father *gave* the revelation to Jesus (ἔδωκεν αὐτῷ) *from* whom (Ἰησοῦ Χριστοῦ) John directly *received* the revelation. John is a recipient of this revelation but is neither the author nor its direct agent. Writers of books that would later be canonized into the NT repeatedly stressed that Jesus was sent by the Father to *reveal* him to humankind (Mt 11:27; Mk 9:37; Lk 10:16; Jn 1:1-14; 4:34; 6:39-44; 8:26-29; 20:21; Gal 4:4; 1 Tim 1:15; Heb 1:2; 1 Jn 4:10) and that he only says what his Father says (Mt 11:27; Lk 10:22; Jn 8:26-29). Jesus, the Son, brings—and in fact *is*—the divine message (Rev 1:1; 2:1, 8 et al.; cf. Jn 1:1-14). Among the collection called the "Apostolic Fathers,"[75] several writings reveal a similar theological impulse. Perhaps most comparably to Revelation, Ignatius of Antioch's letters all include a salutation and/or doxology that includes the Father and Christ. Three of Ignatius's letters directly call Christ "our God" (Ἰησοῦ Χριστοῦ τοῦ θεοῦ ἡμῶν; cf. Ign. *Eph.* sal.; Ign. *Rom.* sal.; 3; Ign. *Smy.* 1) while not conflating him with the Father. As Hurtado put it, these types of passages present "Jesus as both integral to the knowledge of God and 'one' with God, sharing in divine glory, and yet also as a distinguishable figure."[76]

---

[74]Michael F. Bird, *Jesus the Eternal Son: Answering Adoptionist Christology* (Grand Rapids, MI: Eerdmans, 2017), 1.

[75]Unless otherwise noted, English translations of this literature are from *The Apostolic Fathers: Greek Texts and English Translations*, 3rd ed., ed. and trans. Michael W. Holmes (Grand Rapids, MI: Baker Academic, 2007). As Holmes rightly notes, the apostolic fathers collection was written generally in AD 70–150 and are "crucial witnesses" to the development of early Christianity in late antiquity (3). We will engage many of these texts in subsequent chapters.

[76]Larry W. Hurtado, "Observations on the 'Monotheism' Affirmed in the New Testament," in *The Bible and Early Trinitarian Theology*, ed. Christopher A. Beeley and Mark E. Weedman (Washington, DC: The Catholic University of America Press, 2018), 59.

Likewise, the Spirit carries John into the vision to hear God's message (Rev 1:10) and assists Jesus as the message giver to the churches (Rev 2:7, 11). The NT testimony about the Spirit is consistent with these types of descriptions. The Father and Son send the Spirit to deliver God's message post-resurrection via inspiration to continually remind Christians of Jesus' teaching (Jn 14:26; 16:13; Rom 8:26; 1 Cor 2:13; 2 Pet 3:16) by literally dwelling within them (Jn 20:22; Acts 1:8; Rom 8:9; 1 Cor 6:19). In the apostolic fathers, Ignatius's letters contain triadic formulas that include the Spirit (Ign. *Eph.* 9; Ign. *Magn.* 13), as does *Didache* 7 in a triadic baptismal formula. Similar to the Spirit speaking in Revelation 2–3 and John being "in the Spirit" elsewhere, Clement quotes Jeremiah 9:23 as a word "the Holy Spirit says" (1 Clem 13:1). Likewise, the author of Barnabas 12:2 says that the Spirit spoke to Moses and 13:5 says Jacob saw a prophecy "in the Spirit" (εἶδεν δὲ Ἰακὼβ τύπον τῷ πνεύματι). Another early Christian apocalypse, *Ascension of Isaiah*, also describes the Spirit as a revealer (Mart. Ascen. Isa. 3:16-26), while also distinctly placing the Spirit at the left hand of the Father (Mart. Ascen. Isa. 9:36; 11:33). We will look at many of these connections in more depth in subsequent chapters.

Though we will use pro-Nicene trinitarian conceptual tools to aid our interpretation, our primary argumentation for a trinitarian reading of Revelation will come by reading and interacting with the text itself. As N. T. Wright suggests, "Even in [the prologue] John manages to unveil a good deal of what he believes about God and Jesus, and about the divine plan."[77] Leithart further notes the triadic formula of Revelation: "The Father is he who is, was and comes; the Spirit is sevenfold; and Jesus is the witness, firstborn, and ruler. . . . Even the enemies of the church come in parodic threes."[78] Indeed, the way each person works inseparably from the other as the book's message and narrative unfold is plain, so a close reading of the text will notice the trinitarian dynamics already present. We will see both the unity and distinction of the trinitarian persons that affirms what would later be called the *taxis* (order) and inseparable operations, while also

---

[77]N. T. Wright, *Revelation for Everyone* (Louisville: Westminster John Knox, 2011), 5.
[78]Peter J. Leithart, *Revelation 12-22*, The International Theological Commentary on the Holy Scripture of the Old and New Testaments (New York: T&T Clark, 2018), 441. We address the possibility that the "seven spirits" are the Holy Spirit in chap. 4.

avoiding certain novel versions of subordination between the persons that have crept their way into modern trinitarian discourse.[79]

The trinitarian reading proposed here is dependent upon how Revelation describes the divine persons, which reveals that the persons are understood not on individual islands but "in specific relationships or correlations."[80] Perhaps most obviously, we must note that there can be no Father without a Son and no Son without a Father. As Hurtado noted, worship patterns during the NT period left no doubt that "one cannot adequately identify the one without reference to the other."[81] Likewise, the Holy Spirit is only truly understood—to use pro-Nicene terminology—in relation to his procession or spiration, as his mission is ultimately to point back to and perfect the work of the Father and Son. So, binitarianism is untenable given the biblical data because the Spirit's completion of the work of God pressures biblical interpreters into a trinitarian understanding of God's nature and activity. The pro-Nicenes understood the unity-yet-distinction dynamic presented by the biblical text, and thus, as Madison Pierce has suggested, we can say that biblical authors can also describe "a Trinity without *tiers*, but not a Trinity without *taxis*."[82]

Finally, it should be noted that the method used in this book is multivalent in two ways. First, this book operates within several disciplines—biblical studies, systematic theology, church history, and patristics. I consider myself primarily a systematic and historical theologian who loves the

---

[79] For helpful distillations of this debate, see Keith S. Whitfield, ed., *Trinitarian Theology: Theological Models and Doctrinal Application* (Nashville: B&H Academic, 2018); and Millard J. Erickson, *Who's Tampering with the Trinity?: An Assessment of the Subordination Debate* (Grand Rapids, MI: Kregel Academic, 2009). See also Scott Harrower, "Bruce Ware's Trinitarian Methodology," in *Trinity Without Hierarchy*, 307-29; D. Glenn Butner Jr., "Eternal Functional Subordination and the Problem of the Divine Will," *JETS* 58, no. 1 (2015): 131-49; and Thomas H. McCall, *Which Trinity? Whose Monotheism?: Philosophical and Systematic Theologians on the Metaphysics of Trinitarian Theology* (Grand Rapids, MI: Eerdmans, 2010), 175-88 for useful critiques of some of these novel formulations.

[80] Rowe, *Early Narrative Christology*, 21. In dealing with how Luke uses κύριος, Rowe explains that the identity of Jesus in Luke is dependent upon a narrative identity that reveals Jesus' inseparable tie to the identity of God. We will see that John is not dependent on any specific word to accomplish this task but rather espouses trinitarianism through canonical continuity of titles and roles.

[81] Larry W. Hurtado, *God in New Testament Theology* (Nashville: Abingdon, 2010), 43.

[82] Madison N. Pierce, "Trinity Without *Taxis*?: A Reconsideration of 1 Corinthians 11," in *Trinity Without Hierarchy*, 53; emphasis original. Pierce is particularly speaking of how Paul describes the God-Christ relationship in 1 Cor 11, but the point is pertinent for our purposes.

Scriptures and seeks to understand them faithfully and rigorously, so I am attempting to bring together what others may put asunder.[83] Given the aim and scope of this book, each discipline can be engaged with depth and rigor but will be somewhat limited by our narrow focus on a trinitarian reading of Revelation. I therefore will engage with various disciplines while avoiding anachronism or contextual ignorance as much as possible, but nuances are sometimes only able to be covered in footnotes. In each exegetical section in subsequent chapters, I will intentionally interact with commentaries, monographs, and articles from various viewpoints and disciplines, both to highlight their strengths and as a foil to show where my reading differs and hopefully provides a better way forward. That said, this chapter has introduced basic definitions, assumptions, aids, and strategies to clear the ground and set forth a trajectory to those chapters.

Second, this trinitarian reading of Revelation will be explicated in a variety of ways under the umbrella of the theological-canonical approach. The methods noted above from Yeago, Childs, Rowe, and Hill will serve as surfaces on the interpretive kaleidoscope, but we should not expect John to have used a neat-and-clean method.[84] As mentioned above, John used familiar language and concepts—particularly those found in the OT Scriptures—to describe what may have been a borderline indescribable vision. Therefore, the levels of explicitness with which John describes the divine persons may vary based on the particular portion of the vision he is witnessing and will be described in his own vernacular, so to speak, given that his writing comes from "experienced reality."[85] Indeed, as Childs

---

[83] As Ayres put it, there is an "increasing realization [in early Christian studies] that many of the professional distinctions between scholars of 'New Testament,' 'patristics,' 'Church history' and 'systematics' . . . are increasingly problematic"; Lewis Ayres, introduction to *Christian Origins: Theology, Rhetoric and Community*, ed. Lewis Ayres and Gareth Jones (New York: Routledge, 1998), 3. Treier, *Introducing Theological Interpretation of Scripture*, 27, similarly laments, "The Enlightenment and its aftermath finalized [an already developing] metaphysical separation between history and God."

[84] Jan Fekkes, *Isaiah and Prophetic Traditions in the Book of Revelation* (Sheffield, UK: Sheffield Academic Press, 1994), 59-103, details at length John's use of the OT. Fekkes helpfully reminds us that it is impossible to build a neat framework for John's use of the OT, particularly because (1) he employs allusions rather than quotations, and (2) he does not employ allusions in a monolithic way.

[85] Gordon D. Fee, "Paul and the Trinity: The Experience of Christ and the Spirit for Paul's Understanding of God," in *The Trinity: An Interdisciplinary Symposium*, ed. Stephen T. Davis, Daniel Kendall, and Gerald O'Collins (Oxford: Oxford University Press, 1999), 51.

observed: "The issues of symbolism, literary genre, and fluctuating tradition pose a complexity which does not allow for a simple method of 'decoding' the text."[86] So, as Matthew Bates has said, I acknowledge the NT writers did not yet have stable "nomenclature to express the Trinity" but that "the die had been cast" through their understanding of and interaction with the OT.[87] Again, this does not weaken the assertion that a pro-Nicene toolkit can provide helpful ways to understand Revelation's theology, because it helps bring clarity and coherence to John's marvelous vision.

---

[86]Brevard S. Childs, *The New Testament as Canon: An Introduction* (Valley Forge, PA: Trinity Press International, 1984), 504. Richard B. Hays, "Faithful Witness, Alpha and Omega: The Identity of Jesus in the Apocalypse of John," in *Revelation and the Politics of Apocalyptic Interpretation*, ed. Richard B. Hays and Stefan Alkier (Waco, TX: Baylor University Press, 2012), 69, says similarly, "This visionary book deploys a kaleidoscopic profusion of imagery to depict its chief protagonist."
[87]Bates, *Birth of the Trinity*, 40.

Father

The One Seated on the Throne

Our vision of the triune God starts, fittingly, with the Father. His boundless majesty and power are on full display in Revelation as he sits on the throne as the perfectly good, wise, and sovereign creator of all that was, is, and will be. Though nobody could fully comprehend or describe such a marvelous sight, John nonetheless obeys the command to "write what you have seen" (Rev 1:19). As with all who have been granted access to the throne room, John is in awe of his splendor, only able to describe him through images and symbols and familiar scriptural tropes that our finite minds can only begin to ponder. Our glimpse of this divine splendor through John's eyes should bring us all to the same astonishment, saying with Isaiah, "I am ruined because I am a man of unclean lips" (Is 6:5).

John describes his vision of God the Father through two primary concepts: (1) fatherhood with respect to Jesus Christ, and (2) enthronement in the heavenly realms that reveals both transcendence (exalted in glory) and immanence (interacting with people via the seer). Looking at texts such as Revelation 1:1-8; 4–5; and 11:15-19, we will see John's interpretation of these concepts in relation to the vision(s) he received. The resemblance between John's concept of Father and how that concept relates to his Son incipiently resembles some of the patristic writers who followed after Revelation's writing. Alongside the patristic theologians, we will conclude that the Father, Son, and Spirit are ontologically equal as the one simple God, being worthy of divine worship and distinct from the creaturely world. Considering the aim of this book, the most pertinent passages for our discussion will highlight the ways in which God the Father's identity and activity relates to Jesus Christ and to the culmination of history. First, a survey of the patristic trinitarian theology will help explain the concepts of fatherhood and enthronement in patristic theology and highlight tools we will use in interpreting our select texts.

PATRISTIC CONCEPTIONS OF THE FATHER

In pro-Nicene grammar, there is one God who subsists in three persons. The three persons are one in substance (ὁμοούσιος), authority, and eternity and yet distinct in personhood (ὑπόστασις). Their essential or substantial unity is not threatened by their distinction, because the Father, Son, and Spirit relate to one another in a constituted order (*taxis*) that does not imply ontological hierarchy or division of operation or will, since God is simple and therefore not composed of parts. Put another way, God was not put together and cannot be parted out, so splitting or ranking his power or authority or will between the persons would imply division at the level of divinity itself. God would be imperfect, changeable, and unstable—an option that is untenable in light of the biblical witness. Moreover, the persons are all fully and truly God, but the Father is not the Son, the Son is not the Spirit, and the Spirit is not the Father. Basil of Caesarea explained it this way: "When the Lord taught us the doctrine of Father, Son, and Holy Spirit, He did not make arithmetic a part of this gift! He did not say, 'In the first, second, or third' or 'In one, two and three.' . . . There is one God and Father, one Only-Begotten Son, and one Holy Spirit . . . we will not let ignorant arithmetic lead us to polytheism."[1]

In particular, we can speak about their eternal relations: God the Father is unbegotten, the Son is eternally begotten or generated, and Spirit eternally spirates or proceeds. And though there is no ontological or relational hierarchy in the nature of the Trinity (*ad intra*), the Father is in some sense the fount of

---

[1] *D. S. S.* 18.44. Unless otherwise noted, all English translations are from St. Basil the Great, *On the Holy Spirit*, trans. David Anderson (Crestwood, NY: St Vladimir's Seminary Press, 1980), 44. Of course, we reiterate here that Basil's description is *one way* the Trinity was explained in the Nicene or pro-Nicene period, but it is nonetheless a good representation of the pro-Nicene grammar.

the divine nature (as the unbegotten one in the *taxis*)² and the economic missions of triune activity (*ad extra*). Therefore, we understand the distinction of the persons not through a divided will or hierarchical set of attributes (for these are proper to the simple divine nature and do not exist on a gradient scale), but rather through their eternal relations of origin.³ The doctrine of the eternal generation of the Son protects biblical language about the Son's filial relationship to the Father (Jn 3:16) while recognizing the equality of substance and nature (Heb 1:3); eternal spiration likewise protects the Spirit's relationship to the Father and Son and his equality of substance and nature (Jn 14:8-26; 15:26; Acts 5:1-9). So, again, the Father can be in some sense the source of divine nature (as the unbegotten one) and economic action (as the sender) without denigrating the Son's or the Spirit's equality within the divine nature.

Regarding the Father in particular, the Constantinopolitan Creed (381) says, "We believe in one God, the Father almighty, maker of heaven and earth, and of all things visible and invisible."⁴ In the opening line of the creed we see some of the same theological concepts portrayed in Revelation: fatherhood ("God, the Father") and enthronement in glory as Creator ("almighty, maker of heaven and earth"). However, there are theological trajectories that led there.

The designation of "Father" was a source of tension in the first few centuries of Christian thought. The distinction between ontology (or theology) and economy was a major point of emphasis for many patristic theologians, as confusion here led to varying dissident theologies.⁵ Relatedly, since divine speech is a type of accommodation that necessitates God's condescension to his creatures, some patristic theologians reasoned that forgetting the Creator-creature distinction—reading that which is analogical or anthropomorphic as literal—could cause dire theological problems. For example, the Father truly is the

---

²As Lewis Ayres, *Nicaea and Its Legacy: An Approach to Fourth-Century Trinitarian Theology* (Oxford: Oxford University Press, 2004), 113n23, summarizes, "At the end of the 4th century pro-Nicenes assume that distinction: the Father alone is ἀγέννητος (ungenerated) while all three divine persons are ἀγένητος (uncreated)."

³As Adonis Vidu, *The Same God Who Works All Things: Inseparable Operations in Trinitarian Theology* (Grand Rapids, MI: Eerdmans, 2021), 103, nicely summarizes: "The divine persons do not have different natures [but] it can be said that the divine persons have the divine essence in a differentiated way, the Father as unbegotten, the Son as begotten, and the Spirit as spirated."

⁴Πιστεύομεν εἰς ἕνα Θεὸν Πατέρα παντοκράτορα ποιητὴν οὐρανοῦ καὶ γῆς ὁρατῶν τε πάντων καὶ ἀοράτων.

⁵For a helpful survey of this point, see Mark Sheridan, *Language for God in the Patristic Tradition* (Downers Grove, IL: IVP Academic, 2015), 27-44.

Father of the Son, but we should not conclude that the Son was created or biologically produced, since the Father and Son are not bound materially (the divine nature is immaterial) or temporally (God exists outside of time).

We cannot rightly discuss patristic theology without starting with Origen of Alexandria. Origen's theology was enormously influential on later theological debates on both the pro-Nicene and non-Nicene sides of the ledger.[6] As Michel René Barnes says, "Both Arius and Alexander deserve this classification ['Origenist'] to the extent that they both believed in the eternal, separate existence of the second person."[7] Most notably, Origen seemed to wrestle more fully than his predecessors with the ontological implications of the Father, Son, and Spirit's one divine nature, which would influence and later define the orthodox trinitarian affirmations. Though many scholars have accused him of subordinationism,[8] it is anachronistic to hold him accountable to formulations that would be settled long after his death. In any event, before moving on, we must briefly acknowledge the complexity of Origen's views, especially surrounding the charge of subordinationism and his relationship to Arius.[9] I agree generally with Ayres that the charge of subordinationism is somewhat overblown, because (1) Origen's theology, even if "subordinationist" in some sense, takes different paths and emphases

---

[6]We will use the term "non-Nicene" to speak about the various and diverse groups that did not agree with pro-Nicene logic in order to acknowledge their diversity and to avoid assigning motives to their diverse reasonings. I acknowledge that some also use "anti-Nicene" for those who seemed to intentionally challenge Nicaea-Constantinopolitan conclusions; for instance, see these terms used varyingly in Richard Krautheimer, *Three Christian Capitals: Topography and Politics* (Berkeley, CA: California University Press, 1983), 71-92; Ayres, *Nicaea and Its Legacy*, 139-40; Rowan Williams, *Arius: Heresy and Tradition* (Grand Rapids, MI: Eerdmans, 2001).

[7]Michel René Barnes, "The Fourth Century as Trinitarian Canon," in *Christian Origins: Theology, Rhetoric and Community*, ed. Lewis Ayres and Gareth Jones (New York: Routledge, 1998), 49.

[8]As Stephen R. Holmes, *The Quest for the Trinity: The Doctrine of God in Scripture, History and Modernity* (Downers Grove, IL: IVP Academic, 2012), 83, asserts, "It is fair to say that, by the beginning of the fourth century, many or most theologians leaned to one or the other of Origen's tendencies," in reference to Origen's tendencies to discuss both the unity and difference between the Father and Son. Khaled Anatolios, *Retrieving Nicaea: The Development and Meaning of Trinitarian Doctrine* (Grand Rapids, MI: Baker Academic, 2011), 17, notes similarly that Origen influenced the Alexandrians with his idea of eternal generation and the Arians with his idea of real distinctions within the Trinity. Stephen J. Wellum, *God the Son Incarnate: The Doctrine of Christ*, Foundations of Evangelical Theology (Wheaton, IL: Crossway, 2016), 276, says plainly, "In terms of Trinitarian and Christological thought, many later orthodox theologians were highly indebted to him, particularly Athanasius and the Cappadocians."

[9]For a robust treatise on Origen's doctrine of subordination, see J. Nigel Rowe, *Origen's Doctrine of Subordination: A Study in Origen's Christology* (Berne, Switzerland: Peter Lang, 1987).

than Arius's theology; (2) while groups on both sides of the Nicene debate were indebted to Origen, no one adopted his theology wholesale; and (3) the term "subordination" used for third- and fourth-century theologians distorts the fact that many theologians were more concerned with the Father's and Son's unity than with their relative hierarchical positions.[10]

A more precise example of speaking about Origen's relationship to later fourth-century theology is laid out by Ayres: though Origen influenced Athanasius, "Origen directly denies that the Son can come from the Father's *ousia* (οὐσία), as this would imply a material conception of the divine generation," noting that *ousia* language would have been "unsuitable" as compared to *hypostasis* since "Origen is searching for a way to argue that the Father and Son and Spirit each have a distinct existence."[11] Origen unsurprisingly did not employ the same terminology or rhetorical moves with respect to God's ontology and economy if compared to later creedal affirmations—notably his wrestling with the implications of the Father as unbegotten and the Son being begotten;[12] however, his theology was informed by a different contextual and polemical environment than that of the fourth-century debates, so we might expect him to be "retrieved" differently by later theologians, depending on their own context.[13] So, it is better to call Origen "pre-Nicene" instead of "subordinationist" to avoid any anachronism, and then refer to his positions as "pro-Nicene" or "non-Nicene" when compared to their usage in later debates. We will discuss with greater detail in chapter three his view on the Son, but for our purposes here, we should stress the role of the Father in Origen's theology.

Origen's doctrine of creation was an integral part of his theology and served as the scaffolding for his discussions on the Father and Son.[14] Notably,

---

[10] Ayres, *Nicaea and Its Legacy*, 20-21.
[11] Ayres, *Nicaea and Its Legacy*, 24-25. See further agreement with this conclusion in Williams, *Arius*, 134.
[12] Again, his language vacillates between language used by both pro-Nicenes and non-Nicenes. Ayres, *Nicaea and Its Legacy*, 27-28 (emphasis original), notes: "Origen's account of the shared but graded divine existence offers an initially clear, but complex language to describe this relationship.... On the one hand, Origen hesitates ... to talk of the Son as coming from the Father's essence. On the other hand ... to say that the Son is from the Father's will is to *emphasize* the eternal status of the Son as expression of the Father."
[13] Most obviously, Origen's opponents appear to include Monarchian groups that had either modalistic or adoptionistic tendencies, so his arguments with respect to nature, will, and person would naturally differ from the *homoousios* debates of the fourth century.
[14] As Behr notes, "Origen's teaching on creation is notoriously complex and has been the subject of controversy almost from the beginning." See Origen, *On First Principles*, vol. 1., ed. and trans. John Behr, OECT (Oxford: Oxford University Press, 2017), lvi.

Origen shared certain philosophical assumptions with Middle Platonism—or at least used them as apologetic tools—which is a further key for understanding his theology.[15] For instance, he emphasizes in *De Principiis* (*On First Principles*) that God is incorporeal and, therefore, distinct from his creation to the point of invisibility and incomprehensibility.[16] In contrast, creaturely existence is tied to a body either terrestrially or ethereally—a body that will be renewed and reconstituted in eternity, "since it is thought to be a property of God alone, that is, of the Father and of the Son and of the Holy Spirit, to exist without any material substance and apart from any association of a bodily addition."[17] Further, he asserts with Middle Platonism that Father is the source or first cause of all being and, as a matter of consequence, all of creation is dependent upon him as the source of being, "the one who is" (Ex 3:14).[18] These philosophical moves allowed Origen to assert that the Son is begotten and that this birth happens in some unexplainable manner that "must be something exceptional and worthy of God."[19] That said, he tends to privilege the Father to the point of insinuating that the Son derives both his existence and life from the Father as his "right-hand man."[20]

As mentioned above, scholarship on Origen often asserts that he seems entangled in language that resembles logic used by both pro-Nicene and non-Nicene theologians after him. He uses phrases such as the Father "giving [the Son] subsistence"[21] as an act of will,[22] while also attempting to straddle the belief that there was a "'when' when Wisdom was not" even though the Father's substance "was perfectly accounted"[23] (non-Nicene). On the other hand, Origen also says that the Son is "the express figure of [the

---

[15] Ronald E. Heine, "God," in *The Westminster Handbook to Origen*, ed. John Anthony McGuckin (Louisville: Westminster John Knox, 2004), 106-7.
[16] *Princ.* 1.1.5.
[17] *Princ.* 1.6.4. Unless otherwise noted, English translations are from Origen, *On First Principles*, 2 vols., ed. and trans. John Behr, OECT (Oxford: Oxford University Press, 2017); cf. *Princ.* 1.1.
[18] See his argumentation on God and being in *Comm. Jo.* 13; cf. Henri Crouzel, *Origen: The Life and Thought of the First Great Theologian*, trans. A. S. Worrall (San Francisco: Harper & Row, 1989), 183. See also Peter Widdicombe, *The Fatherhood of God from Origen to Athanasius*, rev. ed. (Oxford: Oxford University Press, 2000), 9-43.
[19] *Princ.* 1.2.4.
[20] Rowe, *Origen's Doctrine of Subordination*, 4-5.
[21] *Princ.* 1.2.4.
[22] *Princ.* 4.4.1.
[23] *Princ.* 4.4.1.

Father: The One Seated on the Throne

Father's] substance"[24] and "is a Son by nature" in "an eternal and everlasting begetting, just as brightness is begotten from light"[25] (pro-Nicene). Though later theologians utilized his theology in various ways, we should remember that Origen is not consumed with "subordinationism" as it would later take shape, but rather is seeking to work out the very issues that arise in later debates: How does one speak of the unity and distinction between the persons?[26] This brief survey shows that Ayres is correct in saying,

> Origen's concern is to distinguish Father, Son, and Spirit while maintaining the idea that the latter two reveal and bring to completion the one divine will and action. Origen's account is, then, complex. He speaks of the Son as inferior to the Father, and yet his explanation of this inferiority turns, at many points, into an account of the necessity of the Son within the divine life.[27]

Put another way, Origen was concerned with demonstrating the Father's nature, not with subordinating the Son.[28] This emphasis on God the Father with the Son as an expression of his divine life and activity reminds us that the term "God" itself had still not reached the technical systemization of what it meant to say "God" in pro-Nicene thought. Similarly, Dionysius of Alexandria followed Origen's thought by trying to balance the interconnected relationship with the Father and Son while also protecting the priority of the Father in saying that the Father's name "provides the ground for the union" between the Father and Son.[29]

The fourth century built on this foundation with a gradual but sure development of speaking of "God" as triune—three persons subsisting in one nature. Similarly but more forcefully than Origen, Athanasius—via the term *homoousios*—sought to protect the Father's divine nature while also

---

[24]*Princ.* 4.4.1. quoting Heb 1:3.
[25]*Princ.* 1.2.4. The light metaphor, of course, resonates with Nicene Creed language, "God from God, light from light."
[26]As Ayres, *Nicaea and Its Legacy*, 27, points out, even when his language seems to indicate that the Son was created, "It is difficult to know how we should read this" in light of his broader conversation about the divine relationship to material creation.
[27]Ayres, *Nicaea and Its Legacy*, 28.
[28]Ayres, *Nicaea and Its Legacy*, 26.
[29]*Dion.* 17-18; cf. Widdicombe, *Fatherhood of God from Origen to Athanasius*, 123-25. Interestingly, Dionysius—one of Alexander's and Athanasius's predecessors—suppressed the use of *homoousios* in the third century because Sabellius used the term to eliminate the distinction between the persons; cf. Basil of Caesarea, *Ep.* 9.2.

asserting that the Son's generation still separated him from creation.[30] In many places he warned against violating the Creator-creature distinction by speaking of the Father-Son relationship in eternity in the same way as our conception of human fathers and sons—for example, insinuating that the Son was literally birthed and came into existence. Understanding the Creator-creature divide and limitations of human language and analogy when discussing the Father and Son was an important guardrail.[31] When speaking of the hypostatic union—that the Son is two natures in one person—Gregory of Nazianzus also recommended a reading strategy: in dealing with the tension of Christ's divinity and humanity in Scripture, do not confuse the two natures but rather attribute the "sublime expressions of the Godhead" to his divinity and the "lowlier ones" to his humanity.[32] Ultimately, not employing this strategy—often called "partitive exegesis"—was one of the chief mistakes the pro-Nicenes would accuse non-Nicenes of making.[33]

For example, Arius[34] reasoned that Jesus' begottenness was not only related to his humanity but also to his preexistence, because he was "begotten" and therefore "second" to the Father. That difference between "first" (the Father) and "second" (the Son) requires an essential divide—the Father is uniquely first, and everything else is second and therefore creaturely, including the Son.[35] So, for Arius, in whatever sense Christ is divine, his

---

[30] For example, see *Syn.* 35; cf. Ayres, *Nicaea and Its Legacy*, 171.
[31] For example, see *C. Ar.* 1.14-15.
[32] *Or.* 29.18.
[33] It is worth noting that partitive exegesis, if abused, can have Nestorian consequences. Gregory was wise to preempt that later Christology heresy by continually asserting the *one person* of Christ, even as he at times spoke distinctly about his divine and human natures.
[34] A point of clarification should be emphasized here. When some use the term "Arianism," they mistakenly assume that many or all non- or anti-Nicene groups were disciples or perpetuators of Arius's actual theology. While some groups shared certain theological or exegetical affinities with Arius, many did not even claim awareness of his works; cf. Ayres, *Nicaea and Its Legacy*, 13. Indeed, Krautheimer, *Three Christian Capitals*, 71, notes that some pro-Nicene theologians used the term "Arian" as a pejorative term for those who disagreed with their logic; see also similar notes by Matthew R. Crawford, "The Triumph of Pro-Nicene Theology over Anti-Monarchian Exegesis: Cyril of Alexandria and Theodore of Heraclea on John 14.10-11," *JECS* 21, no. 4 (2013): 538; Barnes, "Fourth Century as Trinitarian Canon," 54; and Stephen M. Hildebrand, *The Trinitarian Theology of Basil of Caesarea: A Synthesis of Greek Thought and Biblical Truth* (Washington, DC: The Catholic University of America Press, 2007), 14-15. So, when we discuss Arius or "Arianism," we are referring to either extant knowledge about Arius's own thought or we are quoting a source using the term.
[35] Anatolios, *Retrieving Nicaea*, 45.

divinity is still associated with a subordinate, creaturely nature.³⁶ To his credit, Arius sought to protect divine simplicity—that God is not made up of parts or composed in any way, as though he was created by something else. For Arius, to say that the Son is of the same substance as the Father would be to deny his simplicity; rather, he thought the idea of *homoousios* insinuated that the Father's essence could be separated into parts and parceled out to the Son. He instead argued for two different—though similar—substances for the Father and Son. Thus, Arius did not take begottenness language to be analogical in the same way as someone like Athanasius. Similarly, we see Eunomius assert that the term "Father" is not related to his nature but rather to the will or agency of begetting the Son.³⁷ For the pro-Nicene theologians, however, the Father and Son's relationship rested in the unity of their nature, not merely the unity of will.

Whereas it seemed possible for Arius to talk about God apart from talking about him only as Father, the trajectory from Origen to Athanasius emphasized the designation as intrinsic to God's nature. Origen at times may have arguably emphasized the fatherhood of God at the expense of the Son, but Athanasius found it impossible to talk about God and related soteriological issues without talking about the Father *and* Son. Athanasius's insistence on the *homoousios* of the Father and Son as core to his polemic was no doubt precipitated by (1) his desire to defend the language of Nicaea³⁸ and, accordingly, (2) feeling the need to highlight Arius's and others' minimization of the Son's divinity.³⁹

---

³⁶Anatolios, *Retrieving Nicaea*, 45.

³⁷*Apol.* 12; cf. Anatolios, *Retrieving Nicaea*, 75.

³⁸Space limits a full engagement with the issues, debates, and relatively lukewarm response to the Nicene Creed (325) during and in the aftermath of the proceedings. That said, I will note at times throughout our subsequent discussions—especially in chap. 3—the major plot points in the development and trajectory before and after Nicaea as they pertain to our immediate concerns for this book. For detailed discussions of the controversy related to the Nicene Creed, see Mark S. Smith, *The Idea of Nicaea in the Early Church and Councils, AD 431–451*, OECS (Oxford: Oxford University Press, 2018), 7-34; and Donald Fairbairn and Ryan M. Reeves, *The Story of Creeds and Confessions: Tracing the Development of the Christian Faith* (Grand Rapids, MI: Baker Academic, 2019), 58-71.

³⁹See, for instance, his glorifying of Nicaea over the "Arian" conspiracies at other council proceedings in *Syn.* 14.3. For useful discussion on Athanasius's *homoousios* polemic against Arius, Aetius et al., see Ayres, *Nicaea and Its Legacy*, 140-44. Smith, *Idea of Nicaea*, 21, notes in particular Athanasius's motivation to use Nicaea as a battleground was likely due in part to his personal disdain for the way he was treated by the councils at Antioch (AD 341) and Sirmium (AD 351).

In his arguments against Arians, Athanasius argued that denying that the Son is divine in the same sense as the Father would deny his eternal fatherhood and undermine the Father's generative nature.[40] If one wants to assert that the Son came into being at some point, one must assert that the Father was not always Father, and thus must have *added* a title or relation to himself at some point in history. This would imply that God is not in fact simple or immutable (incapable of change in both nature and will)—a theological problem even Arius was actually *trying* to avoid. This is notable, for example, in their wrangling over the interpretation of passages like John 1:1 and Proverbs 8:22. At center stage was the question of whether God's "Word" or "Wisdom" was a creation of the Father (albeit somehow divine) or an indication that the Son was of the same substance as the Father. Again, Arius wanted to ontologically separate the Father from the Son as his Word or Wisdom to protect divine simplicity, because the Son being the same substance as the Father implied that the ungenerated Father would have a divided essence, or that the begotten Son relied on the Father's essence rather than having his own.[41] Athanasius (and Alexander), on the other hand, argued that Arius denied simplicity by asserting that if God created the Son as his Word or Wisdom, then he added speech or wisdom to himself at some point later, thus implying that the Father was lacking at some point. For Athanasius, then, we must affirm that the Father and Son are of the same substance, and recognize that this truth is not fully comprehensible to finite human minds.

All of these early Christian theologians felt the tension between the Father as a source or first cause, while also acknowledging his unique relationship to the Son. As the fourth century came to a close, the pro-Nicene theologians would rely not only on *homoousios* but also the concept of eternal relations of origin or *taxis* mentioned above—the Father is unbegotten, the Son is begotten, and the Spirit proceeds. This language is biblical (e.g., Jn 3:16;

---

[40]Widdicombe, *Fatherhood of God from Origen to Athanasius*, 3. As Widdicombe rightly points out later in the book, Athanasius insisted that the Son's ability to save was directly related to his having the same nature as the Father and thus having the same attributes; Arius's theology, in turn, entailed disastrous consequences for the hope of salvation.

[41]He insinuates this in his letter to Eusebius of Nicomedia as he explains the Son's essential distinction from the Father: "The Son is not unbegotten, nor part of the unbegotten one in any way, nor is he from any subsistence." My translation of "ὁ υἱός οὐκ ἔστιν ἀγέννητος, οὐδὲ μέρος ἀγεννήτου κατ' οὐδένα τρόπον, οὐδε ἐξ ὑποκειμένου τινός."

14:26; 15:26) and allows for a distinction among the three eternal persons within the one, eternal divine nature. The Father's begetting of the Son and spirating of the Spirit indicate real relations without division or gradation of power, authority, or will. Once we begin to discuss the economy of God—how he relates to his creation—we can still acknowledge that the Father sends the Son and the Spirit because this is fitting of the *taxis*, without taking this language too far and asserting a hierarchy among the persons, which would deny that the Son and the Spirit exercise the same divine power, authority, and so forth. This protects the important doctrine of divine simplicity by affirming that God is one and immutable (Deut 6:4; Mal 3:6), but that he has always existed in and as three persons who are equally and wholly of the same divine nature and all of its attributional entailments. The pro-Nicenes were willing to live in this mystery demanded by the biblical text, whereas Arius and other non-Nicenes often sought to tie up loose ends that were sometimes unable to be tied.

This tension and the examples listed above are paradigmatic of the issues that arise when reading a text like Revelation, wherein varying titles and descriptions for the Father, Son, and Spirit elicit a range of potential hermeneutical and theological deductions. For example, when we see Jesus' dependence upon or apparent submission to the Father in Revelation, it raises questions about parallel passages wherein Jesus seems to have the same divine nature and act with equal divine power and authority. I will note many of his interactions with Revelation in this chapter and elsewhere.

Finally, we will notice a similarity between Revelation's worship language and throne-room scenes that reveal God as Creator and the ways in which the patristic writers talked about the relationship between the Father and Son. Alexander of Alexandria, for instance, noted that John 1:3 ("All things were created through him, and apart from him not one thing was created that has been created") reveals that the Son is of the same nature as the Father, because a creature cannot be the Creator.[42] This is an extension of the argument noted above, that the unity between the Father and Son is one of nature, not merely will or agency. So, as we will see, the Father on the throne in Revelation is praised as Creator, but we also see Jesus receiving

---

[42] *The Epistle of Alexander* 3:35-41; cf. Anatolios, *Retrieving Nicaea*, 80-81.

the same praise on the same throne. This shows us that for John the seer, the Father may be "first," but his primacy is in relation to what would later be termed *taxis* and/or economic missions, not in relation to nature or essence. This *homoousios* of the Father and Son shows that no one is able to sit on the throne alongside God other than the Lamb, while no other character in Revelation is shown receiving or accepting worship.[43] We get no insinuation from the text that this throne-sharing takes away any glory, honor, and power from the Father; rather, it is a positive statement about the identity of the Son. Moreover, it is also important to note that Jesus receives what Bird calls a "sky-high" christological attribution of also being called "Almighty" in Revelation.[44] In fact, Athanasius cites Revelation 1 to make this very point.[45]

We will now turn to particular passages in Revelation to highlight the Father's nature and activity in Revelation. We will see that John makes grammatical and theological moves that at times resemble Jewish and cultural ideas within his own context, while also highlighting the ways he reimagined or reworked them to make a distinctive theological point. Further, we will note the ways pro-Nicene categories aid a trinitarian reading of Revelation.

Interpretation of Select Passages

The passages covered in this section were selected based on their depiction of the Father as the locus of divine activity and his relationship with Jesus and the Spirit. We will see that though the Father in many senses initiates divine action and relates to Jesus and the Spirit accordingly, *redoublement* helps us see both unity nature and distinction of personhood. Indeed, a trinitarian reading of these passages with an eye toward pro-Nicene conceptual categories highlights the surprising ways in which John elevates Jesus and the Spirit precisely *because* of their relationship to the Father. We will therefore interact with the best interdisciplinary works and ideas on interpreting these passages both to highlight their strengths and show how our method might provide alternate or better readings.

---

[43]I will discuss ways this relates to the Spirit in chap. 4.
[44]Michael F. Bird, *What Christians Ought to Believe: An Introduction to Christian Doctrine Through the Apostles' Creed* (Grand Rapids, MI: Zondervan, 2016), 65.
[45]*Ep. Serap.* 2.2.2.

The source of Revelation (Rev 1:1-8). The letter begins with an epistolary introduction, stating John's name and the circumstances for writing the letter. Most notably for our purposes, John is clear in the introduction about the sender, mediator, and recipients' identities. The phrase in 1b, "The revelation of Jesus Christ which God gave to him to show his servants what things must soon take place,"[46] indicates that God the Father is the ultimate source and sender of the revelation and that Christ is then the transmitter to his servants, who are the ultimate recipients.[47] John Christopher Thomas and Frank Macchia note that Revelation "clearly gives its attention to God as the chief player in the narrative of salvation history."[48] This introduction, then, offers the first cue that John is at some level designating the Father in a particular mode of operation: the one who initiates the revelation (cf. Is 65:1, "I have revealed myself"). As Keener contends, "The preface, or exordium, of a work sets the tone for a work. . . . That God 'is and was and is to come' frames the *source* of the blessing (1:4, 8), hence is a point that John certainly wishes to underline."[49] This opening language in Revelation regarding the Father as the source or locus of divine life already reminds us of the pro-Nicene discussions about his place in the *taxis* and the questions raised about his relationship to the Son. As we will see here and in the next chapter, keeping these tools in mind helps us avoid a potential tendency to subordinate the Son based off the opening lines of Revelation.

That phrase in 1:4a, "was and is and is to come" (ὁ ὢν καὶ ὁ ἦν καὶ ὁ ἐρχόμενος), is found nowhere in the OT or any known early Christian traditions and has caused interpreters of the passage to ponder its use by John in

---

[46]Ἀποκάλυψις Ἰησοῦ Χριστοῦ ἣν ἔδωκεν αὐτῷ ὁ θεὸς δεῖξαι τοῖς δούλοις αὐτοῦ ἃ δεῖ γενέσθαι ἐν τάχει.

[47]David E. Aune, *Revelation 1-5*, WBC 52a (Nashville: Thomas Nelson, 1997), 12. The translation of the genitive into either "of Jesus Christ" or "about Jesus Christ" can be disputed—is this revelation *from* Jesus Christ (the source) or *about* Jesus Christ (the content)? In either scenario—though there is no need for a false dichotomy in the first place—God is the one who gives the revelation. Debating whether God sent the revelation as a co-signer with Jesus or sent a revelation that is centered on Jesus is tangential to our present point.

[48]John Christopher Thomas and Frank D. Macchia, *Revelation*, THNTC (Grand Rapids, MI: Eerdmans, 2016), 406.

[49]Craig S. Keener, *Revelation*, NIVAC (Grand Rapids, MI: Zondervan, 2000), 69; emphasis added. He also notes, as we will discuss in subsequent chapters, that Jesus and the seven spirits' inclusion in this introductory blessing also highlights their importance for the rest of the book.

particular.⁵⁰ Some have argued that John uses this phrase as a polemic against the worship of Aion, thought to be the god who guaranteed Roman rule. Aion's inscription appeared on plates in Aphrodisias near Laodicea—where John or his audience could have encountered them—and read, "I am all that has been and is and will be; and no mortal has lifted my mantle."⁵¹ Others have argued that given John's extensive use of the OT, this phrase is perhaps best understood as a threefold development of Exodus 3:14's phrase "I am who I am" within the Jewish tradition.⁵² If we do not deny that there is a level of anti-imperialism throughout the letter, with a regular and primary emphasis on utilizing OT allusions and themes, it is plausible that John viewed this phrase as the perfect combination of the two purposes and traditions. As Sean McDonough concludes, "Thus while John is obviously indebted to his Jewish heritage for this designation of God, we cannot exclude the possibility that he employed the tradition in a polemical fashion."⁵³

Beale calls the grammatical construction of Revelation 1:4a "the first and most famous solecism [or grammatical error] of the Apocalypse."⁵⁴ Moreover, George Ladd has stated that this phrase is "impossible to translate into idiomatic, equivalent English."⁵⁵ Perhaps more importantly, the Greek construction is awkward as well. Kendall Soulen explains that John purposely uses the nominative case and a "single indeclinable noun" in the words "he who" (ὁ ὤν)—"a grammatical 'error' of the most egregious kind"—to allude to the Tetragrammaton.⁵⁶ We must note repeatedly that John regularly

---

⁵⁰Sean McDonough presents a helpful study of the Jewish and Hellenistic background for this phrase, as well as various options for its employment in Revelation in Sean M. McDonough, *YHWH at Patmos: Rev. 1:4 in Its Hellenistic and Jewish Setting* (Eugene, OR: Wipf & Stock, 2011).

⁵¹McDonough, *YHWH at Patmos*, 54-55, 195-202. Aion could have been viewed also as a cosmic ruler, which would have been a direct affront to John's view of God as Creator (Rev 4:11).

⁵²G. K. Beale, *The Book of Revelation*, NIGTC (Grand Rapids, MI: Eerdmans, 1999), 187. See also Keener, *Revelation*, 69, and Peter Leithart, *Revelation 1–11*, The International Theological Commentary on the Holy Scripture of the Old and New Testaments (New York: T&T Clark, 2018), 87. The LXX is a close parallel.

⁵³McDonough, *YHWH at Patmos*, 202.

⁵⁴G. K. Beale, *John's Use of the Old Testament in Revelation* (Sheffield, UK: Sheffield Academic Press, 1998), 324.

⁵⁵George Eldon Ladd, *A Commentary on the Revelation of John* (Grand Rapids, MI: Eerdmans, 1972), 24.

⁵⁶R. Kendall Soulen, *The Divine Name(s) and the Holy Trinity*, 2 vols. (Louisville: Westminster John Knox, 2011), 1:179. Soulen asserts that this rendering in the LXX would read like a Hebrew proper name to the audience. See also R. H. Charles, *A Critical and Exegetical Commentary on the Revelation of St. John*, vol. 1 (Edinburgh: T&T Clark, 1920), 10, who states that John did this

draws on everything from other texts to grammatical nuance to make theological points, so it would be a stretch to assume that he made such a mistake carelessly, especially in the doxological salutation of a book focused on true and false worship. In fact, John's ability to use correct grammar is readily apparent, as Smalley points out: "That the writer is not ignorant of the Greek language is apparent from the fact that the second ἀπὸ (*apo*) in this verse *is* followed by a genitive plural."[57] Indeed, John uses the genitive correctly twice in this same greeting (Rev 1:4-5).

Allen Callahan is also more cautious than Soulen: "The crudest *koine* Greek speaker would no doubt balk at the prepositional phrase of ἀπό followed by the nominative case in Revelation 1:4. James Montgomery . . . suggested that this phrase 'as it were lifts the Absolute One above grammatical government.' [But] it is important to note that it does not mark the language of the work as a whole."[58]

Callahan agrees with our position that John does not break grammatical rules often or randomly. In fact, he admits that "the seer clearly knows how to follow the rules of the language game when he wants to."[59] However, Callahan indebts this grammatical rule breaking to "some principle yet to be discovered," mainly because there appears to be no LXX precedent for John's choice of words.[60] He is right in noting that these peculiarities are not a result of poor copying of the Hebrew text or inattention to Greek grammar and syntax, but he disregards any hint of theological intentionality on the part of John. However, his assumption that John is not making a theological point unnecessarily flattens out Revelation, which is clearly an interpretation of a divine visionary encounter. John's "poor" grammar is in fact a

---

purposefully. This had led Isbon T. Beckwith, *The Apocalypse of John* (New York: Macmillan, 1919), 424, to say that this construction highlights the majesty, sovereignty, and immutability of God.

[57]Stephen S. Smalley, *The Revelation to John* (Downers Grove, IL: IVP Academic, 2005), 32; emphasis original.

[58]Allen Dwight Callahan, "The Language of the Apocalypse," *HTR* 88, no. 4 (1995): 456.

[59]Callahan, "Language of the Apocalypse," 456-57.

[60]Callahan, "Language of the Apocalypse," 456. Callahan's broader proposal is that John's use of the Septuagint and his "established Greek" vocabulary play a role in his grammatical irregularities, citing LXX precedents and arguing that "any Greek speaker familiar with the Septuagint would have encountered" many of these tendencies. However, Callahan seems most uncertain about this particular phrase because there appears to be no LXX precedent, thus his claim of "some principle yet to be discovered." Alternatively, Michael B. Shepherd, "Daniel 7:13 and the New Testament Son of Man," *WTJ* 68 (2006): 111n49, notes that rather than incorrect grammar based on the expectation of a genitive, the nominative "works quite well as an indication of a quote from the LXX of Exodus 3:14."

vehicle for his theology.[61] Put simply: John appears to choose the title and grammatical construction intentionally; he knows the rules, and he knows how to break them. In that sense, it is not quite right to call this construction an "error."

On the other hand, Beale has called the appeal to the indeclinable noun an "unnecessary" move because "if such is the case, the same kind of grammatical irregularity has the same significance for the Devil's name in 20:2!"[62] Instead, Beale sees the nominative case as reason enough to affirm the Exodus 3:14 reference. We should note in any event that John could use the same grammatical irregularities elsewhere without equating the identities or characteristics of persons or beings. For example, later we will see potential grammatical and analogical parallels between Jesus and angels that do not necessarily amount to either equality or conflation. Further, John compares and contrasts God and evil using similar phrasing in other places, such as Revelation 17:8. The phrase there, "The beast you saw was and is not" (τὸ θηρίον ὃ εἶδες ἦν καὶ οὐκ ἔστιν), in effect creates an anti-Tetragrammaton against Satan, Rome, or whoever embodies the evils that John speaks against.[63]

We can look to Irenaeus for a helpful take on this. In remarks about the Antichrist, Irenaeus employs Revelation 17:8 in the midst of his discussion on the number 666, wherein he seems to take note of an anti-triadic shape in this passage, stating that the Spirit's denial of the Antichrist brings forth John's phrase, "*He was, and is not, and is* about to ascend from the abyss and go to destruction" mirroring Revelation 1:4, 8; 4:8.[64] In the last days, Irenaeus says, the name of the Antichrist "is suppressed, because it is not worthy of being proclaimed by the Holy Spirit," which acts as condemnation of the Antichrist, who will be thrown into the lake of fire by Jesus when he comes "from heaven in the clouds, in the glory of the Father." For Irenaeus, there again appears to be a triadic shape to salvation and judgment—one

---

[61]Or, Ben Witherington III, *Revelation* (Cambridge: Cambridge University Press, 2003), 75; in this passage, "we find both bad grammar and good theology."
[62]Beale, *John's Use of the Old Testament in Revelation*, 326.
[63]Robyn J. Whitaker, *Ekphrasis, Vision, and Persuasion in the Book of Revelation*, WUNT 2, no. 410 (Tübingen: Mohr Siebeck, 2015), 200, also calls this triadic title "yet another example of evil parodying both God and the Lamb."
[64]*Haer.* 5.30.4.

represents a divine prerogative and the other a satanic one. In any event, this language highlights the radical difference between God's character and Satan's character—not to equate them in any way but rather to make a deliberate theological point.[65]

John seems highly deliberate at every turn and thus can use grammar in the same ways to make different theological points, so we should not overlook this solecism and its clear allusion to Exodus 3:14. This means that the reader should take each passage in its theological and argumentative context rather than placing a blanket rule over each instance of the same irregularity across the entire book. Beale ultimately affirms that John is not mistaken in his grammatical construction and intends for his audience to reflect on Exodus 3:14.[66] Though we can affirm that Soulen's argument is slightly more convincing than Beale's, both of them collectively demonstrate that Callahan is mistaken in his assumption that John's solecism is unexplainable.

It is also apparent that this eternal God, at work in the past through the exodus ("who was"), is and will continue to deliver his people ("who is" and "who is coming") even though he is allowing their current suffering.[67] In Revelation 1:8 the phrases "the Alpha and the Omega" and "the Almighty," joined with the same three-pronged "is/was/is coming," reiterates John's elevation of God's sovereignty over history.[68] And since he "is coming," he is reminding his people that from the exodus to the last day he is involved in his creation and is sovereignly moving history toward final, eternal fulfillment.[69] This expression is similar to "the First and the Last," which carries with it a reminder of YHWH's self-identification in Isaiah 41:4, 44:6, and 48:12.[70] For John, the God of creation and history is the source of

---

[65] Leithart, *Revelation 12-22*, 190, notes that the beast may also have a fourfold description ("he was, is, comes, and goes"), but, "Even without knowing *where* he goes, we know he is no real rival to the Triune God, for the Triune God is, was, comes, and *never* departs;" emphasis original.

[66] Beale, *John's Use of the Old Testament in Revelation*, 327.

[67] Grant R. Osborne, *Revelation* (Grand Rapids, MI: Baker Academic, 2002), 60.

[68] As Resseguie notes: "The third title, 'the Almighty,' is an expression of God's absolute control over this world and the world to come, and occurs nine times in Revelation out of ten times in the New Testament . . . God alone is 'the Almighty,' the omnipotent one who is the origin and goal of creation." James L. Resseguie, *The Revelation of John* (Grand Rapids, MI: Baker Academic, 2009), 69.

[69] Richard Bauckham, *The Theology of the Book of Revelation* (Cambridge: Cambridge University Press, 1993), 30.

[70] G. K. Beale and Sean M. McDonough, "Revelation," in *Commentary on the New Testament Use of the Old Testament*, ed. G. K. Beale and D. A. Carson (Grand Rapids, MI: Baker Academic, 2007), 1091. See also a more detailed study in McDonough, *YHWH at Patmos*, 217-20.

divine redemption and vindication. This eternal, immutable, perfect God will not abandon his people because he never has before and has promised to never do so.

According to Jesus in his message to the churches, the Father is also the owner of paradise (2:7) and new Jerusalem (3:12), as the possessive genitive τοῦ Θεοῦ in both passages indicates. "Paradise," which some speculate is a Persian term that was carried over into Jewish religious use, represents Edenic paradise that will become part of the new earth in the eschaton (22:1-5).[71] "New Jerusalem" will also become part of the new earth (καταβαίνουσαν ἐκ τοῦ οὐρανοῦ ἀπὸ τοῦ Θεοῦ) according to 21:2, specifying that it belongs to God and is coming from where God is. Notably, this description of God dwelling among his people in a new temple differs from a similar scene in 1 Enoch, in which Enoch finds out that God will remain in his temple high above the New Jerusalem (90:28-36). The Father in Revelation, however, exercises a sovereign but intimate rule over the re-creation of the earth, bringing all things on heaven and earth together under his throne (21:5).

These descriptions indicate an overwhelming sense of God's transcendent and supernatural authority over heaven and history. God holds a sort of positional authority, though that does not automatically require essential subordination of Jesus or the Spirit. Instead, their relationship must be understood in light of the Father-Son relationship where the attributes, authority, and ultimately the Father, Son, and Spirit are of the same nature.

For example, the καί ἀπό ("and from") construction in John's introduction, καὶ ἀπὸ τῶν ἑπτὰ πνευμάτων ἃ ἐνώπιον τοῦ θρόνου αὐτοῦ καὶ ἀπὸ Ἰησοῦ Χριστοῦ ("and from the seven spirits before his throne and from Jesus Christ"), helps make this clear. Of course, a salutation featuring God the Father and Jesus is not unprecedented in the NT (e.g., Rom 1:7; 1 Cor 1:3; 2 Cor 1:2; Gal 1:3; Eph 1:2; 2 Pet 2). However, lest we exaggerate the Father's "authority" as the one who sends the revelation, we must also consider that these salutations represent a "form of considerable theological significance" that "places Jesus Christ with God on the divine side of the distinction between the divine Giver of blessings and the creaturely recipients of blessings" and "shows how naturally early Christians implicitly included Jesus in the

---

[71]Osborne, *Revelation*, 124.

divine."[72] John appears to be picking up on this tradition, yet his greeting also adds "the seven spirits," an innovative element of including the Spirit in a type of greeting that often only included the Father and Jesus. The role of Jesus and the identity of the spirits will be discussed later, but we can conclude that John's salutation is in line with earlier and contemporary extrabiblical Christian texts that were clearly developing into an incipient trinitarian discourse.[73] This form clearly separates out God, Jesus, and the "seven spirits" from the recipients of the blessings and then is followed up with differentiating missions or activities for each person.

John's grammar in the salutation and the theological pressures he creates for the reader indicate that John self-consciously writes this phrase in this way, which lends itself toward describing God the Father as a distinct person while also tying Jesus and the Spirit to his nature through their worthiness to be included in a doxology or benediction.[74] Moreover, this "Almighty" language is resonant with later patristic conceptions of the Father, as noted above, and we will also see the same designations of "First and Last/Alpha and Omega" applied to Jesus later. We must conclude, then, that he is both elevating the Father in a specific economic mission as a "source" for the economic activity, while revealing Jesus and the Spirit as divine persons acting not merely *on behalf of* the Father in some subordinated role, but inseparably acting because they are of the same nature as the Father.

The throne room (Rev 4:1-11). We will now focus on Revelation 4:1-11, a turning point in the visionary narrative of Revelation. This moment is central to John's Apocalypse, and thus this book cannot avoid interacting with the throne-room scene in each chapter due to its importance for John's trinitarianism. As Scott Swain has noted:

---

[72]Bauckham, *Theology of the Book of Revelation*, 23-24.
[73]See, for example, Ignatius's formulas in Ign. *Eph.*; Ign. *Magn.*; Ign. *Trall.*; Ign. *Rom.*; Ign. *Phil.*; Ign. *Smyrn.*; Ign. *Poly.* A similar Father-Son dynamic is also present in The Epistle to Diognetus. This epistle opens by drawing a strict line between God and the Greek gods and "the superstition of the Jews" (Diogn. 1), which is especially interesting given that Diognetus literally means "son of Zeus" (Διόγνητε). Later, the author lays out an encompassing vision of God as the "omnipotent Creator" who at the same time sent Jesus "as a king sends his son," describing Jesus as being sent "as God [and] as a human to humans" (Diogn. 7).
[74]As Bauckham, *Theology of the Book of Revelation*, 25, rightly notes, "John has no vocabulary equivalent to later trinitarian talk of the divine nature which three divine persons share. But it is impossible for us to do justice to what he does say without speaking somehow of a divine reality in which Jesus Christ and the Holy Spirit (here symbolized by 'the seven Spirits') are included."

Revelation 4-5 presents its teaching on the Trinity in a manner with which we are less likely to be familiar. It does not use the standard terminology of "Father" and "Son" and "Holy Spirit" to identify the three persons of the Trinity. It does not say, "Jesus is Lord." Instead, it presents its teaching on the Trinity in the highly figurative language of apocalyptic literature: there is the throne, there is the Lamb, there are the seven Spirits of God. But it is precisely this factor that makes Revelation 4-5 so instructive regarding the character of the Bible's primary trinitarian discourse. Sometimes, we are lulled into thinking that we understand all too well what the Bible's trinitarian language means. Revelation 4-5 does not allow this. It awakens us from the slumbers of our familiar miscomprehension of biblical language and forces us to pay attention more closely to the actual shape of the Bible's trinitarian discourse.[75]

Further, not only is this scene central to Revelation, but it is also rather distinct among other Jewish and Christian apocalyptic literature.

For example, the author of 1 Enoch presents the most striking resemblance to Revelation's depictions of God's throne. This glorious throne (መንበር) is mentioned nearly thirty times in Enoch's Watchers, describing it in elemental terms (fire, ice, flashes of lightning, shining sun) and as surrounded by angels and other creatures (14:12-20), along with precious stones included in its decorum (18:9-10). The throne is also mentioned briefly in 4 Ezra 8:21-22 and 2 Baruch 21:6, wherein the throne is more generally described as preeminently glorious and from which God exudes unmitigated power. Similar imagery is also picked up in *Ma'aseh Merkabah* (מעשה מרכבה), a major text within the Merkabah mysticism and Hekhalot literature.[76] The fifth prayer reads in part, "May Your name be blessed forever and ever and Your kingdom for eternity. Your dwelling-place is forever and Your Throne is for all generations. Your eminence is in heaven and earth and Your dominion over those above and below."[77] All of these

---

[75] Scott R. Swain, "'To Him Who Sits on the Throne and to the Lamb': Hymning God's Triune Name in Revelation 4-5," *RFP* 4, no. 2 (2019): 5-6.
[76] David E. Aune, *Apocalypticism, Prophecy, and Magic in Early Christianity: Collected Essays* (Grand Rapids, MI: Baker Academic, 2008), 57, notes: "In spite of differences in emphasis (apocalypses tend to focus more on eschatological and cosmological themes, while Merkavah literature focuses on the mysteries of heaven and the throne of God), there is tentative agreement [among scholars] that Merkavah mysticism emerged from Jewish apocalypticism."
[77] English translation from Michael D. Swartz, *Mystical Prayer in Ancient Judaism: An Analysis of Ma'aseh Merkabah,"* Texts and Studies in Ancient Judaism 28 (Tübingen: Mohr Siebeck, 1992).

images are undoubtedly rooted in their own Jewish foundations, with ample images of God's throne from which to draw (Ex 24:9-11; 2 Chron 18:18; Is 6:1-4; Ezek 1). While God's transcendence is on clear display in these visions, it is notable that the seers are granted access to the throne room and are given instructions to relay the message to others. Further, John repeatedly uses the title "Almighty" (ὁ παντοκράτωρ) when describing God and describes his throne room in similarly lucid ways. The invocation of this title shows his affinity for his Jewish heritage, in which "God Almighty" (צבאות) was an important title and name for YHWH.[78] However, John's description is distinct in various ways, primarily its focus gradually centering on the Lamb—a figure unknown in other literature.[79]

When the vision begins, one first notices the imagery of walking through an open door into the divine realm, which reflects a common cultic motif in Hellenistic and Roman divine epiphanies, especially in John's setting of Asia Minor.[80] The introduction to this portion of the revelation shows John "invited into heaven [which] enables him to see from a heavenly perspective . . . in which God rules justly and his sovereignty is acknowledged by his creatures" and is "the starting point of the whole process of judgement and salvation by which God's sovereignty is explicitly restored on earth (the appearance of the Lamb in Rev. 5)."[81] This portion of the vision is a shift in perspective from earth to heaven, placing "the past, present, and future in the context of God's overall plan for history, making sense of what happens on earth because earthly events are seen from an above point of view."[82] The passive perfect participle ἠνεῳγμένη leads us to assume that God himself opened the door and initiated John's entrance into the heavenly realm.[83]

Many interpreters have seen this portion of Revelation as a type of heavenly liturgy performed in God's heavenly abode, in which God the

---

[78]In the LXX, παντοκράτωρ is often a rendering for צבאות.
[79]Aune, *Apocalypticism, Prophecy, and Magic in Early Christianity*, 128-31. See also David A. deSilva, "The Testament of Levi and Revelation 4:1-11," in *Reading Revelation in Context: John's Apocalypse and Second Temple Judaism*, ed. Ben C. Blackwell, John K. Goodrich, and Jason Maston (Grand Rapids, MI: Zondervan Academic, 2019), 52-58.
[80]Whitaker, *Ekphrasis*, 106. See also Wilfred J. Harrington, *Revelation*, SP 16 (Collegeville, MN: Liturgical, 1993), 78.
[81]Michael Gilbertson, *God and History in the Book of Revelation* (Cambridge: Cambridge University Press, 2003), 83.
[82]Resseguie, *Revelation*, 106.
[83]Smalley, *Revelation to John*, 113.

Creator is worshiped and celebrated for guiding Israel's salvation history and providing the deliverance through the Passover lamb.[84] As Michael Gorman concludes, "[John] appears unable to maintain pure epistolary form as he quickly ascends into the sphere of worship, composing (or perhaps reciting) first a doxology (1:5b-6), then an acclamation (1:7), and then a divine self-identification (1:8) that foreshadows the heavenly worship of God in chapter 4. It is no ordinary letter; it is a liturgical letter."[85]

While acknowledging that some elements of paschal liturgy envelope Revelation 4–5, Beale has noted that this theory does not take into account fully the clear allusions to Daniel and Ezekiel.[86] Revelation 4:2-3, for example, appears to have a background in OT throne room theophanies,[87] most notably Ezekiel 1 and Daniel 7,[88] Isaiah 6,[89] as well as other apocalyptic works like 1 Enoch.[90] However, as Robyn Whitaker points out, John has altered the OT prophetic tradition found in the throne-room scenes of Ezekiel, Enoch, and Isaiah.[91] In particular, Whitaker notes that John has omitted anthropomorphic descriptions such as robes, feet, face, and eyes: "It is not a didactic illustration of what God (or heaven) looks like, but rather a description of God's attributes and character as the enthroned one."[92] The invitation by God to "come up here" in 4:1 also brings to mind God's call to

---

[84] See for example Pierre Prigent, *Apocalypse et Liturgie* (Neuchâtel: Delachaux et Niestlé, 1964), 46-79; and Massey H. Shepherd Jr., *The Paschal Liturgy and the Apocalypse* (Richmond, VA: John Knox, 1960), 77-91. While Robert A. Briggs, *Jewish Temple Imagery in the Book of Revelation* (New York: Peter Lang, 1999), 54, argues that the temple "is almost certainly an altogether visionary one with no connection to any 'real' sanctuary on earth or to one in heaven," this undermines the following chapters in which judgment reigns from heaven down to earth, as well as Revelation's conclusion in which this very temple appears to come down to earth physically to join the physically and bodily resurrected saints.

[85] Michael J. Gorman, *Reading Revelation Responsibly: Uncivil Worship and Witness: Following the Lamb into the New Creation* (Eugene, OR: Cascade, 2011), 26.

[86] Beale, *Book of Revelation*, 313.

[87] As Aune deftly notes in *Revelation 1-5*, 284: "The throne of God, a symbol of sovereignty, is the central feature of the OT, Jewish, and early Christian conceptions of heaven, and is modeled after the throne rooms of earthly kings."

[88] Beale, *Book of Revelation*, 319-20.

[89] Thomas and Macchia, *Revelation*, 136-37.

[90] Keener, *Revelation*, 169. He notes in particular that the use of Daniel became "characteristic" of early apocalyptic visions. Harrington, *Revelation*, 78, also mentions Ezek 1:1 and 1 En. 14:15.

[91] Whitaker, *Ekphrasis*, 107-8.

[92] Whitaker, *Ekphrasis*, 109-10. See also Harrington, *Revelation*, 81; and Smalley, *Revelation to John*, 115.

Moses to receive his revelation (Ex 19:20) in the first type of throne-room vision of the OT (Ex 19:24; 24:10-12).[93]

Further, John's reference to precious jewels here and in Revelation 21 illustrates the splendor and glory of God,[94] a relatively unique image among early Jewish apocalypses outside of Ezekiel 1,[95] though we noted above this similarity with 1 Enoch. In conjunction with these allusions, θρόνος (throne) is used seventeen times in Revelation 4–5 and is "the center of [John's] heavenly cosmology," which emphasizes that God's "hand superintends everything for [God's suffering people's] good and his glory . . . demonstrated by the fact that all the judgments in chs. 6-16 issue from God's throne."[96] Ricardo Foulkes reflects on this connection well, further highlighting that while John joins the other prophets in visiting the throne, "this vision surpasses the creativity of its predecessors' descriptions."[97] Indeed, John's vision is more extended and vivid than that of the OT prophets and includes in clearer detail the work of Christ and the Spirit. However, while the Lamb later appears at the throne working in similar ways (as we will see), John first describes a vision of the throne with God the Father being praised as the creator, initiator, and sustainer of salvation history.[98] McDonough helpfully asserts that the pairing of the repeated Tetagrammaton ὁ ἦν καὶ ὁ ὢν καὶ ὁ ἐρχόμενος (4:8) and ἦσαν καὶ ἐκτίσθησαν (4:11, "they were and were created") is a poetic device meant to reiterate and heighten the view of God's unmatched glory.[99]

On a distinct but related note, Elisabeth Fiorenza argues that for this section, the "central image is political" because it begins a cycle of passages highlighting God's throne and the lordship of God and the victorious Christ:

---

[93]Keener, *Revelation*, 170.
[94]Smalley, *Revelation to John*, 115, concludes that "the stones in 4:3 anticipate the fuller list of precious stones in Rev. 21.11, 18-21, where the glory of God is revealed throughout the new creation, and not only in heaven."
[95]Aune, *Revelation 1-5*, 285. See also Keener, *Revelation*, 171.
[96]Beale, *Book of Revelation*, 320.
[97]Ricardo Foulkes, *El Apocalipsis de San Juan* (Buenos Aires: Nueva Creación, 1989), 54. My translation of "esta visión sobrepasa en creatividad las descripciones de todos sus predecesores."
[98]As Laszlo Gallusz asserts, "The worshipping of the figure and the reference to his title, κύριος ὁ θεὸς ὁ παντοκράτωρ ('Lord God Almighty'), unmistakably identify him as the Father God"; see Laszlo Gallusz, *The Throne Motif in the Book of Revelation*, LNTS 487 (London: Bloomsbury, 2014), 104.
[99]McDonough, *YHWH at Patmos*, 212-13.

The central figure of the whole vision is clearly God enthroned in great splendor and surrounded by a court of angelic principalities and powers. Just as the Roman emperor was depicted as surrounded by his friends and advisors when dispensing justice, so is God seen here in the role of judge. Just as the Roman emperor surrounded by the court was depicted as holding a *libellus*, a petition or letter in the form of an open scroll, so God is seen as holding a *biblion*, a scroll with seven seals.[100]

Fiorenza's anti-imperial angle is worth considering. In Greco-Roman contexts, the throne-room scene of Revelation 4–5 compares to the structure and activity of the imperial courts, with God and Christ perhaps serving as a parody of Satan and Caesar.[101] Recounting Alexander the Great's conquest of Persia, Alexándrou Anábasis reports that his embassies were themselves crowned while also bestowing golden crowns on Alexander "as if they had come on a sacred embassy to honour some god."[102] As Aune notes, Roman historian Herodian tells a similar story about the emperor Maximus, who received golden crowns from his white-robed delegates as dedications.[103] Though the twenty-four elders in Revelation do not offer their crowns to God and Christ, the resemblance between these accounts is noticeable, especially considering that there is no Jewish parallel. Moreover, the hymnic worship offered to God and Christ certainly has parallels in Jewish literature—one thinks of language in places like Isaiah 6:3 or Psalm 18:3—but some Roman emperors such as Gaius Caligula and Nero were not shy about receiving deity-level prayers and hymns. Most notably, according to Aune, "the importance of the consensus omnium as a constitutional basis for imperial legitimacy was strongly emphasized during the period following the fall of Nero."[104] When comparing this to Revelation, we may surmise that

---

[100] Elisabeth Schüssler Fiorenza, *Revelation* (Minneapolis: Fortress, 1991), 59. Harrington, *Revelation*, 79, concurs: "'Throne' is a political term, implying political polemic: a claim as to who *really* rules" (emphasis original). Gorman, *Reading Revelation Responsibly*, 40-48, makes a similar point about Revelation as a whole, stating that John intends to challenge the "God and country" imperial cult or civil religion of the Roman Empire.

[101] Aune, *Apocalypticism, Prophecy, and Magic in Early Christianity*, 99-100.

[102] *Anab.* 7.23, as quoted in Aune, *Apocalypticism, Prophecy, and Magic*, 107.

[103] Aune, *Apocalypticism, Prophecy, and Magic*, 107-13.

[104] Aune, *Apocalypticism, Prophecy, and Magic*, 114; cf. Klaus Oehler, "Der Consensus als Kriterium der Wahrheit in der antiken Philosphie und der Patristic," *Antike und Abenland* 10 (1961): 103-17, who notes especially Caesar Augustus's appeal to his authority due to the consensus acknowledgement by his subjects.

John uses these imperial cultic practices as a foil to describe the throne room in heaven as a consensus of beings recognizing God and Christ as the true divine sovereigns.

Thrones are certainly political symbols, so even if John were not attempting to critique Caesar, the implications would be unavoidable if one talks about an enthroned deity, which is a common picture of God and his rule. Nonetheless, it is highly doubtful that John was unaware of this cultural connection. As Wright stresses, "A throne room, surrounded by senior counsellors, would instantly remind John's readers of a very different court: that of Caesar."[105] It is likely, then, that John is highlighting the sovereignty of God as a polemic that both continues the Jewish tradition about YHWH and also challenges Roman royal imagery of a throne encircled by worshiping subordinates.[106]

Bauckham seconds this argument, noting that the whole scene combines cultic and political imagery; cultic in its rich OT allusions to the divine throne room and political in its explicit assertion that God governs the world from his throne, which poses an affront to Rome's "pretended divine sovereignty."[107] It is God, then, who initiates judgment, not Caesar. John is simply reminding his audience of the truth they already are conditioned to believe—that YHWH is the creator and supreme ruler of the universe, the true King of kings.[108] As Moisés Mayordomo notes, "God's absolute rule is concentrated in Heaven; here—and not Rome—is the 'administrative' point of order of world affairs."[109] Further, Leithart thinks this passage also carries with it overtones of Daniel 2:

---

[105] N. T. Wright, *Revelation for Everyone* (Louisville: Westminster John Knox, 2011), 45.
[106] Fiorenza, *Revelation*, 58.
[107] Bauckham, *Theology of Revelation*, 33-35.
[108] As Bauckham, *Theology of Revelation*, 47-48, asserts, "This is the understanding of God as Creator which was characteristic of Judaism and which early Christianity shared without question."
[109] Moisés Mayordomo, "Gewalt in der Johannesoffenbarung als theologisches Problem," in *Die Offenbarung des Joannes: Kommunikation im Konflikt*, ed. Thomas Schmeller, Martin Ebner, and Rudolf Hoppe (Freiburg im Breisgau: Herder, 2013), 132. My translation of "Im Himmel konzentriert sich Gottes absolute Herrschaft; hier—und nicht Rom—ist der alles 'verwaltende' Ordnungspunkt des Weltgeschehens." Mayordomo compares God in Revelation to the "politically perfect Hobbesian Leviathan" ("in politischer Hinsicht der vollkommene Hobb'sche Leviathan"), a reference to the classic book *Leviathan* by Thomas Hobbes (1651) in which Leviathan represents a perfect, peace-bringing, sovereign government. Further, this note is illustrative of the point but does not contend that Hobbes's theology is stridently pro-Nicene in form.

According to Daniel, "God has shown King Nebuchadnezzar what must take place in the last days." The crucial difference is the time reference. Daniel predicts the distant future; John sees and hears things that will happen "soon." What was sealed in the time of Daniel is unsealed for John. . . . Daniel interprets a dream about the latter days that end with the collapse of the imperial statue; John receives a vision about the same realities, but with the assurance that his catastrophe is *imminent*. The entire world system is about to collapse.[110]

Those around the throne are composed of two groups: the twenty-four elders and the four creatures or beasts. John noticeably separates the elders from the creatures rather than saying something generic such as, "There were all sorts of beings around the throne." Though digging into the backgrounds and imagery for the elders is beyond the scope of this book, the elders were likely humans—whether individual heavenly saints or representative of all of God's elect,[111] or perhaps representative of the twenty-four courses of priests in the OT (1 Chron 24:4).[112] However, the point for our purposes is that those around the throne are made up of all types of worshipers from the various "species" of God's creatures who are subject to the enthroned God and his Christ.

A more symbolic angle to the creatures or beasts is possible. For example, Irenaeus viewed the four living creatures or beasts in 4:6-8 as a fourfold christological fulfillment of the OT. In *Against Heresies*, Revelation first appears as Irenaeus explains the church's foundation on the fourfold Gospel of Matthew, Mark, Luke, and John.[113] These four "columns" stand on the unifying ground of the Holy Spirit. He goes on to explain the importance of the number four, highlighting its significance in the "four regions of the world" and then turning to the four-faced cherubim at God's throne (Ps 80; Ezek 1; 10), which he parallels with the four living creatures in Revelation 4:7. John the seer synchronizes these passages by saying that the faces of these creatures represent something about the dispensation of the Son of God as he fulfills various aspects of the OT through the four Gospels. Irenaeus concludes that the fourth creature (the eagle) is "the gift of the Spirit flying

---

[110]Leithart, *Revelation 1-11*, 71, emphasis original.
[111]Witherington, *Revelation*, 117.
[112]Keener, *Revelation*, 171-72.
[113]*Haer.* 3.11.8. Unless otherwise noted, English translations are from Robert M. Grant, *Irenaeus of Lyons* (New York: Routledge, 1997).

upon the church." He ties together all of this by claiming that Revelation's description alludes to Christ's "glorious generation from the Father" as described in John 1:1. In sum, Revelation 4:7 illustrates for Irenaeus how the church rests on the multifaceted power of Christ and the Spirit, who join the church to the Father. Commenting on Irenaeus's "inventive interpretation" of this passage, Christopher Hall notes that Irenaeus pulls from the Gospels a view of Christ that includes descriptions of his holiness, divinity, and revelation of the Father.[114] While we may not follow Irenaeus down this particular interpretive path, it is illustrative for our purposes to see multiple ways theologians have noticed and attempted to make sense of the trinitarian dynamic in Revelation.

Another proposal is that these living creatures might represent the cherubim at the throne or ark of the covenant in the tabernacle.[115] It is also possible that the living creatures are associated with God's judgment doled out in Revelation 6 and 15.[116] John's allusions to OT throne scenes and Roman royal traditions indicate that these beings are intended to be seen as actual individuals or groups of people or creatures who surround God's throne, placing him on the receiving end of all worship. As John R. Gilhooly rightly reminds us, the throne-room scene does not merely depict "choirs of angels singing anthems to God" but rather "they are properly understood as confessions of praise to God."[117]

Regardless of one's nuanced interpretation of the scene, John's vision shows significant commotion traveling to and from God's throne, which can only indicate how pervasive his power and activities truly are. As James Resseguie points out, "John prefers expansive titles to describe God's infinite nature [in order to] heighten the fullness of God's character. John's favorite description appears to be 'the one seated on the throne,' focusing the reader's

---

[114]Christopher A. Hall, *Learning Theology with the Church Fathers* (Downers Grove, IL: IVP Academic, 2002), 209-10.

[115]J. Massyngberde Ford, *Revelation*, AB 38 (Garden City, NY: Doubleday, 1975), 74-75. Ford notes that John does an "impressive thing" in translating *zōa* as the plural of *zoon hayyōt* and eliminating terms like cherubim, seraphim, watchers, or angels, "only [presenting] to us spirits and living forces."

[116]Smalley, *Revelation to John*, 121.

[117]John R. Gilhooly, *40 Questions About Angels, Demons, and Spiritual Warfare* (Grand Rapids, MI: Kregel Academic, 2018), 39. Gilhooly bases this on the fact that throne-room scenes like Isaiah 6:3 and Revelation 4–5 do not use the Hebrew or Greek verbs for "to sing."

attention on who rules this world in contrast to counterfeit rulers that claim sovereignty."[118]

It is notable that before the exaltation and worship of Jesus in Revelation 5, we see the Father receiving praise somewhat independently as the source of divine activity. The Father as the source of divine activity resembles later creedal language, and this will become more apparent in the next chapter, when we discuss further the Son's sharing God's throne and receiving worship alongside him. For now, we will consider one final passage that highlights the relationship between the Father and Jesus.

Sharing his kingdom (Rev 11:15-19). This passage begins with a phrase seemingly derived from Psalm 2:2 ("the Lord and his anointed"), commonly viewed as a messianic prophecy in the early church.[119] It is peculiar, however, because it is unclear as to whether "our Lord" (κυρίου ἡμῶν) or "his Christ/Messiah" (χριστοῦ αὐτοῦ) is the one who "owns" the kingdom and will reign forever and ever.[120] The genitive case introduces the primary issue, indicating that perhaps Jesus belongs to God in some sort of ontological or functional hierarchy. Here I will show that the treatment of the genitive in much of modern scholarship ignores a larger picture of John's presentation of the relation between the Father and Son in Revelation, a presentation more fairly captured by employing pro-Nicene tools.

There are several possible ways of dealing with this issue. On the one hand, this passage could mean that the kingdom and reigning could be God's, with Jesus as a sort of subordinate agent. On the other hand, the singular form could be indicating God and Christ as an inseparable unity.[121] According to Beale, it could also be that "Christ gives up the historical phase of his rule and then assumes an eternal rule alongside but in subjection to his Father."[122]

While each case has its merits, perhaps there is not such a distinct dichotomy. As we will see in subsequent chapters, the throne does not belong

---

[118]Resseguie, *Revelation*, 107.
[119]Smalley, *Revelation to John*, 289, notes this usage of Ps 2:2 in Acts 4:26-28; Lk 2:26; and Odes Sol. 29:6.
[120]Beale, *Book of Revelation*, 611.
[121]Traugott Holtz, *Die Christologie der Apokalypse des Johannes* (Berlin: Akademie-Verlag, 1962), 202; cf. Beale, *Book of Revelation*, 611.
[122]Beale, *Book of Revelation*, 611.

solely to the Father but is shared by Jesus and arguably by the Spirit. That logic indicates that there is a shared rule and that Jesus holds a unique position as one able to sit on the throne with the Father, while all creatures in Revelation ultimately reside "around" or "before" the throne. This is not at odds with the parallel assumption that the processions and missions allow personal, relational, and economical distinctions between the Father and Jesus even as they are fully and truly God. It is not unreasonable to posit that Jesus is very much a divine nature with divine authority and power to create and judge (which have been alluded to elsewhere in Revelation, as we have already and will later note) while at the same time having the role in salvation history of being "slaughtered" and handing the kingdom over to the Father (cf. 1 Cor 15:24-28). The Father who sent the Son and the Son who died on the cross share authority over the kingdom; their distinctive acts in history are inseparable. The genitive χριστοῦ αὐτοῦ does not require subordination in nature or authority but rather can also describe their constitutive relationship to one another, because one is only a Father if he has a child (Son) and vice versa, and the biblical shape of salvation includes each of them (e.g., Mt 28:18-20; Jn 3:16; 5:17; 6:38-44; 15:10). For a man to refer to his son as "his child" or "his helper" does not indicate that the son is subhuman, so it follows that "his Christ" also does not require an ontological subjection. A common non-Nicene mistake was to conflate order and power; the pro-Nicene theologians would parse this distinction through discussions of eternal generation, divine simplicity, *taxis*, and acknowledging the limits of analogical language.

A further observation amplifies such a conclusion. Commentators have pointed out that in verse 17 the formula "was/is/is to come" is missing the final phrase, possibly because the "is to come" is now the present, now becoming the "is."[123] This passage concludes Revelation 11 and leads into Revelation 12, in which John begins to describe a war in heaven between Michael and Satan ("the dragon"). As Kovacs and Rowland note, "The war in heaven and Satan's ejection are both familiar themes in Jewish and Christian sources, as is the two-level drama, in which heavenly and earthly events are

---

[123]For example, Ford, *Revelation*, 172; M. Eugene Boring, *Revelation*, Interpretation (Louisville: Westminster John Knox, 1989), 148. As Witherington, *Revelation*, 160, puts it, "The end has arrived, and the coming has become a reality."

juxtaposed and closely related."[124] We can gather from the transition between Revelation 11 and 12 that John wants to highlight God's transcendent reign over both heaven and earth and that the earthly war between the church and Rome reflects the war taking place in heaven between God's army and Satan. Just as God's kingdom is at war in the unseen realms, this struggle also is manifested on earth. No longer is this battle a future expectation—it is playing itself out right before the audience's eyes, with God and his Christ as the eventual victors (cf. Ps 2:2).

Witherington rightly points out the seemingly rough transition between Revelation 11 and 12. He argues that this transition is due to two factors: (1) the difference in source material, and (2) John using Revelation 12–14 as a type of flashback. Regardless of the reasons for the seeming abruptness of the transition, we would agree with Witherington that, as noted above, "John believes that these realities exist and they dramatically affect the course of human history . . . that war in heaven mirrors war on earth."[125] Though not a continuous narrative, John nonetheless reiterates in 12:10 the idea that God and "his Christ" (τοῦ θεοῦ ἡμῶν καὶ ἡ ἐξουσία τοῦ χριστοῦ αὐτοῦ) share authority, power, and judgment over not only Rome but also the cosmos. Christ's role in establishing God's kingdom inevitably includes salvation for the faithful and judgment for the wicked.[126]

Moreover, the genitive form "his Christ" is used in relation to God, so the kingdom authority is said to belong to Christ (ἡ ἐξουσία τοῦ χριστοῦ αὐτοῦ). This is a striking indication that Christ cannot simply be viewed as a subordinate vicegerent with allocated power. The indication here is that Christ not a surrogate for divine power; rather, divine power pertaining to the Father actually belongs to Christ properly and naturally, as it does to the Father. As chapter three will suggest, the sharing of the Father's throne as the representation of his authority and power seems to indicate that they are of the same nature, albeit subsisting as distinct persons. Indeed, the twenty-four elders praise God at the end of 11:17, saying, "You have taken your great power and begun to reign" (εἴληφας τὴν δύναμίν σου τὴν μεγάλην); however, an

---

[124]Judith Kovacs and Christopher Rowland, *Revelation*, Blackwell Bible Commentaries (Oxford: Blackwell, 2004), 134.
[125]Witherington, *Revelation*, 166-67.
[126]Bauckham, *Theology of Revelation*, 67.

essential component to the inauguration of his kingdom is the Messiah's victory over sin and Satan. Indeed, the aforementioned truncated phrase, "who is and who was," likely "indicates that God's coming has already happened with the paschal event; the establishment of his eschatological rule is his coming . . . realized in the present, in-between time."[127] Given this, we can say that the kingdom highlighted in the vision belongs to God as the sovereign ruler over creation in general and all empires in particular, but also belongs to Christ as evident in his exaltation (Rev 1:9-19), death (Rev 1:5-6; 5:12), opening of the seals (Rev 6), and placement on God's throne (Rev 4-5; 7:17). Further, the genitive need not serve as a demotion for Christ because he self-identifies as τὸ ἄλφα καὶ τὸ ὦ, ἡ ἀρχὴ καὶ τὸ τέλος ("the Alpha and the Omega, the beginning and the end") in 21:6 and 22:13, which the Father also says of himself in 1:8.

This passage, then, highlights the established role of God the Father as enthroned and transcendent, without exclusion of the Son or Spirit. Hence, this emphasizes our trinitarian reading: John's portrayal of the Father, Son, and Spirit remains a discussion of God who is *triune*, equal in divine power, authority, and activity.

Conclusion

In Revelation 1:1-8 we saw that God is portrayed by John as the source and giver of the revelation of Jesus Christ. He is sovereign over not only the exodus from Egypt but also the final exodus from sin and suffering. In Revelation 4:1-11 we saw that God sits on his throne, receiving worship and honor alongside the Christ, the Lamb. He is praised as the creator of the universe and the true King of kings, which, as we have noted, is standard monotheism and monolatry found, for example, in the Pentateuch, Isaiah, and Second Temple literature. In Revelation 11:15-19 God is the one to whom Jesus hands over the kingdom and thus brings God's promises to their culmination. When John in these passages discusses their role in creation, salvation, and worship, we see the relationship between the Father and Son that mirrors the logic employed by the patristics, namely that the Father and Son's nature and actions are an indication of one divine substance

---

[127]Resseguie, *Revelation*, 168.

(*homoousios*) and yet personal distinctions (*hypostases*). We saw that a theological-canonical method which draws on pro-Nicene tools helped us work through issues related to the triadic dynamic native to John's writing.

We must say, then, that the Father and Christ are shown in the context of Revelation as two divine persons existing in a constitutive relationship, but that the Father's ordered relationship in the *taxis* and economic mission is seen in his initiation of the revelation, his seat on "his" throne, salvific activity flowing from the throne, his reception of worship, and his role as the eternal creator and sustainer of history. This meshes well with later pro-Nicene trinitarian conceptions wherein God and Christ (the Son) are relationally distinct in the way that the text describes their inseparable operations and distinct missions in the redemptive drama. These missions are relationally constituted by fatherhood and filiality combined with a shared divine authority and will, highlighting that they are ontologically equal as is clear by their sharing of the divine nature, while being distinct from the creaturely world and therefore worthy of divine worship.

THREE

Son

The Slain Lamb and Risen King

OUR VISION OF THE TRIUNE GOD now fittingly centers on the Son, the slain Lamb and risen King. Throughout the Gospels, we see Jesus Christ at his birth, his baptism, his ministry, his death, his resurrection, his transfiguration, and his ascension. In Revelation, this Lamb who shed his blood for the sins of his people now stands in his heavenly session, sitting on the throne with his Father and speaking alongside the Spirit, worthy to reign fully and equally as the sovereign ruler of all he created. In his unmitigated glory, he is worthy to offer comfort, enact justice, and ultimately bring to bear our longing for God's new creation.

Jesus is the central figure in John's vision, causing scholars to expend considerable effort trying to understand John's portrayal of him and requiring this chapter to be longer than the others. Several questions arise when considering the identity of Jesus in Revelation: To what degree is he a human, semidivine, or a fully divine agent? Is he preexistent? Does he receive worship, and if so, is it the same worship the Father receives? Is Jesus depicted as an ontological equal to the Father, or is he subordinated in some sense? How does his designation as the Son of Man or slaughtered Lamb relate (or not relate) to the use of these themes in Jewish writings? In what ways did the somewhat varying definitions of monotheism (or, put another way, conceptions of how God is one) influence the way John characterizes Jesus' relationship with God?[1] These concerns will be addressed in this chapter through a close reading of Revelation, particularly in light of patristic theology and exegesis.

We have already discussed in the previous chapter ways that the Father relates to the Son and Spirit in Revelation; now our discussion will highlight how Jesus is truly divine and how he relates to the Father and the Spirit with respect to unity and distinction. I will show primarily that John's message can be read through a trinitarian lens with the pro-Nicene toolkit, especially in the ways Jesus is of the same nature as the Father and demonstrates his full divinity as he exercises divine power and unashamedly receives worship, while also moving history toward its final culmination as the economic securer of the triune God's redemption of all things. I will also examine how Jesus acts on behalf of or because of God the Father, further revealing the trinitarian dynamic that later patristic authors recognized. Further, I will describe how Jesus acts upon or in relation to the Spirit in such a way that reveals that they are of the same nature, yet with distinct personhood and missions.

We will also see how Revelation prefigures and provides ingredients for later patristic development of the doctrine of the Trinity, particularly with respect to the tension between Jesus' divine nature and his relationship to the Father and Spirit. Moreover, we will note how pro-Nicene tools help us conceptually grasp John's theology and smooth out rough exegetical issues. First, though, it is important to address the recent conversation surrounding "high/low Christology," which informs much of the conversation about the identity of Jesus in Revelation.

CHRISTOLOGY IN CONTEXT

A major concern with a trinitarian reading of Revelation relates to the definition and scope of divinity in the first century and how these concepts played into the early Christians' worship patterns and theological confessions. Given the priority of monotheism in the Jewish community,[2] any

---

[1]For a fuller overview of modern scholarship on christological monotheism in relation to the Jewish and Greco-Roman context of the first century, see Brandon D. Smith, "What Christ Does, God Does: Surveying Recent Scholarship on Christological Monotheism," *CBR* 17, no. 2 (2019): 184-208. Some of the references below will be indebted to my research in that article. For a detailed survey, see Loke, *Origin of Divine Christology*.
[2]While the stock definition of "monotheism" might be "the belief that only one God exists," we briefly noted above that there existed some sort of diversity in ancient monotheism. Larry W.

cultic activity in which Jesus was venerated as a deity certainly would not have been taken lightly. For example, Josephus clearly notes a strict line between God and men, implying that not even emperors were allowed to cross it.[3] Further, given the first-century Hellenistic world in which early Christology developed, concepts and language about divinity might also involve Hellenistic categories. Aune, for example, has noted that Revelation represents "a high Christology" given that divine predicates used for God are also attributed to Christ. However, he argues that divine language such as "Alpha and Omega" (1:8; 21:6-13) does not originate in the Jewish tradition but in Hellenistic and Egyptian magic traditions.[4] With this in mind, it is worth briefly exploring divinity in the first-century world in which Revelation was written, primarily to show the complexities behind the question of Jesus' divinity as we seek to engage John's trinitarianism.

The Greco-Roman world had a long history with concepts of divinity and deification.[5] In Suetonius's work on the twelve Roman Caesars, he lists those who were deified post-mortem by their divine names—Divus Julius, Divus

---

Hurtado, "'Ancient Jewish Monotheism' in the Hellenistic and Roman Periods," *Journal of Ancient Judaism* 4 (2013): 379-400, uses the term "ancient Jewish monotheism" to offer a more precise definition to the flavor of Jewish monotheism (that YHWH was exclusively to be worshiped), given that (according to Hurtado) many Jews seemed to believe other gods existed. He concludes that Roman-era Jewish monotheism stipulated that the worship of any other deity by Jews or anyone else was idolatry. Bernhard Lang, using the term "monolatry" to explain the same general idea, argues that "soteriological monotheism is older than dogmatic monotheism," asserting that the hope in YHWH as the only savior (not necessarily the only deity) was forged in Jewish political crisis, and only later did the church fathers emphasize the existence of only one God. See Bernhard Lang, "No God but Yahweh! The Origin and Character of Biblical Monotheism," in *Monotheism*, ed. Claude Geffré and Jean-Pierre Jossua (Edinburgh: T&T Clark, 1985), 41-49. See also Nathan MacDonald, *Deuteronomy and the Meaning of 'Monotheism,'* 2nd ed., FAT 2, no. 1 (Tübingen: Mohr Siebeck, 2012), who argues that the idea of a strict Jewish monotheism that rules out lesser deities is an anachronistic idea inherited from the Enlightenment. Richard Bauckham, *Jesus and the God of Israel: God Crucified and Other Studies on the New Testament's Christology of Divine Identity* (Grand Rapids, MI: Eerdmans, 2008), 62-71, accuses him of not taking seriously enough YHWH's uniqueness in Jewish thought. As we will further observe in the Bousset-Hengel debate, there is a diversity of understanding among modern scholars about the diversity of Jewish understanding of monotheism.

[3]*A.J.* 18.256; cf. *Flavius Josephus: Against Apion*, trans. John M. G. Barclay, *Flavius Josephus: Translation and Commentary* 10 (Leiden: Brill, 2013), 208.

[4]David E. Aune, *Apocalypticism, Prophecy, and Magic in Early Christianity: Collected Essays* (Grand Rapids, MI: Baker Academic, 2008), 361-64. Aune gives examples that include Greek magical papyri using "ΑΩ" as a summation of the divine name, which appears to imitate similar Egyptian formulations for a deity's name.

[5]Though we only have space to briefly discuss a few examples, other citations of divine honors and inscriptions to emperors worth considering include: *Halikarnassos* 39; *Teos* 97; Orientis Graeci Inscriptiones Selectae 655.

Augustus, Divus Claudius, Divus Vespasian, and Divus Titus.[6] To be clear, deification in the Greco-Roman world was not monolithic. As Bird has summarized, "Deity was stratified by gradations, so there was a spectrum of divinity."[7] Augustus, for example, was not only deified but could conceivably add to his divine honors in a way that elevated him to a "son of God" above even the Olympian gods.[8] We also see this type of divine paternal relationship with respect to the great Greek god Zeus/Jupiter, who was said to be father of the gods and is called "Father Zeus" or "shining father" (Ζεῦ πάτερ) in some places.[9]

Further, "worship was the reciprocal response by inhabitants to someone who provided salvation and benefaction."[10] Put another way, if the emperor provided benefits to his subjects, then he could expect accolades from his subject up to the point of divine titles, temples, and worship. Again, Greco-Roman deification culture was not cut-and-dry. For instance, Seneca's *Apocolocyntosis divi Claudii* (*The Pumpkinification of the Divine Claudius*) was a satire on Claudius's supposed divinity, highlighting his failures and mercilessness and showing him eventually banished by the gods to Hades. Nonetheless, the tendency to deify mythic figures and rulers has led scholars to assert that Jesus' divinity was merely another instance of deification extant in Hellenistic environments. As the most prominent modern purveyor of this assertion, we will now explore Wilhelm Bousset's influence on this discussion and the results of his major work, *Kyrios Christos*.[11]

Bousset primarily argued that Jesus' divine status developed "once Christianity passed over into the Hellenistic milieu with the transition from Jerusalem to Antioch."[12] For Bousset, the titles given to Jesus by his followers were not indicative of his ontological divinity per se, but rather they were

---

[6]Suetonius, *De vita Caes.*; see *The Twelve Caesars*, trans. Robert Graves (London: Penguin, 1957).
[7]Michael F. Bird, *Jesus the Eternal Son: Answering Adoptionist Christology* (Grand Rapids, MI: Eerdmans, 2017), 41.
[8]*1 Olympia* 53. See further explanation in Bird, *Jesus the Eternal Son*, 41; Paul Zanker, *The Power of Divine Images in the Age of Augustus*, trans. Alan Shapiro (Ann Arbor, MI: University of Michigan Press, 1988), 304; Greg Carey, "Early Christianity and the Early Empire," in *The State of New Testament Studies*, ed. Scot McKnight and Nijay K. Gupta (Grand Rapids, MI: Baker Academic, 2019), 9-34.
[9]*Il.* 7.446; 19.121; *Theog.* 47; 457; 838. Justin Martyr notably uses the stories of Zeus/Jupiter and his sons to talk about the "superiority" of the Father and Son; cf. *1 Apol.* 22; *2 Apol.* 6.
[10]Bird, *Jesus the Eternal Son*, 41.
[11]Wilhelm Bousset, *Kyrios Christos* (Nashville: Abingdon, 1970).
[12]Bousset, *Kyrios Christos*, 13.

indicative of his followers' later tendency to honor him in the way the Greeks deified their heroes.[13] Bultmann followed Bousset generally, but he specifically argued for a "demythologized" account of Jesus, noting that though he was a historical person, the divine attributes and exalted titles given to him by his followers were mythological accounts influenced by Jewish apocalypticism and Hellenistic Gnosticism.[14] For instance, he did not affirm the divinity of Christ in Revelation but instead accused Revelation of being "weakly Christianized Judaism" that limits "the significance of Christ" and merely gives "the passionate eschatological hope a certainty which the Jewish apocalyptists lack."[15] In a similar vein, Wolfgang Schrage tended to highlight the titular and mediatorial expressions in Paul that he viewed as clear examples of subordinationist thought over and against equating Christ with God.[16] However, given that the Hellenistic concepts operated on a gradation of ontological divinity, this assertion does not prove that Jesus only received cultic honors without the corresponding ontological implications.

The Greeks acknowledged, for example, a distinction between "eternal and unbegotten" deities (such as Apollo) and mortals who were eventually deified.[17] Moreover, the first-century world was a decidedly integrated culture of Jewish and Hellenistic concepts, leaving doubt that Jesus' Jewish followers would have easily rejected a divine ontology with respect to Jesus based on some sort of "pure" Jewish monotheism.[18] As Hengel has shown, early Christian worship was Jewish in nature but nonetheless existed within the context of a wider Jewish-Hellenistic milieu. Hengel proved that Bousset suggested a false dichotomy between the influences of Judaism and Hellenism on Christology in the context of the early church. While Hengel granted that some early Christology relied on Greek ideas given the

---

[13]Indeed, Bousset, *Kyrios Christos*, 210, even admits the appearance of divine Christology in Paul, for instance, and yet ultimately downplays this language since there are no direct indications of his deity, such as using the word θεός for Christ.

[14]See, for example, Rudolph Bultmann, *Primitive Christianity in Its Contemporary Setting* (Meridian, NY: Living Age, 1958), 162-63.

[15]Rudolf Bultmann, *Theology of the New Testament*, trans. Kendrick Grobel (Waco, TX: Baylor University Press, 2007), 175.

[16]For example, see Wolfgang Schrage, *Unterwegs Zur Einzigkeit Und Einheit Gottes: Zum 'Monotheismus' Des Paulus Und Seiner Alttestamentlich-Judischen Tradition*, Biblisch-Theologische Studien 48 (Neukirchen-Vluyn: Vandenhoeck & Ruprecht, 2002), 158.

[17]Plutarch, *Pel.* 16:5; cf. Bird, *Jesus the Eternal Son*, 68.

[18]Larry W. Hurtado, "New Testament Christology: A Critique of Bousset's Influence," *TS* 40 (1979): 309.

influence of Hellenism in Jerusalem, he still emphasized that early Christians' understanding of Jesus' identity and vocation was heavily influenced by their own experience and by their Jewish conceptual heritage.[19]

Hurtado and Bauckham would be the most prominent torchbearers of Hengel's task of challenging the claims made by Bousset and Bultmann. Hurtado's work in tracing early Christian devotional patterns and Bauckham's theological category of "divine identity" brought considerable clarity to the notion that though Hellenistic categories may have helped shape early Christology, the earliest Christians were ultimately rooting their basis for Jesus' divinity in Jewish categories, not Greek ones. In fact, on the basis of their work, Wright has concluded that it is "almost inconceivable that one could go back to the older days of Bousset and Bultmann."[20] That said, recent scholars have reached a different conclusion.

Ehrman, for example, argues that monotheism in the first century was not as strict as Hurtado or Bauckham claim. Using examples from Second Temple Judaism and the Greco-Roman world, he asserts that deification was not uncommon in first century.[21] Hurtado acknowledged that chief angel figures traversing between heaven and earth existed in Jewish literature, giving the earliest Christians a level of permission to elevate Jesus to an exalted status, but noted that Jesus was exalted to a much higher status than any figure beforehand.[22] With respect to Jesus' inclusion in the throne-room scenes of Revelation 4–5, Hurtado asserts: "Nearly all scholars recognize in Rev. 5 clear indications of the writer's Christian views, especially in the description of the Lamb (5.6-12), the content of the hymns (5.9-10, 12-13), and the fact that they are sung *to the Lamb* as to God, and even in the sealed book which can be opened only by the Lamb (5.1-5, 7-10)."[23]

Ehrman challenges Hurtado for taking this type of final step in elevating Jesus above other exalted figures: "If humans could be angels (and angels

---

[19]See Martin Hengel, *Judaism and Hellenism: Studies in Their Encounter in Palestine During the Early Hellenistic Period* (London: SCM, 1974).

[20]N. T. Wright, *Paul and the Faithfulness of God*, 2 vols. (Minneapolis: Fortress, 2013), 2:647.

[21]Bart D. Ehrman, *How Jesus Became God: The Exaltation of a Jewish Preacher from Galilee* (San Francisco: HarperOne, 2014), 12-39.

[22]Larry W. Hurtado, *One God, One Lord: Early Christian Devotion and Ancient Jewish Monotheism*, 3rd ed. (New York: T&T Clark, 2015), 17-52.

[23]Larry W. Hurtado, "Revelation 4–5 in the Light of Jewish Apocalyptic Analogies," *JSNT* 25 (1985): 109, emphasis original.

humans), and if angels could be gods, and if in fact the chief angel could be the Lord himself—then to make Jesus divine, one simply needs to think of him as an angel in human form."[24]

For Ehrman, then, there were many acceptable options in the spectrum of what constituted monotheism in the first century. In fact, he concludes that Jesus' deification among his followers proves that monotheism was a flexible concept.[25] Collins similarly contends that the notion of a "strict" monotheism by the time of Jesus "had already been 'stretched' or even ignored in much of the literature of Second Temple Judaism."[26] Moreover, as we will see later, she contends that John portrays Jesus as an angelic exalted figure in Revelation, similar to Ehrman's point above.

Hurtado conceded that exalted figures and chief angels "stretched" the definition of monotheism, though he disagreed with Ehrman and Collins that Jesus should be classified in this way. Bauckham, however, argues that the distinction between Creator and creature is a sharp line that Jewish monotheists would not cross. Challenging Hurtado directly, Bauckham believes the chief-angel discussion has been exaggerated, given that Jesus was clearly exalted above any type of divine agent.[27] Bauckham asserts that Jesus is included in the "divine identity," which places him on the "Creator side" of the Creator-creature divide.[28] He asserts that Revelation in particular draws a clear distinction between Jesus and angels, most notably his place on the throne vis-à-vis the angels, his worthiness to open the scroll, and his co-deliverance of the revelation.[29] As we mentioned at the beginning of this book, Dunn's views on this topic vary somewhat depending on the biblical book, but he acknowledges that the divinity of Jesus in Revelation is obvious.[30]

---

[24]Ehrman, *How Jesus Became God*, 61.
[25]Ehrman, *How Jesus Became God*, 50-55.
[26]Adela Yarbro Collins, "The Worship of Jesus and the Imperial Cult," in *The Jewish Roots of Christological Monotheism: Papers from the St. Andrews Conference on the Historical Origins of the Worship of Jesus*, ed. Casey C. Newman, James R. Davila, and Gladys S. Lewis (Waco, TX: Baylor University Press, 2017), 236.
[27]Richard Bauckham, "Devotion to Jesus Christ in Earliest Christianity: An Appraisal and Discussion of the Work of Larry Hurtado," in *Mark, Manuscripts, and Monotheism: Essays in Honor of Larry W. Hurtado*, ed. Chris Keith and Dieter T. Roth, LNTS 528 (London: T&T Clark, 2015), 182-86.
[28]Bauckham, *Jesus and the God of Israel*, 182-232.
[29]Richard Bauckham, "The Worship of Jesus in Apocalyptic Christianity," *NTS* 27, no. 3 (1981): 329-30.
[30]James D. G. Dunn, *Did the First Christians Worship Jesus?: The New Testament Evidence* (Louisville: Westminster John Knox, 2010), 130-32.

It is also worth noting that scholars have recently picked up some of Bousset's ideas. David Litwa claims that "early Christians imagined and depicted Jesus with some of the basic traits common to other Mediterranean divinities and deified men,"[31] charging Hurtado's focus on the Jewishness of Jesus-devotion with overlooking the clear Hellenistic influence.[32] Since early Christians combined both Jewish and Greco-Roman descriptions for Jesus, Litwa's view ultimately acknowledges that their vision of Jesus contained connotations of both ontological and associational deification. Michael Peppard also sees a heavy influence derived from Greco-Roman deification ideas. For him, the early Christians called Jesus the "son of God" not because they were making later creedal claims about his divinity but rather to hold him up as divine counter-Caesar who challenged the deification honors given to Roman emperors.[33] While Crispin Fletcher-Lewis is closer to Hurtado and Bauckham on this issue, he still acknowledges that "the treatment of 'divine' human beings in the wider Gentile world *do* offer likely precedents for *some aspects* of the worship of Jesus and his inclusion within the divine identity."[34] We will see various places in Revelation where these issues come to bear, and we will deal with them later in this chapter.

Patristic Conceptions of the Son

I will address a few major questions in this section. How was trinitarian language about Jesus articulated as early Christianity entered the patristic period? In what ways could both pro-Nicenes and non-Nicenes use Revelation for their own arguments? In what ways did Revelation contribute to patristic debates in the sense of providing pressures, framework, and grammar? Reciprocally, how does later patristic language provide conceptual aids in understanding John's theology?

By way of introduction, we should summarize pro-Nicene trinitarian grammar as we did in the previous chapter, this time with respect to its

---

[31]David M. Litwa, *Iesus Deus: The Early Christian Depiction of Jesus as a Mediterranean God* (Minneapolis: Fortress, 2014), 215.
[32]Litwa, *Iesus Deus*, 1-16.
[33]Michael Peppard, *The Son of God in the Roman World: Divine Sonship in Its Social and Political Context* (Oxford: Oxford University Press, 2011), 95-123.
[34]Crispin Fletcher-Louis, *Jesus Monotheism, Volume 1: Christological Origins: The Emerging Consensus and Beyond* (Eugene, OR: Cascade, 2015), 248; emphasis original.

Christology. God the Son is fully divine and thus singular in will, power, and authority with the Father and Spirit. He is eternally begotten of and sent by the Father (Jn 3:16; 7:28-29; 20:21) and with the Father created all things before his incarnation (Jn 1:1-3; Heb 1:10-12). Though there is no ontological or relational authority in the nature of the Trinity (*ad intra*), the Son *in the mission of his incarnation* is the securer of redemption and obedient to the Father according to his human nature and will (*ad extra*) (e.g., Phil 2:5-11). So, within the *taxis*, he is begotten and eternally generated from the Father, and the Holy Spirit proceeds or spirates from the Father.[35]

In particular, the Constantinopolitan Creed (381) says it this way: "And in one Lord, Jesus Christ, the only Son of God, eternally begotten of the Father, God from God, Light from Light, true God from true God, begotten, not made, of one substance with the Father, through him all things were made."[36] The Son is eternally generated, and thus he is "from" the Father but was not begotten in time or "after" the Father. Further, the pro-Nicenes sought to preserve divine simplicity—that the divine essence is uncreated, undivided, and not composed of parts—at the same time acknowledging the distinct personhood of the Father, Son, and Spirit who are of the one, undivided divine essence.[37] We will see how later trinitarian theologies and pro-Nicene formulations used passages from Revelation over and against theologies that affirmed variations of subordinationism or modalism, though we will acknowledge where non-Nicenes might have conceivably found footing. Let us now turn our

---

[35]Space does not permit a full engagement with the *filioque* debate. I have not included the *filioque* here since it is not original to the creed. That said, I am sympathetic toward the Western tradition's tendency to say "from the Father and Son," if for no other reason than my interpretation of Jn 15:26 and related themes. For a good summary of the debate, see Stephen R. Holmes, *The Quest for the Trinity: The Doctrine of God in Scripture, History and Modernity* (Downers Grove, IL: IVP Academic, 2012), 147-64.

[36]καὶ εἰς ἕνα Κύριον Ἰησοῦν Χριστὸν τὸν υἱὸν τοῦ Θεοῦ τὸν Μονογενῆ, τὸν ἐκ τοῦ Πατρὸς γεννηθέντα πρὸ πάντων τῶν αἰώνων, Φῶς ἐκ Φωτός, Θεὸν ἀληθινὸν ἐκ Θεοῦ ἀληθινοῦ, γεννηθέντα οὐ ποιηθέντα, ὁμοούσιον τῷ Πατρί, δι' οὗ τὰ πάντα ἐγένετο.

[37]Pui Him Ip, "Re-imagining Divine Simplicity in Trinitarian Theology," *IJST* 18, no. 3 (2016): 274-89, makes a compelling case that divine simplicity was foundational to trinitarian theology as early as Justin Martyr, Athenagoras, and Origen, but obviously articulated in different ways. For a thorough yet concise survey of divine simplicity and its exegetical, theological, and historical foundations, see Steven J. Duby, *Divine Simplicity: A Dogmatic Account*, T&T Clark Studies in Systematic Theology 30 (New York: T&T Clark, 2016). For a further outworking of divine simplicity in Christian doctrine, see Duby, *God in Himself: Scripture, Metaphysics, and the Task of Christian Theology*, SCDS (Downers Grove, IL: IVP Academic, 2019).

attention to the development of trinitarian Christology in the patristic period.

Centuries before the pro-Nicenes, Irenaeus offered perhaps the most structured interpretive rule of his time—a rule that would carry on long after his death.[38] He used this "rule of faith" or "truth" (κανών της αληθείας) in his polemics against Gnostics, such as the Valentinians[39] and Marcion,[40] as a way to show how to properly interpret Scripture over and against their teachings. These Gnostics erred by espousing allegorical readings that sought to find the secret or hidden meaning beneath the text (Valentinians) and/or picking and choosing some parts of Scripture over others (Marcion). Perhaps the most succinct summary of this rule can be found in *Epideixis* 6, which is worth quoting at length in order to see the whole triadic vision:

> And this is the order of our faith, the foundation of [the] edifice and the support of [our] conduct: God, the Father, uncreated, uncontainable, invisible, one God, the Creator of all: this is the first article (κεφάλαιον) of our faith. And the second article: the Word of God, the Son of God, Christ Jesus our Lord, who was revealed by the prophets according to the nature of the economies of the Father, by whom all things were made, and who, in the last times, to recapitulate all things, became a man amongst men, visible and palpable, in order to abolish death, to demonstrate life, and to effect communion between God and man. And the third article: the Holy Spirit, through whom the prophets prophesied and the patriarchs learnt the things of God and the righteous were led in the path of righteousness, and who, in the last times, was poured out in a new fashion upon the human race renewing man, throughout the world, to God.[41]

---

[38]John Behr, *The Way to Nicaea* (Crestwood, NY: St Vladimir's Seminary Press, 2001), 113; Craig A. Carter, *Interpreting Scripture with the Great Tradition: Recovering the Genius of Premodern Exegesis* (Grand Rapids, MI: Baker Academic, 2018), 99.

[39]He begins *Haer.* by immediately charging the Valentinians with hermeneutical absurdity. Though beyond the scope of this book, Ayres's claim that these exegetical practices included the adaptation of ancient literary-critical techniques that worked against allegorical interpretations found in Valentinian biblical commentaries is persuasive; see Lewis Ayres, "Irenaeus vs. the Valentinians: Toward a Rethinking of Patristic Exegetical Origins," *JECS* 23, no. 2 (2015): 153-87.

[40]Marcion's method of elevating Paul over the Gospel writers and diminution of Israel's God caused Irenaeus to charge him with hating God and separating himself from the apostles' authority, given to them by Christ himself; cf. *Haer.* 3.14.1-15.1.

[41]*Epid.* 6. Unless otherwise noted, English translations are from St. Irenaeus of Lyons, *On the Apostolic Preaching*, trans. John Behr (Crestwood, NY: St Vladimir's Seminary Press, 1997), 42-43.

As Stephen Presley points out, Irenaeus's hermeneutical principle "elevates the theological networking of Scripture under the administration of God in three persons"[42] and asserts "any time Scripture uses a title or appellation for God . . . the interpreter must assume a unified divine referent behind each one."[43] This networking or unity of Scripture's theology flew in the face of Gnostic tendencies to bring their own theological presuppositions to the text. This rule also served as a foundation for "the baptism of our regeneration [which] takes place through these three articles" who are united in their work, for "without the Spirit it is not [possible] to see the Word of God, and without the Son one is not able to approach the Father."[44] For Irenaeus, then, we should not take pieces of Scripture that we like and create artwork of a dog or fox; rather, we should follow the interpretive "key" or "hypothesis" (ὑπόθεσις) of Scripture itself that reveals the interconnected witness, thus revealing the true picture of the King.[45] While Irenaeus was not pro-Nicene, we cannot fully understand their conclusions without him; as Ayres has convincingly argued, the rule of faith was a core hermeneutical piece of development in later pro-Nicene theology, and Irenaeus's exegetical practices against the Valentinians "provided the stimulus" and "laid the foundations of the classical patristic exegesis of later centuries."[46]

As we introduced in the previous chapter, Origen's influence on the theological journey to Nicaea cannot be understated. Origen spoke of the λόγος as a second divine person (ὑπόστασις) in a divine hierarchy who is eternally generated (μονογενής)[47] from the Father. Further, Origen delved deeper into implications of what would later be called the hypostatic union—the reality of Christ's divinity and humanity—highlighting that he was God's power

---

[42]Stephen O. Presley, "The *Demonstration* of Intertextuality in Irenaeus of Lyons," in *Intertextuality in the Second Century*, ed. D. Jeffrey Bingham and Clayton N. Jefford, The Bible in Ancient Christianity (Leiden: Brill, 2016), 197.

[43]Stephen O. Presley, "Biblical Theology and the Unity of Scripture in Irenaeus of Lyons," *CTR* 16, no. 2 (2019): 8.

[44]*Epid.* 7.

[45]*Haer.* 1.8.1-1.9.4.

[46]Ayres, "Irenaeus vs. the Valentinians," 187.

[47]Notably, Origen does not expound on this word other than using it as a title, but we can infer what he means by it generally—generated or begotten; see, e.g., *Princ.* 1.2. For a helpful discussion, see Lewis Ayres, "At the Origins of Eternal Generation: Scriptural Foundations and Theological Purpose in Origen of Alexandria," in *Retrieving Eternal Generation*, ed. Fred Sanders and Scott R. Swain (Grand Rapids, MI: Zondervan Academic, 2017), 149-62.

(δύναμις) present at creation and yet also became a human baby who cried and eventually died like actual humans do.[48] The move from the Son and Spirit as mediating presences to a more precise unity-yet-distinction paradigm was a notable transition as the pro-Nicene theologies began to take shape.

Once again, we must begin with Origen before we discuss the Christology of the pro-Nicenes. Holmes notes that for Origen "the theological question of the Trinity is not whether to worship Father, Son, and Spirit, but how to understand the triune life of God."[49] So, for example, he sought to show that Father and Son are not two Gods by "exploring the differing ways in which Father and Son are one and two."[50] When speaking of Christ, Origen affirms the distinction between "the nature of his divinity as he is the only-begotten Son of God" and "the human nature, which in the last times he took on account of the economy."[51] Leaning on biblical titles such as Wisdom (σοφία) and Firstborn (πρωτότοκος), he reasons that the Son must have always existed: "And how can one, who has learnt to know and think piously about God, think or believe that God the Father ever existed, even for a single moment, without begetting his Wisdom?"[52] He acknowledges, then, that "God is always the Father of his only-begotten Son, who is indeed born of him, and derives from him what he is, but without, however, any beginning."[53] Further, he concludes that begetting must include a birth, so the Father must beget or generate the Son eternally.[54] Origen openly struggles with how to describe the Father and Son's ontological relationship, because he feels the tension between their clear inseparability with their equally clear distinction from one another.[55] It appears that Origen cannot escape the philosophical implications that the begotten one must be less than the begetter while also acknowledging the necessarily ontological relationship between the Father and Son.[56] This wrestling ends with a non-Nicene type of concession, in

---

[48] *Princ.* 2.6.1-2.
[49] Holmes, *Quest for the Trinity*, 75.
[50] Holmes, *Quest for the Trinity*, 75.
[51] *Princ.* 1.2.1.
[52] *Princ.* 1.2.2.
[53] *Princ.* 1.2.2.
[54] *Princ.* 1.2.4.
[55] Holmes, *Quest for the Trinity*, 76-77.
[56] The idea that begottenness must indicate something about being or origin is not foreign in Greek philosophy; cf. Plato, *Phileb.* 26 and Aristotle, *Metaph.* 4.2.

which Origen compares 1 John 1:5 (in the Father there is no darkness at all) with John 1:5 (Jesus is the light that shines in darkness) to imply that this distinction of light reveals a differentiation in essence—"they are not the same."[57] Origen's back-and-forth language about the Father and Son's relationship reminds us why both pro-Nicenes and non-Nicenes were able to find support from Origen for their respective positions.

I will include other comments from Origen in the section below, but a representative example of his interaction with Revelation and the Trinity shows up in his commentary on John's Gospel. In his *Commentary on John*, Origen considers the multitude of titles given to Jesus. He challenges the idea that "Son of God" is special or unique in relation to all of Jesus' scriptural designations. Instead, he aims to consider how all of the scriptural titles paint Jesus not merely as "an expression of the Father occurring in syllables" but in regard to "what manner he has essence,"[58] which is an explicitly ontological claim. Moreover, as Rebecca Lyman notes, "Origen's attempt to explain the incarnation of the Logos in terms of a pre-existent human soul was one of the first constructive Christologies, and anticipated many problems in later theology regarding the proper union of divine and human nature."[59]

Interestingly, Revelation 1:17-18 ("I am the first and the last, the living one. I was dead but look—I am alive forever and ever") is one of the key phrases as he describes a divine Christology in John's Gospel.[60] In a

---

[57] *Comm. Jo.* 2.149; cf. Holmes, *Quest for the Trinity*, 77.

[58] *Comm. Jo.* 1.151. While it is fair to question whether his trinitarian thought was a form of subordinationism, his wrestling with divine essence and hierarchy of origin and function was in many ways ahead of his predecessors, as well as a precursor for his contemporaries and successors. This does not mean that he was not engaged in language contemporary with his time, such as the use of "angelomorphic Christology." However, similar to the note above regarding Tertullian, Origen seemed able to distinguish between the various ways "angel" or "messenger" is used in the Bible as a title or designation and the idea of Christ having an angelic nature *stricto sensu*; see Bogdan G. Bucur, *Angelomorphic Pneumatology: Clement of Alexandria and Other Christian Witnesses*, VCS 95 (Leiden: Brill, 2009), xxvi-xxvii. Charles A. Gieschen, *Angelomorphic Christology: Antecedents and Early Evidence*, Arbeiten zur Geschichte des antiken Judentums und des Urchristentums 42 (Leiden: Brill, 1998), 195-96, notes that Origen sometimes refers to angels in the Bible as Christ or the Holy Spirit, but Gieschen's point does not require of Origen a belief in "angel Christology."

[59] J. Rebecca Lyman, *Christology and Cosmology: Models of Divine Activity in Origen, Eusebius, and Athanasius* (Oxford: Clarendon, 1993), 69.

[60] *Comm. Jo.* 1.132. Rowan Williams, *Arius: Heresy and Tradition* (Grand Rapids, MI: Eerdmans, 2001), 134, notes that in the same commentary Origen "sharply repudiates the idea that the Son is generated out of the Father's *ousia*, as this implies that the Father and Son are material realities."

fragment on the Apocalypse, Origen uses Revelation 1:17-18 to acknowledge that the Son is YHWH at Sinai "in his very substance" (ὁ ὄν οὐσία) because he shares the divine name.[61] This example highlights the potential for Revelation to carry with it ontological claims for Jesus that were later articulated by the pro-Nicenes.

Origen's influence in many ways serves as the backdrop for the lead-up to the Council of Nicaea in AD 325. Arius partially echoed Origenian logic in his *Thalia* when he asserted that Jesus was divine, though not of the same essence as the Father, because he was a created being. Athanasius summarized Arius as follows:[62]

> The Son did not always exist. Everything created is out of nothing, all existing creatures, all things that are made; so the Word of God himself came into existence out of nothing. There was [a time] when he did not exist; before he was brought into being, he did not exist. He too had a beginning to his created existence.... For he is not equal to God, nor yet is he of the same substance.... Or again: there exists a trinity in unequal glories, for their subsistences are not mixed with each other. In their glories, one is more glorious than another in infinite degree.[63]

The primary language to notice is that, for Arius, the Son is not *homoousios* with the Father. This distinction eventually became a rallying point for debates against non-Nicenes, since Arius and Eusebius wielded for their own purposes previous scriptural terminology used by Alexander of Alexandria, such as "power of God" and "Son of God," but *homoousios* was a term they refused.[64] Even before he began to hone his *homoousios* polemic, Athanasius had already departed from his predecessor Alexander on this point: whereas Alexander conceived of the Word as an ontological

---

[61]*Schol. Apoc.* 20, as quoted in Williams, *Arius*, 142. The comparison between the above footnote and this footnote, both citing Williams, shows the disparity with which Origen used ontological language.

[62]As Williams, *Arius*, 99, points out, it is difficult to ascertain when Athanasius is directly quoting Arius and when he is summarizing him. Given that our fullest sense of Arius's theology comes from Athanasius, I have chosen to use the word "summarized" to reflect that we are often unsure what is a quotation and what is Athanasius's interpretation.

[63]*C. Ar.* 1.5-6; *Syn.* 15, as quoted in Williams, *Arius*, 100-102. As noted above, the text of *Thalia* is disputed since it exists primarily in quotations from other authors.

[64]*Decr.* 19-20. See the helpful summary in Barnes, "The Fourth Century as Trinitarian Canon," 49. Of course, as Barnes rightly notes, *homoousios* was later a "lightning rod" for some since it had a history of use in modalism, had materialist connotations, and was not a scriptural term.

intermediary, Athanasius downplayed any intermediary status of the Son and instead emphasized that the Son's existence comes from the Father's own nature.[65]

As we have seen, Arius could still elevate the Son above humanity in numerous ways (he is glorious, heavenly, preexistent, and united in will with the Father); however, the Son's nature as a created being still relegated him to a lesser substance and glory. In response to this line of thought, Athanasius wrote in his defense of the Council of Nicaea (*De Decretis*) that Arius's "corrupt and futile" arguments—which included calling *homoousios* an unscriptural term—were akin to those who denied Jesus' divinity in the Gospel of John:

> Only the Pharisees, despite the appearance of signs that shone brighter than the sun, still grumbled in their ignorance, saying: "Why do you, a human being, make yourself to be God?" (Jn 10:33). They were senseless and truly blind in their understanding. What they should have said, on the contrary, is: "Why do you, being God, become a human being?" For his works showed that he is God, so that they might worship the goodness of the Father, and marvel at his dispensation (*economian*) for our sake. . . . Despite the Savior manifesting his own divinity many times in many ways and preaching the Father to all, they, like those who kick against the goad, contradicted him with silly talk, only so that they may find a pretext to separate themselves from the truth, as the divine proverb says.[66]

He then notes that "the party of Eusebius" began to argue amongst themselves when they realized they were wrong in denying that the Son is "from the essence" (*ek tēs ousias*) and "one in essence" (*homoousios*) and that the Son of God is not a creature nor work nor one of the things that have come to be, but that the Word is offspring from the essence of the Father (*gennēma tēs ousias tou patros*).[67]

This Creator-creature distinction was an important point for Athanasius as he discussed implications of divine simplicity and one nature of the Father and Son. His employment of the term ἴδιος (proper, own) also

---

[65]Lewis Ayres, *Nicaea and Its Legacy: An Approach to Fourth-Century Trinitarian Theology* (Oxford: Oxford University Press, 2004), 46.

[66]*Decr.* 1. Unless otherwise noted, English translations are from Khaled Anatolios, *Athanasius*, The Early Church Fathers (New York: Routledge, 2004).

[67]*Decr.* 3. Transliteration in Anatolios's translation.

helped him speak about the attributes and qualities "proper to" the Son's divine and human natures.[68] We will see that some of the passages in Revelation that we will discuss below could have contributed to an Arian or other non-Nicene understanding of the Son if one takes the route of Jesus as a subordinated agent or chief angel. However, Revelation 1:1-8 helped Athanasius make the case that Jesus was *homoousios* with the Father, primarily illustrating that he shares titles like "he who is and who was and who is to come" and "Almighty."[69] As Behr notes about the Father and Son sharing the "Almighty" title,

> The name "Father" is older (that is, logically prior) to the title "Almighty," for the God who is identified as the Father of Christ, the Son of God, is almighty through his creative work through his Son, the Word by whom, and the Wisdom in whom, all things are made, sharing the title "Almighty" with the Son and exercising his omnipotence through the weakness of the cross such that all things are, in the end, brought into subjection to Christ as his creation, in which God will indeed be "all in all."[70]

So, for Athanasius, this sharing of the divine title in Revelation insinuated an ontological union.

More broadly, Athanasius held to the Son's eternal generation as a key affirmation of the biblical witness. Athanasius made several basic theological moves based on a few key texts. For our purposes here, we will walk through his argument in *Contra Arianos* 1.14 as a representative example of his larger project.[71] We will see here that Athanasius's case for eternal generation helps buttress the biblical doctrine of the Son's full divinity.

He begins by addressing one particular "Arian" rebuttal: if the Son is uncreated and eternal, he must actually be the Father's brother. For these groups, for the Son to be truly a son, he must come after the Father in some sort of sequence; his "begottenness" or "generation" must have had a beginning. Athanasius replies,

---

[68]See, for instance, *C. Ar.* 1.58. Ayres, *Nicaea and Its Legacy*, 114-15 provides a helpful summary.
[69]*C. Ar.* 1.4; 3.23; *Syn.* 3.49.
[70]John Behr, "One God Father Almighty," *Modern Theology* 34, no. 3 (2018): 330.
[71]Unless otherwise noted, English translations are from *Nicene and Post-Nicene Fathers*, vol. 4, ed. Philip Schaff and Henry Wace, trans. John Henry Newman and Archibald Robertson (Buffalo, NY: Christian Literature, 1892).

For the Father and the Son were not generated from some pre-existing origin, that we may account them brothers, but the Father is the origin of the Son and begot Him; and the Father is Father, and not born the son of any; and the Son is Son, and not brother. Further, if He is called the eternal offspring of the Father, He is rightly so called. For never was the essence of the Father imperfect, that what is proper to it should be added afterwards; nor, as man from man, has the Son been begotten, so as to be later than His Father's existence; but He is God's offspring, and as being proper Son of God, who is ever, He exists eternally.[72]

Put another way, Athanasius is happy to concede some sort of "origin" in the Son's existence from the Father—for they are truly and always Father and Son—but it must be an *eternal* begottenness/generation/birth. If the Father is eternal, then Son must share the same nature in order to be called a true Son. If the Son is a created being, a creature like us, he is not truly the *only begotten* Son of the Father; instead, he is just another generic son, like humans are. But to call Christians "sons and daughters" of the Father is to talk about their adoption as sons through the true Son (e.g., Rom 8). If the Father begat the Son in time, then the Father would have somehow added to himself by *becoming* a Father, which would indicate that the perfect God—lacking nothing—would have added to himself. This would mean that God was imperfect or lacking, and that he can change or add titles and/or attributes to himself.

One major issue with Arius—and similar groups after him—was their inability to distinguish between reading Scripture literally and analogously, at least on this issue. For them, the Son can only be a son if he is younger or somehow comes after the Father in time. But the Creator-creature distinction limits our ability to make one-to-one comparisons between how humans beget children and how the Father does. God is Creator, and thus stands outside of creation and is not bound by the rules of creation. As Athanasius says, "For, whereas it is proper to men to beget in time, from the imperfection of their nature, God's offspring is eternal, for His nature is ever perfect."[73]

Athanasius then appeals to three passages that help affirm his point:

> But if He is Son, as the Father says, and the Scriptures proclaim, and 'Son' is nothing else than what is generated from the Father; and what is generated

---

[72]*C. Ar.* 1.14.
[73]*C. Ar.* 1.14.

from the Father is His Word (John 1:1-3), and Wisdom (1 Cor 1:24), and Radiance (Heb 1:3); what is to be said but that, in maintaining 'Once the Son was not,' they rob God of His Word, like plunderers, and openly predicate of Him that He was once without His proper Word and Wisdom, and that the Light was once without radiance, and the Fountain was once barren and dry?[74]

This is a crucial point made by many theologians throughout these debates: to say that the Son was created is to say that the Father at some point was mute ("Word"), dumb ("Wisdom"), and dull ("Radiance of God's glory"). Further, they must say that the "fountain of salvation" (Is 12:3; Jn 7:37-38) was once dry. When we think of how God is described throughout Scripture—eternal, perfect, unchanging, complete—it would seem to do serious damage to the biblical portrait of God if one said that the Son was created.

Instead, the Bible describes that the Son is God, was always with God, and created all things with God (Jn 1:1-3). So whatever we say about the Son's "begottenness," we must say that it is an eternal "birth," distinct from our finite creaturely conceptions of birth. There is a reality—albeit a mysterious reality—that the Father and Son are fully and truly Father and Son, both are fully and truly God, and yet they are not each other.

We know somewhat intuitively when Scripture says that God "reaches down with his mighty right hand" or "turns his ear toward us" that God does not literally have arms and ears in these passages—we know it is an analogy to tell us about his activity. In the same way, eternal generation affirms the Son's uniqueness as the only begotten Son of the Father, without implying he was created or is somehow of a lower status than the Father.

As Mark DelCogliano reminds us, "All theologians in the fourth century agreed that the Son had been begotten from the Father. They disagreed over what this meant and what it implied."[75] Michel Barnes calls this the "X from X" formula that all sides in the early Nicene debates agreed upon.[76] Indeed, the Council of Nicaea was not Alexander the Orthodox versus

---

[74] *C. Ar.* 1.14.
[75] Mark DelCogliano, "Basil of Caesarea on John 1:1 as an Affirmation of Pro-Nicene Trinitarian Doctrine," in *The Bible and Early Trinitarian Theology*, ed. Christopher A. Beeley and Mark E. Weedman (Washington, DC: The Catholic University of America Press, 2018), 136. See also Ayres, *Nicaea and Its Legacy*, 3-4.
[76] Michel René Barnes, *The Power of God: Dunamis in Gregory of Nyssa's Trinitarian Theology* (Washington, DC: The Catholic University of America Press, 2001), 119.

Arius the Heretic; rather, dissident and varying theologies with similar theological priorities coexisted leading up to, during, and after the creed was approved.[77]

Nonetheless, as we discussed in the last chapter, Arius notably promoted a different understanding than the later pro-Nicenes of the terms "unbegotten" and "begotten" with respect to the Father and Son. He said that the Father is unbegotten and therefore is uniquely *first*, and begottenness implies that the Son is created and therefore of a *second* substance or rank.[78] Gregory of Nazianzus, using a litany of titles and references from the Gospel of John[79] and elsewhere (including "Word," "he who is in the beginning," "truth," "life," "light," "Lord," "Almighty") clarified the pro-Nicene understanding of Jesus as the "only-begotten Son":

> Plainly these, and all the expressions synonymous with these, refer to the Son. None of them is a later acquisition, none became attached at a later stage to the Son or to the Spirit any more than to the Father, for perfection does not result from additions. It was never the case that he was without his Word, that he was not Father, that he was not true, or that he was without wisdom and power, or that he lacked life, splendor, or goodness.[80]

Gregory reasoned that because the Scripture used so many of the same titles for the Father and Son, to separate them ontologically would imply an imperfection in God, because the addition of attributes and titles would mean that God had changed and thus would challenge doctrines such as divine simplicity and immutability. Following the X-from-X formula, creedal grammar would use phrases for the Son such as "light from light" and "true God from true God"—and since they shared these things, the only

---

[77] Ayres, *Nicaea and Its Legacy*, 78-80, notes the complexities of trying to map historically the orthodox or heretical trajectories leading up to Nicaea because various groups appealed to their own convictions regarding the implications of doctrinal summaries, hermeneutical methods, and baptismal creeds, yet formal ways of determining "orthodox" and "heretical" were not fully developed and sometimes what was once considered orthodoxy would later be rendered heresy.

[78] Khaled Anatolios, *Retrieving Nicaea: The Development and Meaning of Trinitarian Doctrine* (Grand Rapids, MI: Baker Academic, 2011), 45, summarizes this well.

[79] It is noted that in a work on Revelation, we have referenced the Gospel of John in particular several times in this section. The reason for this is simple: the pro-Nicenes were indebted to the Gospel of John and utilize its language often. These references only serve to help explain their foundational logic, but we will see as this chapter progresses similar ways that they use Revelation.

[80] *Or*. 29.17.

explanation is that they had *always* shared them. Basil of Caesarea also noted that the phrase "in the beginning was the Word" means that the Son has a coeternal nature with the Father and that being the Father's "Word" meant that he must be tied to his whole thought and heart, just as our words represent the essence of who we are.[81]

As we mentioned above, the logic of titles, roles, and descriptions that necessitate a sharing of essence are buffered in the creed by the phrases "God from God, light from light, true God from true God." Origen introduced a version of this logic in *Princ.* 1.2.11, when he reasoned that Wisdom 7:25-26, Hebrews 1:3, and Colossians 1:15 shared a christological-exegetical thread. He used the book of Wisdom's language of "a pure emanation of the glory of the Almighty" and "a reflection of the eternal light" to understand how Christ is the image of the Father. So, as the Father is light, so the Son is the image and revealer of that light—light from light.[82] Similarly, the pro-Nicenes asserted that just as the Father is God, so the Son is God; just as the Father is true God, so the Son is true God—this is not merely honorific but fully and totally ontological without any range of gradation. As Ayres explains, talking about the Son's generation from the Father "implies not just 'mirroring' of the Father by the Son—as the reflection of an object shares only the appearance of that object—but a real sharing of nature and qualities."[83]

R. P. C. Hanson also notes that *ousia* (substance) was not used in trinitarian contexts in the second and third centuries,[84] though we should note that Irenaeus seemed concerned with those who deny any *ousia* (in this context, meaning "an existence proper to a quality or attribute") in the Son.[85] Tertullian, for example, often used the Latin phrase *una substantia* (one substance), and even the word *consubstantialis*. That said, while Tertullian reasoned that the Son is "substantial" because nothing unsubstantial can come from the Father, *una substantia* was not used monolithically in his writings; in fact, *substantia* is used in reference to what the Father and Son

---

[81] *Homilia in illud: In principio erat Verbum* 3; *Contra Eunomium* 2.14-15; cf. DelCogliano, "Basil of Caesarea on John 1:1."
[82] Ayres, *Nicaea and Its Legacy*, 23.
[83] Ayres, *Nicaea and Its Legacy*, 42.
[84] R. P. C. Hanson, *The Search for the Christian Doctrine of God: The Arian Controversy, 318-381* (Grand Rapids, MI: Baker Academic, 2005), 190.
[85] G. L. Prestige, *God in Patristic Thought* (Eugene, OR: Wipf & Stock, 2008), 189.

share, that which distinguishes them, and the two natures of Christ.[86] Origen notably never used *ousia* and preferred *hypostases*.[87] However, by the middle of the third century we have some debatable evidence that the affirmation and denial of *homoousios* was present in the debates between Dionysius of Rome and Dionysius of Alexandria.[88]

Given our continued emphasis on the complexity of early trinitarian language and its trajectories, it should not surprise us that leading up to the fourth-century debates, the terms *hypostasis* and *ousia* were still not uniformly defined. As Hanson points out, *hypostasis* was more generally used to describe "distinct realities" rather than "persons" who are of the same substance as the pro-Nicenes would later use it.[89] G. L. Prestige notes that *hypostasis* was sometimes used interchangeably with *ousia* during the fourth century as well, depending on whether one was in the West (Latin) or East (Greek).[90] For example, the Western church often used *hypostasis* "as a literal representation of the Latin *substantia*."[91] *Tomas ad Antiochenos*, written after the proceedings of the Council of Alexandria (362), serves as a prime example. The letter mentions an exchange between the presiding bishops, some of whom preferred to describe God as three hypostases. Given that this language was also preferred by "Arians," the group assured Athanasius that they did not intend to say that there are three Gods or three sources but rather one Godhead and one source, in alignment with the Nicene confession of *homoousios*. On the other side, some insisted on speaking of one *hypostasis*, which led to their explanation that they did not teach the Son and Spirit as merely names or unsubstantial qualities of the Father, but rather they were using *hypostasis* and *ousia* interchangeably.[92] Athanasius appears to have

---

[86] Ayres, *Nicaea and Its Legacy*, 73 n30.
[87] As Ayres, *Nicaea and Its Legacy*, 24-25, points out, the solitary instance that Origen may have used *ousia* (a fragment from a Hebrews commentary) is almost definitely a later addition, especially since he explicitly rejected the term elsewhere due to its materialistic Gnostic implications (*Comm. Jo.* 20.157). *Hypostases*, on the other hand, allowed him "to describe the participation and hierarchy existing among the three that are most definitely three."
[88] Hanson, *Search for the Christian Doctrine of God*, 191.
[89] Hanson, *Search for the Christian Doctrine of God*, 190. We saw an example of this with Origen.
[90] Prestige, *God in Patristic Thought*, 188. This led to the Nicene Creed using "one hypostasis" language. We note here that the so-called West/East divide can be wrongly exaggerated in these discussions, and I will attempt to avoid this tendency throughout the discussion.
[91] Prestige, *God in Patristic Thought*, 188.
[92] Prestige, *God in Patristic Thought*, 181-84, provides a helpful summary of this interaction. For a complementary summary, see Hanson, *Search for the Christian Doctrine of God*, 639-45.

orchestrated a compromise between the two parties: "And all, by God's grace, and after the above explanations, agree together that the faith confessed by the fathers at Nicaea is better than the said phrases, and that for the future they would prefer to be content to use its language."[93] Indeed, as Sara Parvis notes, Athanasius's "instinct" to allow for terminological breathing room "was eventually to be crucial in restoring some kind of unity to Eastern doctrinal confession"[94] because he recognized, unlike more rigid leaders such as Marcellus,[95] "that doctrinal definition should be kept to the minimum necessary, to leave room for various possible interpretations within the parameters of orthodoxy."[96] Similar to the conclusions of the Council of Nicaea, Athanasius may have been willing to allow a minimalist, common affirmation of Nicaea's principles of unity and diversity in order to secure a general consensus against their opponents.[97]

The incipient trinitarianism of Revelation does not use any of the phrases or expressions covered above; however, the logic and method used by these early Christian theologians can be useful for understanding John's trinitarianism. In particular, we will see how Revelation points toward the affirmation that the Father, Son, and Spirit are presented as sharing the nature and activities of God—prefiguring later language about ontological unity and relational distinction. Indeed, understanding the development of trinitarian language and the methodological moves therein keeps readers from overlooking the trinitarianism of John's theology.

Finally, we should also note the role of God's power (δύναμις) in early Christian conceptions of God. Revelation's throne-room scene(s) and Jesus' exertion of divine prerogatives pressure readers to consider the pro-Nicene

---

[93] Athanasius, *Tom.* 6. Gregory of Nazianzus offers a similar conciliatory tone in *Or.* 39:11, allowing for differing terms with respect to personhood—e.g., "*hypostases*" or "properties"—so long as the words point toward the same meaning.

[94] Sara Parvis, *Marcellus of Ancyra and the Lost Years of the Arian Controversy 325-345* (Oxford: Oxford University Press, 2006), 243.

[95] Of course, it is worth nothing that Athanasius and Marcellus both used "Arian" pejoratively in speaking about those opposed to their Nicene formula (Anatolios, *Retrieving Nicaea*, 28). However, while their polemical tactics were ultimately similar, Marcellus was not fond of the term *homoousios* and was eventually removed from his see for teaching a version of modalism.

[96] Parvis, *Marcellus of Ancyra and the Lost Years of the Arian Controversy 325-345*, 244.

[97] See, for example, Ayres, *Nicaea and Its Legacy*, 171-77; and Anatolios, *Retrieving Nicaea*, 21-23, for a discussion on Athanasius's attempts at "rapprochement" against opponents of *homoousios*.

logic of connecting the Father's power with the Son's position as incarnate savior, unique throne-sharer, and agent in creation. Athanasius, for example, reported that the idea of God's power was a useful tool in the battle against the "Arians," given that it indicated the unity between the Father and Son; in short, δύναμις was a characteristic of God that was shared exclusively with the Son.[98] This logic is also notably picked up by Marcellus, who charges Eusebius and Asterius with teaching that the Son is a separate power (and thus a separate essence) from the Father.[99]

Gregory of Nyssa often used the expression "one power" in the 380s rather than the common language of "one essence" or "one substance"[100] in his trinitarian formula because, as Barnes summarizes, "*Power* was a scripturally-based term, authoritative in the tradition, given content and nuance by philosophy, and—by the fourth century—having a rich history in trinitarian theology."[101] In particular, Gregory was keen on utilizing this phrase as part of his defense for the divinity of Christ, arguing that he has the divine attribute of power and, as Lucas Mateo-Seco puts it, "The Word could become man because He is all powerful."[102] Not only was the power of God in Christ shown at his incarnation, but it was fitting for the Son also to be active in creation. The act of creation was not a capability to be delegated but rather an indication of the essential unity between nature and power.[103] Gregory emphasized this logic in particular as he debated Eunomius's subordinationist language. As Barnes notes, for Eunomius, "The causal sequence of Father, Son, and Spirit indicates kinds of being . . . Gregory's reply is that there is neither 'more' or 'less' to being and that sequence cannot determine the degree of being."[104] In one place, Gregory asserts:

---

[98]Barnes, *Power of God*, 125; cf. Athanasius, *Ep. Afr.* 5.
[99]Barnes, *Power of God*, 137.
[100]Though, as we will see in chap. 4, this language is used in *Letter 38*, which was once attributed to Basil of Caesarea.
[101]Barnes, *Power of God*, 1, emphasis original. For a further explanation of Gregory's use of δύναμις and his reliance on Platonism for the concept, see Johannes Zachhuber, "The Soul as *Dynamis* in Gregory of Nyssa's *On the Soul and Resurrection*," in *Exploring Gregory of Nyssa: Philosophical, Theological, and Historical Studies*, ed. Anna Marmodoro and Neil. B. McLynn (Oxford: Oxford University Press, 2018), 142-59.
[102]Lucas Francisco Mateo-Seco, "Christology," in *The Brill Dictionary of Gregory of Nyssa*, ed. Lucas Francisco Mateo-Seco and Giulio Maspero, trans. Seth Cherney, Vigiliae Christianae Supplements 99 (Leiden: Brill, 2010), 145.
[103]Barnes, *Power of God*, 262-63.
[104]Barnes, *Power of God*, 264.

The Son is the Father's power (*1 Cor* 1.24). Those therefore who are saved through the Son are saved by the Father's Power. . . . Whether you look at the whole world, or at the parts of the world which constitute the whole, all these are the Father's works, produced by his Power, and thus the scripture is true in both ways, when it says both that the Father makes all things, and that without the Son no existing thing comes to be; for the activity of the Power points back to him whose Power he is. Since therefore the Son is the Father's power, all the works of the Son are the works of the Power.[105]

Ultimately, Gregory notes that the Father and Son are inseparable and equal in "being" because they have the same power without gradation, shown clearly through their works in creation. Further, the power of the Spirit (δυνάμει τοῦ πνεύματος) completes and perfects this work.[106]

We will now turn to particular passages in Revelation to highlight these theological concepts and relationship between John's writing and other texts. We will see that John uses grammatical and theological tools that at times resemble Jewish and Greco-Roman ideas within his own context, while also highlighting the ways he reimagined or reworked such ideas to make a distinct theological point about Jesus' divine nature and his carrying out of divine prerogatives. Further, we will see how the above patristic authors and concepts are similar to those in Revelation, particularly as we consider a trinitarian reading that acknowledges the unity and distinction between the persons, which is shown clearly through his sharing of divine titles and the divine throne, his reception of worship, and his worthiness and authority to carry out divine activity.

Interpretation of Select Passages

The passages covered in this section were chosen based on their depiction of Jesus as divine and/or their portrayal of his relationship with the Father and Spirit. Through a close reading of these texts, we will see John's incipient trinitarianism through textual clues and theological deductions. We will see that John's Christology entails a view of Jesus that prefigures later pro-Nicene concepts of unity and distinction among the persons. We will

---

[105]*Contra Eunomium* 3.4.33-35. English translation from Gregory of Nyssa, Contra Eunomium *III: An English Translation with Commentary and Supporting Studies*, ed. Johan Leemans and Matthieu Cassin, Vigiliae Christianae Supplements 124 (Leiden: Brill, 2014).
[106]*Ad Ablabium* 3.1.50.

therefore interact with the best interdisciplinary works and ideas on interpreting these passages both to highlight their strengths and show how our method might provide alternate or better readings.

The Word of God and the testimony of Jesus Christ (Rev 1:1-8). Revelation's opening phrase includes an immediate reference to Jesus. As the parallel phrases τὸν λόγον τοῦ Θεοῦ (to the word of God) and καὶ τὴν μαρτυρίαν Ἰησοῦ Χριστοῦ (and to the testimony of Jesus Christ) in 1:2 indicate, John testified (ἐμαρτύρησεν) to a revelation that is both from and about Jesus, albeit initiated by God.[107] This "unveiling" (ἀποκάλυψις) brings to mind the biblical idea of God's righteousness, judgment, and salvific plans being unveiled "through abrupt intervention" (Rom 2:5; 8:19; Eph 3:3).[108] In terms of trinitarian reading, the interplay between God and Christ does not require a subordination that some non-Nicenes later argued, but rather reading through the concept of *redoublement* helps us notice the unity and distinction between the Father and Son. As we will see, Jesus is not merely an angelic guide taking John on a heavenly journey but rather he reveals the vision, similar to how God reveals to prophets in the OT. Leithart reminds us of the NT precedent: "Because the Father has given all to his Son, the Son reveals himself and the Father, making known their mutual and exclusive knowledge of one another (Matt. 11:25-27). . . . We should not infer that reception implies subordination."[109] Athanasius says of 1:8, "The Godhead of the Son is the Father's. It is indivisible. Thus there is one God and none other but he. So, since they are one, and the Godhead itself one, the same things are said of the Son, which are said of the Father, except his being said to be the Father."[110]

Moreover, Jesus is also referred to as the inaugurator of the new covenant (1:5) who sacrifices his own life for the salvation of God's people (Mt 26:27-28; Acts 20:28; Rom 3:25; Eph 1:7; Heb 9:12-14; 1 Pet 1:2). In 1:7 he is "pierced" (αὐτὸν ἐξεκέντησαν), a noticeable allusion to Zechariah 12:10 (MT), which

---

[107]G. K. Beale, *The Book of Revelation*, NIGTC (Grand Rapids, MI: Eerdmans, 1999), 183. Beale asserts that these genitive phrases offer "an intentional ambiguity and therefore a 'general' genitive which includes both subjective and objective aspects." As mentioned in the previous chapter, this portion of the greeting seems to indicate God's giving of the revelation whose source and content both center on Christ. We also discussed this in the previous chapter.

[108]Peter Leithart, *Revelation 1-11*, The International Theological Commentary on the Holy Scripture of the Old and New Testaments (New York: T&T Clark, 2018), 69.

[109]Leithart, *Revelation 1-11*, 73.

[110]*C. Ar.* 3.4.

"contains an ambiguity in that God is the one who is pierced, yet he apparently identifies himself with an associate."[111] Put into this context, John gives the impression that somehow when Jesus the man is pierced, God is pierced—a description that communicates shared divine attributes.

This theme continues, with Jesus appearing as the conduit of God's revelation (1:1), the one who addresses each church with the message (1:11; 2:1), and the one through whose blood Revelation's recipients were freed from sin (1:5). Jesus is continually displayed as more than a mere messenger—he is the one who himself "is coming" (1:7), a designation similar to God's name in 4, "he who is and who was and who is coming."[112] The "first and last" language in 1:17 portrays Jesus clearly designating himself as the coming God,[113] and his use of ἐγώ εἰμι (I am) recalls his statement in John 8:58, "Before Abraham was, I am" (πρὶν Ἀβραὰμ γενέσθαι, ἐγώ εἰμι), for which the Jews tried to stone him for claiming to be God.[114] Jesus also self-identifies as "the Alpha and the Omega" in 22:13, signifying his own sovereignty over history. Hays asserts that "the mysterious coinherence of the identity of God and the identity of Jesus . . . is nowhere expressed more remarkably than in Revelation's deployment of the divine title 'the Alpha and the Omega.'"[115] This language of blood-bought freedom, God's sovereign deliverance, and the divine name bring to mind the exodus story, showing that "Christ has established a counterkingdom—a kingdom opposed to the influence of the

---

[111] Beale, *Book of Revelation*, 198.

[112] R. Kendall Soulen, *The Divine Name(s) and the Holy Trinity*, 2 vols. (Louisville: Westminster John Knox, 2011), 1:181. Soulen remarks, "Jesus Christ is, quite literally, the one who comes 'in the name of the Lord.'"

[113] Richard Bauckham, *The Theology of the Book of Revelation* (Cambridge: Cambridge University Press, 1993), 19.

[114] G. K. Beale, *John's Use of the Old Testament in Revelation* (Sheffield, UK: Sheffield Academic Press, 1998), 327-28, further notes that Jn 8:58 uses the same striking language as Rev 1:4, and in the same awkward grammatical form: "There are much better, even more correct, ways of the saying the same thing . . . 'before Abraham was born, *I already existed*' [or] 'before Abraham was born, *I existed from generations of old.*' . . . Such an unusual use of ἐγώ εἰμι in John 8:58 probably highlights it as an allusion to Isaiah 43.10, 13 specifically, and generally to the numerous repetitions of ἐγώ εἰμι with reference to God in Isaiah 41-52." So, God and Jesus use the same form of ἐγώ εἰμι in Rev 1:4 and Jn 8:58, and then Jesus himself uses it again (albeit slightly modified) in Rev 1:17. John's language strongly indicates that Jesus is to be identified as God himself, both in John's use of OT allusions and in the very words of Jesus himself in canonical context.

[115] Richard B. Hays, "Faithful Witness, Alpha and Omega: The Identity of Jesus in the Apocalypse of John," in *Revelation and the Politics of Apocalyptic Interpretation*, ed. Richard B. Hays and Stefan Alkier (Waco, TX: Baylor University Press, 2012), 74.

Son: The Slain Lamb and Risen King 95

dragon and the beast, the Pharaohs of this narrative."[116] This lends itself to the conclusion that Christ is portrayed as sovereign and a deliverer over Roman and all other forms of worldly emperorship, just like his Father. Given that John opens the letter with the connection between God and Christ, it is no surprise that it continues and even develops here.

Collins has made a strong case against this conclusion, asserting that Revelation "seems to portray the risen Jesus as an angel or at least in angelomorphic terms" rather than the high Christology associated with the Gospel of John and Hebrews.[117] She suggests that the message-delivering angel in 1:1 could be Jesus since John states in the same verse that God gave the revelation to Jesus.[118] But as we mentioned above, Jesus is identified more with God's nature than an angel's in the prologue (1:1-8). Also, it seems uncharacteristic of John to tie the angel and Jesus together in the same sentence in such a vague manner. While John certainly portrays Jesus with angelic qualities—the mighty angel in 10:1 is also described coming from the clouds with a shining aura—John also uses specific language befitting of a deity when he portrays Jesus with a golden sash and white hair in 1:13-14,[119] characteristics that also apply to the Ancient of Days in Daniel 7.[120] Thomas Hieke concludes, "It is the risen Jesus Christ in whom all the images about heavenly and human-like beings coincide. It also becomes clear that Jesus Christ forms an inseparable unity with the Ancient One, the Lord God, the Father. This is 'new' and 'a revelation'; however, the attributes and imagery are familiar to all those who are acquainted with the Scriptures."[121]

John also later reports Jesus freely receiving worship, while angels intentionally do not (Rev 19:10; 22:9). As we will see below, these passages and others help us see that John uses celestial or awe-stricken descriptions for

---

[116]James L. Resseguie, *The Revelation of John* (Grand Rapids, MI: Baker Academic, 2009), 67. For an exploration of Revelation as a document of counter kingdom or civil disobedience, see Thomas B. Slater, *Revelation as Civil Disobedience: Witnesses Not Warriors in John's Apocalypse* (Nashville: Abingdon, 2019).

[117]Adela Yarbro Collins and John J. Collins, *King and Messiah as Son of God: Divine, Human, and Angelic Messianic Figures in Biblical and Related Literature* (Grand Rapids, MI: Eerdmans, 2008), 189. Yarbro Collins wrote the latter four chapters of the volume, according to the introduction.

[118]Collins and Collins, *King and Messiah as Son of God*, 190.

[119]Robyn J. Whitaker, *Ekphrasis, Vision, and Persuasion in the Book of Revelation*, WUNT 2, no. 410 (Tübingen: Mohr Siebeck, 2015), 86.

[120]Ben Witherington III, *Revelation* (Cambridge: Cambridge University Press, 2003), 81.

[121]Thomas Hieke, "The Reception of Daniel 7 in the Revelation of John," in *Revelation and the Politics of Apocalyptic Interpretation*, 57.

Jesus while not conflating his nature with that of an angel. We will continue this discussion below as it pertains to other passages in Revelation, but suffice to say for now that the aforementioned logic of Tertullian and Origen to speak of Jesus in angelic terms without the necessary ontological equation is worth considering here and elsewhere.

The divine Son of Man (Rev 1:9-20). In this passage John describes a vision of Jesus that includes vivid images drawn from Daniel 7. As Benjamin Reynolds has summarized, this section is setup by John quoting "the Old Testament to indicate that Jesus Christ (1:5-6) is both the cloud-riding 'one like a son of man' envisioned by Daniel (7:13) *and* the 'pierced' messenger of God prophesied by Zechariah (12:10)."[122] Given the reference to the Son of Man and accompanying descriptions, this passage is inserted into debates around the nature of the Son of Man figure in John's vision. Our primary concern here is whether John presents this figure as divine or angelic.

Collins continues her assertion of Jesus' angelomorphism when she notes that the appearance of the risen Christ in 1:12-16 does not explicitly portray him as either divine or an angel, but the "features of that description are attributed elsewhere to angels."[123] As a defense for this conclusion, she notes that John does not apply "Son of Man" as a title for Jesus but instead disobeys grammatical rules to call him "one like a son of man," which is closer to the Hebrew and LXX and unlike the double-articular Gospel references.[124] Her point is that John, in effect, recovers the Jewishness of the term by dropping the article that the Gospel tradition added. By removing the article, Collins infers that John is going back to the historical context of Daniel 7:13 wherein the "one like a son of man" is more likely a messiah or an angel than a divine being. Collins asserts that this portion of Revelation "may, but need not, imply divinity."[125] If we consider this illustration alone, Collins has a point. One cannot say definitively that Jesus is any sort of divine figure simply because he is given Son of Man characteristics, however exalted they may appear.

---

[122]Benjamin E. Reynolds, "The Parables of Enoch and Revelation 1:1-20: Daniel's Son of Man," in *Reading Revelation in Context: John's Apocalypse and Second Temple Judaism*, ed. Ben C. Blackwell, John K. Goodrich, and Jason Maston (Grand Rapids, MI: Zondervan Academic, 2019), 37.
[123]Collins and Collins, *King and Messiah as Son of God*, 190-91.
[124]Collins and Collins, *King and Messiah as Son of God*, 191. In 1:13 she points out that the phrase ὅμοιον υἱὸν ἀνθρώπου probably is either a translation of the Aramaic in Daniel 7:13 or the Hebrew in Daniel 10:16, and that υἱὸν is in the accusative though it should be in the dative or genitive.
[125]Collins and Collins, *King and Messiah as Son of God*, 192.

Son: The Slain Lamb and Risen King 97

The connections John draws between Daniel 7 and Jesus are indeed in reference to the Son of Man figure, but he does not stop there; he also folds Jesus into the nature of YHWH through Daniel 7 and select other OT allusions. The meaning of "Son of Man" is not found simply by mapping Daniel 7 and/or the Gospel tradition directly onto this text but rather by paying attention to how *John* uses the allusion to make his own theological point about the relationship between Jesus and YHWH. Yet we may appeal to Markus Zehnder, who has argued that Son of Man as a divine figure was a recognized concept in postbiblical Jewish Second Temple literature, "[so] we are compelled to deduce that the use of the expression 'Son of Man' in some of its instances in the NT, insofar as it relates to Daniel 7:13, points to a conception of Jesus as more than an exemplary ideal human being but as a divine figure."[126]

Put another way, Collins may be correct that John reverted to the Jewish rendering, but he did so with the intent to show Jesus as a divine figure—the Ancient of Days characteristics are one piece of a fuller argument for Jesus' identity. As Paul notes, John "incorporates aspects of Daniel's earlier vision of the Ancient of Days, so that John sees Jesus as both divine and as the messenger of the divine."[127]

Michael Shepherd notes, "The great weakness of the angelic interpretation [of the Son of Man figure in Dan 7] is that nowhere in the Hebrew canon do angels receive dominion and worship (Dan 7:14)."[128] This is true enough, and *even if* descriptions of Jesus are or appear to be angelic in nature, this does not reduce or dismiss his divinity. As Bucur has rightly said, John can use "angelic characteristics in descriptions of God or humans, while not necessarily implying that the latter are angels *stricto sensu*."[129] Origen, for instance, explicitly refers to Revelation 1:8, 4:8, 21:6, and 22:13 in his defense of Christ's divine attributes:

---

[126] Markus Zehnder, "Why the Danielic 'Son of Man' Is a Divine Being," *BBR* 24, no. 3 (2014): 347.

[127] Ian Paul, *Revelation* (Downers Grove, IL: IVP Academic, 2018), 67. Though not commenting on Revelation directly, J. Ross Wagner, *Reading the Sealed Book: Reading Old Greek Isaiah and the Problem of Septuagint Hermeneutics* (Waco, TX: Baylor University Press, 2013), 62, argues alternatively that such constructions were nothing more than translation phenomena, in which the later LXX translations brought Greek recensions into conformity with the Hebrew, which "assured a monolingual [Hellenistic Jew] audience . . . these scriptural texts faithfully represent their Hebrew parents."

[128] Michael B. Shepherd, "Daniel 7:13 and the New Testament Son of Man," *WTJ* 68 (2006): 103.

[129] Bogdan G. Bucur, "Hierarchy, Prophecy, and the Angelomorphic Spirit: A Contribution to the Study of the Book of Revelation's *Wirkungsgeschichte*," *JBL* 127, no. 1 (2008): 175.

And that you may understand that the omnipotence of Father and Son is one and the same, just as God and the Lord are one and the same with the Father, listen to the way in in which John speaks in the Apocalypse: *These things says the Lord God, who was and is and is to come, the Almighty*. For *he who is to come*, who else is that than Christ? And as no one ought to be offended that, while the Father is God, the Saviour also is *God*, so also, since the Father is called *Almighty*, no one ought to be offended that the Son of God is also called *Almighty*.[130]

Origen's commentary shows that John's allusion to the Tetragrammaton—with "Almighty" as the proxy for the divine name—is one of the starkest examples in Scripture of Christ being directly identified with YHWH.[131]

While other early Christian writers mentioned thus far have quoted Revelation 1:4, 8; 4:8 in relation to the divinity of Christ or the Spirit, Athanasius offers a clearer pro-Nicene comment on the passage in his *Apologia Contra Arianos*. In a chapter on the eternal and uncreated nature of the Son, Athanasius notes that the Apocalypse refers to Christ as the one "who is and who was and who is to come," which indicates the eternality of Christ.[132] This was one biblical text in a long line of texts that Athanasius used to prove from Scripture that Arius was wrong in saying, "There was a time when the Son was not." Elsewhere, when discussing how Scripture describes the Father and the Son sharing the same essence, he once again finds this language in Revelation 1:4, 8, 4:8 helpful, noting that a phrase like "he who is and who was and who is to come" shows that what is said of the Son is also said of the Father.[133] He also uses this argument in *Letters to Serapion*, in which he directly quotes 1:8 and says, "The Father is Almighty; the Son is also Almighty, as John said."[134]

---

[130]*Princ.* 1.2.10, emphasis original. As Prigent has noted about Clement of Alexandria, Origen, and others: "The earliest commentators" on this passage concluded that "in spite of appearances, it is always Christ who utters this self-designation"; see Pierre Prigent, *Commentary on the Apocalypse of St. John*, trans. Wendy Pradels (Tübingen: Mohr Siebeck, 2001), 123.

[131]As Holmes, *Quest for the Trinity*, 75, notes, "As for so many in the Christian tradition, God's ontological primacy and simplicity is established for Origen not by rational speculations about the necessary nature of the divine, but by reading Exodus 3:13-14." We have already noted above the less-than-tidy ontological and economic language used by Origen in his writings.

[132]*C. Ar.* 1.4.

[133]*C. Ar.* 3.23; *Syn.* 3.49.

[134]*Ep. Serap.* 2.2.2. English translation from Athanasius the Great and Didymus the Blind, *Works on the Spirit*, trans. Mark DelCogliano, Andrew Radde-Gallwitz, and Lewis Ayres (Yonkers, NY: St Vladimir's Seminary Press, 2011).

In another place, Athanasius explains that the only way the Son could receive worship is if he is "the Father's own Son by essence."¹³⁵ Here he points out that in Revelation 22:9, when John moves to worship an angel, he is told only to worship God. For Athanasius, this statement proves that Jesus is the divine Son of God because angels worship him (Heb 1:6). He argues that though the angels are in greater glory than humans, they are clearly in subordination to Jesus. This means, then, that Jesus must have the same divine glory as the Father since the angels say "worship God alone," and yet they worship Jesus. As Sarah Underwood Dixon rightly concludes, "The angel asserts that John must worship God alone, and the context makes clear that the worship of the exalted Christ is an appropriate and indeed required expression of his monotheistic devotion."¹³⁶

Finally, though Hebrews 1:5-14 seems to indicate a distinct superiority of Jesus over the angels, it was not uncommon in early Christian communities to use polymorphism to indicate the transcendence of Jesus over the material realm and the restrictions of mortality.¹³⁷ So, even if Collins is correct—and we have shown the weakness of her argument—the use of angelomorphism and polymorphism in early christological reflection does not by necessity lessen the divinity of Jesus in John's telling of the vision. All of this said, the context of the passage leans more toward Jesus as coequal with the Father than as a mere angelic being, especially if we notice John's intertextual clues and some broader illuminating pro-Nicene tools. A few examples will clarify the point.

We should first notice that in 1:10-11 Jesus gets John's attention with an authoritative "voice like a trumpet," much like YHWH's voice in Exodus 19:16. John seeing the voice (βλέπειν τὴν φωνὴν) is reminiscent of Israel "seeing" YHWH's voice in Exodus 20:18 and Moses seeing it in Deuteronomy 7:11 (LXX).¹³⁸ This also resonates with the Lord's command to other prophets to

---

¹³⁵*C. Ar.* 2.23. English translation from Anatolios, *Athanasius*.
¹³⁶Sarah Underwood Dixon, "The Apocalypse of Zephaniah and Revelation 22:6-21," in *Reading Revelation in Context*, 180.
¹³⁷For more on polymorphism in early Christianity, see Paul Foster, "Polymorphic Christology: Its Origins and Development in Early Christianity," *JTS* 58, no. 1 (2007): 66-99.
¹³⁸Leithart, *Revelation 1-11*, 108. This phrase βλέπειν τὴν φωνὴν ἥτις ἐλάλει also could be taken from Dan 7:11 (LXX). Beale, *Book of Revelation*, 85, notes that John is purposeful in his use of Daniel in the surrounding context but may have "spontaneously used this language without much forethought" because Dan 7:11 speaks about the beast's "boastful words." If

write down the revelation (Jer 30:2; Dan 12:4). The order of events in 1:17 mirrors the sequence found in Daniel 10:8-20: "(1) The prophet observes a vision, (2) falls on his face in fear, (3) subsequently is strengthened by a heavenly being, and (4) then receives further revelation."[139] As mentioned above and reiterated here, it is no surprise that John gets the impression in his vision of Jesus that he is, in fact, a prophet himself receiving words from God and not a mere angel.[140] Indeed, it appears that Jesus is almost literally God's Word—"an *embodied* Voice."[141]

Further, when John turns "to see the voice that was speaking," he sees "one like a son of man," wearing a robe and golden sash, with hair "white as snow," eyes "like a blazing fire," glowing feet, and "a voice like the sound of rushing waters" (1:13-16). The implication is striking—Jesus is portrayed as both the Son of Man *and* explicitly connected with the divine characteristics of the Ancient of Days mentioned in Daniel's account.[142]

Other contemporary apocalypses at times use this same blended description for the divine-human Son of Man; however, John is unique in his introductory description of Jesus' authoritative voice, and as Revelation continues, he uses it as a building block for Jesus as having the same nature as YHWH with the culmination being his throne-sharing with the Father in Revelation 4–5. In 1 Enoch, it appears Enoch or the Son of Man is allowed to sit on God's throne in eschatological judgment (1 En. 5:13; 55:4; 61:8), though it is debatable if he exercises judgment or merely observes it from an exalted position near God. Indeed, Moses appears to be able to sit on God's throne in *Exagoge* 68–80, indicating his status as a righteous man worthy of sitting on God's throne; however, this event is portrayed as an honorific bestowal because Moses' uprightness rather than Moses sharing God's throne in a strict sense. In 2 Enoch 22:8, Enoch is dressed in garments that radiate divine glory,

---

subconscious, this furthers the hypothesis that John inescapably alludes to the OT/LXX throughout the Apocalypse.

[139]G. K. Beale and Sean M. McDonough, "Revelation," in *Commentary on the New Testament Use of the Old Testament*, ed. G. K. Beale and D. A. Carson (Grand Rapids, MI: Baker Academic, 2007), 1092. Leithart, *Revelation 1-11*, 109, notes the similarities between this passage and the commissioning scenes of Ezekiel, Daniel, and Isaiah.

[140]Leithart, *Revelation 1-1*, 75 surmises that though John the Baptist is not the author of Revelation as some have suggested, he may consider himself a prophet like John the Baptist given the structural parallels between Jn 1 and Rev 1.

[141]Leithart, *Revelation 1-11*, 108; emphasis original.

[142]Witherington, *Revelation*, 81.

yet his throne appears to be seated *near* God's throne rather than directly *on* it. In 3 Enoch 10:1, Enoch-Metatron appears to have reached the peak exaltation of the Enoch tradition. And yet his throne is *like* God's throne; he does not share the same throne. Rabbi Akiva (ca. AD 50–135), a major contributor to the *Mishnah*, interpreted Daniel 7:9 as teaching the existence of two thrones: one for God and one for the Davidic Messiah. Rabbi Yosi challenged this interpretation, asserting that multiple thrones existed so that God could dole out judgment on one throne and mercy on another.[143] Jesus in Revelation, however, receives heavenly hymns sung to him alongside God—not from a separate throne, but on the same throne at the same time as God (Rev 4–5).

John may also be giving Jesus OT angelic characteristics, such as wearing a long robe (Ezek 9:2) and golden sash (Dan 10:5 LXX=MT)[144] and having bronze feet (Dan 10:6 LXX). However, Jesus' white-as-wool hair and flaming eyes in 1:14 are then paralleled with that of the theophany in Daniel 7:9-14. John is also amazed at Jesus' blazing eyes and face "like the sun shining in all its brilliance," akin to the description of the angel in Daniel 10:5-6 LXX. While the Daniel parallel is still there, John's description of his voice as "like the roar of many waters" (ὡς φωνὴ ὑδάτων πολλῶν) reads more like God's voice in the MT of Ezekiel 1:24 and 43:2.[145] Robert Gundry asserts that John is using angelic descriptors for Jesus but concludes that (1) Jesus is not merely another angel compared to others in Revelation, and (2) deification language also is present.[146] So, whether Daniel is actually describing an angelophany or theophany in 10:5-6, John seems to intentionally attach divine characteristics to Jesus, which does not allow the reader to associate Jesus with a mere exalted being or angel.[147] As we noted above, the LXX rendering of Daniel 7:13 is disputed with respect to whether the Son of Man and the Ancient of Days are the same figure, but it seems likely that they are two associated figures. Indeed, even if one wants to assert that Jesus is not

---

[143] Carol A. Newsom and Brennan W. Breed, *Daniel: A Commentary* (Louisville: Westminster John Knox, 2014), 247. Similar issues arise with Mk 14:62, which we will mention briefly below.

[144] Though, as we saw above, Whitaker says that this may be a description of deity.

[145] Beale, *Book of Revelation*, 210.

[146] Robert H. Gundry, *The Old Is Better: New Testament Essays in Support of Traditional Interpretations* (Eugene, OR: Wipf & Stock, 2010), 377-97. Citing Jesus' description of himself in Revelation 3:14, he notes that Jesus was "acting out of a sense that God was his Father in a distinctive way."

[147] Loren T. Stuckenbruck, *Angel Veneration and Christology: A Study in Early Judaism and in the Christology of the Apocalypse of John*, WUNT 2, no. 70 (Tübingen: Mohr Siebeck, 1995), 213.

identified with God in the way we have asserted thus far, we can safely rule out either an angelic ontology for Jesus or some sort of mere melding of two figures into one. Instead, we can acknowledge that God and Jesus are two figures while noting that John sees a close connection (but not conflation) between their identities when he applies Ancient of Days language to Jesus.

In any event, we have seen that it would be out of character for John to suddenly demote Jesus here, so his divinity cannot be ignored. Looking back as a trinitarian reader, the Daniel 7 and 10 parallel is pregnant with ingredients for the idea of a hypostatic union because these texts allow us to reflect upon a union of divinity and humanity in the one person of Jesus, which makes sense of the Ancient of Days language in Revelation being applied to him while not diminishing the identity of the Ancient of Days with God. Leithart lucidly observes the connection between the epilogue and this passage: "The structural link between the Trinitarian blessings (vv. 4-6) and the vision of Jesus (vv. 12-16) highlights the fact that the revelation of Jesus is the unveiling of Triune life."[148] Thus, he is not just the exalted Son of Man; he is associated with the divine nature and divine actions of YHWH from the beginning of the letter until now. As Dennis Johnson says,

> We might infer that this merely indicates that Christ reflects the glory of the One who sent him . . . but the white hair of the Son of Man says more than this. In the symbolic vocabulary provided by Daniel's vision, John sees "one like a son of man" who is distinguished from and identified with the Ancient of Days—a mysterious combination but consistent with the fact that he lays claim to the title "the first and the last" (1:17). . . . The Son of Man is God, infinite in wisdom and holiness.[149]

Johnson goes on to explain that John's reaction to interacting with Jesus in 1:17—"I fell at his feet like a dead man" (ἔπεσα πρὸς τοὺς πόδας αὐτοῦ ὡς νεκρός)—is similar to Daniel's response to hearing God's voice (Dan 10:9).[150] Of course, one could argue that John falls down at the feet of nondivine beings elsewhere (ἔπεσα προσκυνῆσαι ἔμπροσθεν τῶν ποδῶν τοῦ ἀγγέλου; 22:8) and therefore his response does not prove the deity of Jesus. However,

---

[148]Leithart, *Revelation 1-11*, 68.
[149]Dennis E. Johnson, *Triumph of the Lamb* (Phillipsburg, NJ: P&R, 2001), 59. See also Leithart, *Revelation 1-11*, 111-12.
[150]Johnson, *Triumph of the Lamb*, 61.

in a book so concerned with true and false worship, John does not record Jesus deflecting worship away from himself like the angels do.[151]

Further, John says that Jesus put his right hand on him (τὴν δεξιὰν αὐτοῦ ἐπ' ἐμὲ), indicating an act of authority over John and bringing to mind Jesus' authoritative position at God's right hand (Acts 7:55-56; Rom 8:34; Eph 1:20; Col 3:1; Heb 1:3).[152] It is also Jesus' right hand that holds the "seven stars," which reminds us of God's control of the stars in the OT (Gen 1:16; Pss 8:3; 136:9). One cannot mistake the evident connections in authority, activity, and appearance that John continues to make between God and Jesus. As Aune observes, the "first and the last" language,[153] the Ancient of Days descriptions being applied to Jesus, and "the Living One" title as a probable "double entendre" of the God of Israel as "the living God" (Deut 5:26; 1 Sam 17:26; Jer 10:10; Dan 6:27) "implies some kind of equal status for God and Jesus Christ."[154] These connections undercut Collins, showing that John highlights Jesus' divine nature in this passage and the Apocalypse as a whole.

Collins has rejected the idea that Jesus himself linked his identity with that of the Son of Man in Daniel 7:13, instead arguing that Jesus "closely associated" himself with Daniel's Son of Man.[155] In fact, according to her, it is probably the fault of his followers that his Son of Man teachings were altered from mere association (what Jesus likely actually taught) to direct identification ("in the reflection of some of Jesus' followers").[156] However, Mark 12 challenges her assertion. There, Jesus associates himself with the "lord" of Psalm 110, which incites similar questions about his claims to exaltation as a man greater than even the Son of David. These divine Son of Man characteristics are not merely characteristics John claims to have seen but are also quotes he attaches to Jesus himself. It is likely that his followers were aware

---

[151] Alan David Hultberg, "Messianic Exegesis in the Apocalypse: The Significance of the Old Testament for the Christology of Revelation" (PhD diss., Trinity Evangelical Divinity School, 2001), 326-27.

[152] Leithart, *Revelation 1-11*, 120.

[153] Attributed to God in Isaiah 44:6 LXX: οὕτως λέγει ὁ θεὸς ὁ βασιλεὺς τοῦ ισραηλ ὁ ῥυσάμενος αὐτὸν θεὸς σαβαωθ ἐγὼ πρῶτος καὶ ἐγὼ μετὰ ταῦτα πλὴν ἐμοῦ οὐκ ἔστιν θεός.

[154] Aune, *Apocalypticism, Prophecy and Magic in Early Christianity*, 206-7.

[155] Adela Yarbro Collins, "The Origin of the Designation of Jesus as 'Son of Man,'" *HTR* 80, no. 4 (1987): 406.

[156] Collins, "Origin of the Designation of Jesus as 'Son of Man,'" 406.

of Jesus' claims. Bird argues, "As Jesus' own idiomatic from of self-reference, the phrase [Son of Man] is used as a cipher for the eschatological mystery that surrounds his mission. He can even use it tacit references to his divinely given regal-like authority and let the designation link him to a role of suffering and rejection in the divine plan."[157]

Obviously, John offers his own spin on the Son of Man tradition in comparison to other Jewish and Christian literature, but it seems improbable to assert that Jesus himself did not claim to be the Son of Man and that John would not have access to the Gospel tradition associated with the term.[158] In any event, John clearly identifies Jesus with this figure—this same Jesus whom John later sees on God's throne.

Now, if we take Collins's argument to the Apocalypse, one would assume that John is also mistaken in his exegesis of Daniel because he misunderstood Jesus (or at least the Gospel tradition) in the first place. However, it seems that John cannot make sense of his vision unless Jesus both *is* the heavenly Son of Man and is somehow *identified* with God's very nature. His vacillating descriptions of Jesus as the Son of Man and Ancient of Days reveal this. In 14:14, after receiving worship alongside God, Jesus is again ὅμοιον υἱὸν ἀνθρώπου ("one like a son of man") wearing a golden crown and wielding a sharp sickle as a divine judge.[159] Moreover, the verbal connection between Revelation 14:14 and Isaiah 19:1 (LXX), where "the Lord is seated on a swift cloud" (κάθηται ἐπὶ νεφέλης κούφης) and surrounded by multitudes, implies a throne-room scene.[160] John appears to take the divinity of Jesus for granted here, since he has already explained that the Son of Man role is in some sense a divine one. John interprets the OT here and throughout Revelation, joining other NT

---

[157] Michael F. Bird, *Are You the One Who Is to Come? The Historical Jesus and the Messianic Question* (Grand Rapids, MI: Baker Academic, 2009), 98.

[158] Bird, *Are You the One Who Is to Come?*, 96, makes this case against Collins's assertion that Revelation reflects a pre-Synoptic tradition. Boyarin, "What Enoch Can Teach Us About Jesus?," 58-59, suggests that Revelation was likely written after the Gospels, and yet John does not follow their lead in using the term in the titular form.

[159] Beale, *Book of Revelation*, 776-800. While beyond the scope of this book, Beale discusses the debate surrounding 14:14-19, concluding that the background of "sickle" (δρέπανα) in Isaiah 2:4; Joel 4:10; and Mic 4:3 coupled with the grape harvest metaphors of Is 18; Jer 28:33; 32:30 LXX et al. lean toward a picture of war and judgment.

[160] Brian J. Tabb, *All Things New: Revelation as Canonical Capstone* (Downers Grove, IL: IVP Academic, 2019), 52. Tabb in part uses this argument to challenge Aune's (*Revelation 6-16*, 841) assumption that the Son of Man here is an angelic being.

writers by following "the lead *given by Jesus himself* concerning his presence in the ancient events."[161] John is not mistakenly reinterpreting his Lord—he is correctly interpreting his vision alongside and in light of the Christian tradition. His interpretation makes sense when we consider our earlier point that John draws on the Son of Man vision in Daniel in a similar fashion as apocalypses such as 1 Enoch and 4 Ezra but ultimately creates a distinctly Christian version that identifies the Son of Man as Jesus and then elevates him from a divine messenger to sharing the throne with God himself (Rev 4–5).

Additionally, John records in 1:16 that Jesus has a "sharp, double-edged sword coming from his mouth." In 19:15 he declares eschatological war on God's enemies with a sword protruding from his mouth. Williamson notes the similarities between this passage and Isaiah 11:4:

> Isaiah 11:4 says that the Messiah "shall strike the ruthless with the rod of his mouth, / and with the breath of his lips he shall slay the wicked"—a text that St. Paul applies to Christ's defeat of the man of lawlessness at the end of history (2 Thess 2:8). Isaiah 49:2 says that the Lord made the mouth of his Servant a "sharp-edged sword." This description of the risen Christ combines both images, and the sword in his mouth represents the all-powerful word of God by which God created the world and brings judgment (Wis 18:1; Rev 19:13).[162]

Compare this with Genesis 1 (God speaking creation into existence) and John 1 (the Word creating all things): both associate God's word with creation. Also compare with Revelation 12:5, wherein a son is born of a woman and raised up to "rule" (ποιμαίνειν) with an "iron rod" (ῥάβδῳ σιδηρᾷ). This may indicate the fulfillment of the prophecy in Isaiah 11:4 and also in 49:2, wherein YHWH is shown to be acting in divine judgment, further solidifying the Son's divine-nature-sharing role as eschatological judge.[163] It seems

---

[161] Graeme Goldsworthy, *The Son of God and the New Creation* (Wheaton, IL: Crossway: 2015), 123, emphasis original. Though Goldsworthy's work here only tackles the last few chapters of Revelation, he shows that Jesus repeatedly and inescapably teaches about his own divinity, using the OT as his apologetic. With Goldsworthy's method, the narrative of Revelation can be folded in quite easily and successfully.

[162] Peter S. Williamson, *Revelation*, Catholic Commentary on Sacred Scripture (Grand Rapids, MI: Baker Academic, 2015), 53. Ford notes that the combination of a sword proceeding from his mouth and his ruling with an iron rod (19:15) also appear together in Pss. Sol. 17:24, 27; cf. J. Massyngberde Ford, *Revelation*, AB 38 (Garden City, NY: Doubleday, 1975), 314.

[163] Beale and McDonough, "Revelation," 1092. For a prodigious survey of the throne room as a divine courtroom, see Alan S. Bandy, *The Prophetic Lawsuit in the Book of Revelation* (Sheffield, UK: Sheffield Phoenix Press, 2010).

that the churches in Asia could only deduce that eschatological hope was coming through him.

The pro-Nicene concepts of *redoublement* and partitive exegesis help us attend to the ways John uses both divine and human descriptions for Jesus' nature and activity, while also tethering him to the Father's nature and activity. As many patristic theologians noticed, the Son's identity as the Word indicates preexistence at the very least, and further reflection led many of them to assume that the Father's Word must have the same divine nature; he could never be without his Word, and his Word carries the same divine power.[164] Contrary to many modern scholars' alternatives, a trinitarian reading and pro-Nicene logic alleviates some of this passage's thorny language and imagery.

The eschatological judge (Rev 2:18). To Thyatira, Jesus calls himself "Son of God" and repeats the Son of Man language mentioned above. Collins also challenges the divinity of Jesus here, saying that 2:18 is the only instance in which the Apocalypse explicitly calls Jesus the "Son of God."[165] Unsurprisingly, Collins sees this Daniel 10 allusion as describing "an angelic heavenly messiah."[166] Yet the bulk of the Thyatiran message offers more to consider.

First, Jesus tells the church that he will "strike dead" or "kill" Jezebel's children. The Greek phrase ἀποκτενῶ ἐν θανάτῳ compares to Ezekiel 33:27 (LXX), which is followed by the phrase "and they will know that I am the Lord" (Ezek 33:29 LXX). As Beale notes, "And they will know that I am the Lord" is used approximately fifty times in the LXX of Ezekiel, mostly referring to "God being known as a result of judgment, as in Revelation 2:23, which also highlights further the divine nature of Jesus' judicial function."[167]

This probable allusion reinforces the idea that he is the righteous, divine judge who "searches mind and heart" and "gives to each according to his deeds" (2:23). This formula of omniscience is startlingly parallel to the Lord's

---

[164]See, for example, *C. Ar.* 1.14.
[165]Collins and Collins, *King and Messiah as Son of God*, 202.
[166]Collins and Collins, *King and Messiah as Son of God*, 202. She refers to other instances where Jesus is described as a "son," such as "the son of David" in 5:5 and 22:16 and the son of the woman in chap. 12. Since these are somewhat ambiguous and symbolic, she suggests that the language "ought not be pressed." This an unfortunate pass on her part because the message to Thyatira gives ample clues to the divinity of Jesus.
[167]Beale, *Book of Revelation*, 264.

words in Jeremiah 17:10 as well.[168] In Jeremiah 17:10 ("I examine the mind") and here, God on the one hand declares his ability to know their hearts and minds, and on the other hand he promises to reward or punish based on this knowledge. While angels throughout Jewish literature exercised varying roles as agents in God's judgment of the world, Jesus here appears to be taking the actual judging upon himself while claiming in some sense the identity of YHWH, a role that angels never undertake in the MT. The υἱὸς τοῦ θεοῦ language by John is, then, placed in John's narrative constellation as both a reference to Jesus' function as the Messiah and his filial status as the divine Son.

Second, John's use of the Son of Man language has already been shown to reflect the divine (ontological union with YHWH) more than the angelic (a merely heavenly mediator), even if polymorphism is involved. John marries together his visionary experiences with a scripturally soaked imagination to communicate through marvel, metaphor, and midrash the Son's participation in what is uniquely true of YHWH while also underscoring his divine commission from God and communion with his church. Put another way, we can reasonably surmise that when υἱὸς τοῦ θεοῦ is placed in John's narrative constellation and in the orbit of his intertextuality, the title combines ontology and economy. On ontology, we see his power and authority as the divine judge; on economy, we see his inseparable operation with the Father as they enact judgment together. John's abundant use of OT intertextuality here and elsewhere reminds us that the OT contains the necessary subject matter to make sense of his triadic vision, reminding us that God's providential inspiration features the OT and NT as a complementary witness to the one triune God.

Dispensing the Spirit (Rev 3:1-6). To Sardis, the vision records Jesus employing a slight twist on his greeting to Ephesus, as the one "who has the seven spirits of God and the seven stars." "The one who" language here resembles language for the Father that we have noted elsewhere. Bruce Metzger supposes that this phrase indicates his "sovereign control over churches and

---

[168]Ford, *Revelation*, 402-6, notes that the title "Son of God" indicates a more unique filial relationship to God than the "Son of Man" title, and though John could be referring to either a priestly or political messiah or to an angelic figure like Michael or Melchizedek, the allusion to God's own omniscience is evident in his searching eyes.

the source of spiritual power."[169] But to take this a step further, Jesus' control over the seven spirits may have a more specific application, signifying his inseparable activity with the Holy Spirit. This connection to the Spirit is especially pertinent considering that he speaks to the church(es) alongside the Spirit (3:6).

Further, as Thomas and Macchia point out, the mention of the "book of life" (βίβλου τῆς ζωῆς) in 3:5 alludes to language that appears in Exodus 32:31-33. In Exodus the book belongs to YHWH; here Jesus "has [the same] authority to expunge names from the book of life. For this book belongs to [Jesus]."[170] This same language appears again in Revelation 13:8 and 17:8, reiterating Jesus' eternal authority over the beast and his minions.

While one could argue that Jesus is exerting borrowed or channeled power from God, the plain language of the text describes Jesus' ability to enact divine prerogatives by his own authority, even with the Father present, for there is no competition between him and Jesus in terms of authority and activity. In terms of *redoublement*, Jesus does not need to acquiesce in this situation, because he has the same right and ability as God to eternally judge and to send the Spirit by virtue of his divine nature. In turn, this reminds us of Jesus as the dispenser of the Spirit in John 15:26 and 20:22, which is important of itself, because in Israel's sacred traditions only YHWH bestows the Spirit. The doctrine of inseparable operations is clearly present in this way.

The holy one and the keys of David (Rev 3:7). To Philadelphia, John records Jesus describing himself as "the holy one, the true one, who has the key of David." As Ford notes, holiness and truthfulness "are essential attributes of God in the OT, where He is designated the Holy One (Isa 1:4, 5:9, etc.) or the God of Truth (cf. Exod 34:6, Isa 65:16, etc.).... These titles are used for God in Revelation 6:10, but are applied here to the speaker of the prophecies."[171] So it seems rather clear that Jesus is introducing himself in divine terms, both within the grammar of the OT and even within the theocentric framework of Revelation itself. More than a simple description of an attribute, Jesus uses these terms to describe his *name*, giving the impression

---

[169] Bruce Metzger, *Breaking the Code: Understanding the Book of Revelation* (Nashville: Abingdon, 1993), 39.

[170] John Christopher Thomas and Frank D. Macchia, *Revelation*, THNTC (Grand Rapids, MI: Eerdmans, 2016), 116-17.

[171] Ford, *Revelation*, 414.

Son: The Slain Lamb and Risen King

that he is ontologically divine. *Redoublement* allows us to reject the notion that these titles are merely borrowed or derivative (as we have seen McGrath and others argue in various ways already), instead noticing that these titles indicate not mere activity but also nature. As we saw, the pro-Nicenes were quick to defend divine simplicity as necessary to maintain the oneness and immutability of God, and the idea that the Father could dole out some of his attributes or power to Jesus would indicate that he has a cup of divinity, as it were, that he could empty. Instead, it is more faithful to the text and theological consistency to lean into the biblical portrait—God is one and simple, and yet each person is fully God and therefore *just is* everything it is to be God.

Beale and McDonough note that the "keys of David" alludes to Isaiah 22:22, with "David" substituted for "death and Hades," as well as being heavily influenced by the "open doors that shall not be closed" language of Isaiah 45. They also rightly point out that Isaiah 22 itself points back to the prophecy of Isaiah 9:6, which predicts this future Israelite ruler to be an "Eternal Father."[172] More than just the exalted Messiah on David's throne, Jesus exercises the eternal sovereignty of God over the kingdom of all kingdoms. Christ alone can open the door;[173] he has the authority to admit people into God's kingdom or send them away to eternal punishment.[174] Indeed, the fact that the inscription promised for them contains God's and Jesus' name indicates shared authority between them.

Moreover, Irenaeus used this passage to lay out a case that the Father created all things by means of the Son ("the Word") and the Spirit.[175] Reiterating that God did not need to create anything, Irenaeus explains, "For always with him are his Word and Wisdom, the Son and the Spirit, through whom and in whom he made everything freely and independently, to whom he also speaks when he says, 'Let us make man after our image and likeness.'"[176]

Irenaeus suggests the preexistence and distinct personhood of the Son and Spirit. He then explains that Christ was given power to sovereignly

---

[172]Beale and McDonough, "Revelation," 1096-97.
[173]Joseph L. Mangina, *Revelation*, BTCB (Grand Rapids, MI: Brazos, 2010), 65.
[174]Craig R. Koester, *Revelation and the End of All Things* (Grand Rapids, MI: Eerdmans, 2001), 66.
[175]*Haer.* 4.20. Anthony Briggman, *Irenaeus of Lyons and the Theology of the Holy Spirit* (Oxford: Oxford University Press, 2012), 104-47, has pointed out that Irenaeus's way of describing the Spirit's role in creation is a clear indication that he believed the Spirit to be divine.
[176]*Haer.* 4.20.1.

judge the dead and the living, quoting Revelation 3:7 ("the one who has the key of David") to support this claim. Irenaeus asserts that this sovereign power is shown because "in heaven he had the first place as Word of God" and on earth he was "a just man" who committed no sin.[177] For Irenaeus, the words of Jesus in Revelation help us see that his divine judgment serves a sole purpose: to restore fallen creation by pointing back to that Father, so that "man reached imperishability, enveloped by the paternal light."[178] This language of coequal power also reminds us of Gregory of Nyssa's logic—if they each have this divine power, then we must conclude that they are of the same nature. *Redoublement* helps us understand that one does not have to choose between nature and activity, since the activity is an indication of the nature and vice versa. Unity and distinction are not at odds but are rather complementary ways to affirm what Scripture affirms, and remain silent where Scripture leaves the mystery.

The Amen, faithful and true, the beginning (Rev 3:14). To Laodicea, John records Jesus referring to himself as "the Amen, the faithful and true witness, the beginning of God's creation." Similar to his address to Philadelphia, John records Jesus giving himself the divine characteristic of truthfulness as a name. This is a tripartite statement that elucidates one central point—Jesus is to be trusted because of his divine perfection and holiness. The background for Jesus being ὁ μάρτυς ὁ πιστὸς καὶ ὁ ἀληθινός ("a faithful and true witness") harkens back to "the notion of God and of Israel as a 'faithful witness' to the new creation in Isaiah 43:10-12."[179] Also, as God's "Amen" (Ἀμήν; cf. 2 Cor 1:20), he is as reliable as God himself because God is the God of truth.[180] This is because he *is* God. Laodicea should cry out, then, as the people in Jeremiah, that YHWH, "the faithful and true witness," would hold them accountable for breaking his commands (Jer 42:5).

To say that Jesus is the "beginning of God's creation" is not merely to say he is the first created being; rather, he is the "origin" or "ruler" (ἀρχὴ),

---

[177]*Haer.* 4.20.2.
[178]*Haer.* 4.20.2.
[179]Beale, *Book of Revelation*, 297. On p. 300 Beale expands on this comment, suggesting that this phrase comes from Is 43:10 LXX ("'You [Israel] are my witnesses and I am a witness,' says the Lord, 'and my servant whom I have chosen'") and its parallel in vv. 11-12. We should also note that Ps 89, for example, applies this type of witness language to Israel's king.
[180]Leon Morris, *Revelation*, TNTC (Downers Grove, IL: IVP Academic, 1987), 81. Morris points to Is 65:16, where "the God of truth" is literally "the God of Amen."

paralleling John 1:1-3 and Colossians 1:15-17. As the ἀρχὴ, he is tied closely to the power and presence of God in the creation of all things and the one who has set in motion God's plan for a new creation. Put another way, his presence and power at creation insinuate his power and presence over the events of new creation. We are reminded of the point made by the patristics, such as Origen: this "firstborn" language is not indicative of his own creation but rather his position as the "first principle" on whom creation is dependent and subordinate.[181] He is able to exert divine power because he is a divine being. Moreover, this proper noun of "Amen" is used only here in the NT, echoing God's name in Isaiah 65:16[182] and "in the beginning" language in Genesis 1. As Alexander Stewart says:

> So, when we look at the messages to the churches, they seem to fall into two major categories. On the one hand, there is a warning of judgment. Ephesus, Pergamum, Thyatira, Sardis, and especially Laodicea fall under this rubric. Applying the exhortative formula found in the Deuteronomic tradition and the prophets Joel, Zechariah, Isaiah, and Ezekiel, John calls them to repentance lest they fall under the punitive judgment of God.[183] On the other hand, there is always a promise of salvation. Especially seen in the messages to Smyrna and Philadelphia, the encouragement to remain faithful is the driving force toward their hope of eternal redemption.[184] But regardless of each message's tone, there is always a hopeful promise at the end, seen in the substantive participle τῷ νικῶντι (2:7) or some variant of it—"to the one who overcomes" or "conquers." In addition to God's existence before the beginning of creation, John affirms that names had been written in the Lamb's book of life from the foundation of the world [and that] God had initiated salvation even before the world was created and before things went terribly wrong.[185]

The conquering saint is promised that he will have authority over the nations (2:26) and will not have his name blotted out of the Book of Life (3:5).

Further, it may seem to complicate our thesis that in Revelation 3:21 Jesus says that the Laodiceans will sit on thrones with him; however, as Loke points

---

[181] See Ayres, *Nicaea and Its Legacy*, 29, for a brief overview of the debates over Origen's idea.
[182] Thomas and Macchia, *Revelation*, 126.
[183] Robert L. Muse, "Revelation 2-3: A Critical Analysis of Seven Prophetic Messages," *JETS* 29, no. 2 (1986): 158.
[184] Muse, "Revelation 2-3," 159.
[185] Alexander E. Stewart, *Soteriology as Motivation in the Apocalypse of John*, GBS 61 (Piscataway, NJ: Gorgias, 2015), 95.

out, "according to Jewish tradition only God can direct such a seating."[186] So even in the midst of warning or commendation, hope is offered, and there is a call to perseverance. Persevere, Jesus says, and he will be faithful and true to his promise of salvation as the eschatological divine judge. As the ἀρχή who holds the same power and authority as the Father, he has the power to bring new creation in an inseparable act with the Father (and Spirit).

The lamb on the throne (Rev 5:1-14).[187] As we mentioned in chapter two, Revelation 4–5 makes up a sort of heavenly liturgy, wherein God's people are around the throne of God praising him as though they are gathered in a sanctuary. This liturgy-sanctuary imagery continues when the slaughtered lamb appears on the throne and receives worship. A slaughtered lamb in the sanctuary of God shows that, as Müller puts it, "the saving significance of Christ's blood stands in the background as the early Christian conception of Christ's atoning death,"[188] which would again evoke images of God's deliverance through the Passover lamb in Israel's story. Jesus' identification with the lion of Judah (Gen 49:9) may also point to his designation as a divine ruler and executor of salvation and judgment, as this symbol often represented God's power.[189] Of primary importance, however, is the vision's centering focus on God's throne and the role Jesus plays in relation to the throne. Moreover, we will need to notice the ways in which Jesus' divine nature and divine activity are not placed at odds but rather are complementary in their relation to each other and to God.

While John's throne-room vision is similar to other apocalyptic visions in terms of God's central role (Is 6; Ezek 1-2) and his work through a Messiah figure (1 En. 90; 4 Ezra 10:60-12:35; T. Levi 18), none are worshiped alongside God, which shows the distinctly *Christian* expression of John's writing that challenges some notions of Jewish monotheism.[190]

---

[186]Andrew Ter Ern Loke, *The Origin of Divine Christology* (Grand Rapids, MI: Eerdmans, 2015), 170. Loke makes this comment in relation to Jesus' self-identification as the Son of Man in Mk 14:62.

[187]We will also discuss Rev 3:21; 7:9-17; 21:22-22:1 as illustrative counterparts to this passage.

[188]Ulrich B. Müller, *Die Offenbarung des Johannes* (Gütersloh: Gütersloher Verlagshaus Gerd Mohn, 1984), 158. My translation of "der Heilsbedeutung des Blutes Christi deutlich, daß im Hintergrund die urchristliche Vorstelung vom Sühnetod Christi steht."

[189]Ford, *Revelation*, 88.

[190]Russell S. Morton, *One Upon the Throne and the Lamb: A Tradition Historical/Theological Analysis of Revelation 4-5* (New York: Peter Lang, 2007), 193-96. Morton aptly calls this John's "transformation of the heavenly council scene."

Indeed, as we have noted already, John is not beholden to these traditions or comparable texts; instead, we regularly see a family resemblance due to John's use of the apocalyptic genre, yet with his own theological project on clear display. In his discussion on the centrality of the throne motif in Revelation, Gallusz notes:

> While the throne motif conveys primarily the idea of God's royal authority and unrivalled power in Revelation, it balances, at the same time the emphasis on divine transcendence with an immanent aspect. On the basis on the high Christology of the book, it is possible to speak of the convergence of God and the Christ-figure Lamb. . . . It reveals that God is related to the world not only as a transcendent sovereign king, but also as a Lamb, slaughtered for the redemption of fallen humanity.[191]

After being described as sitting on God's throne (5:6), the lamb in 5:12-14 receives equal worship alongside God from the mouths of every being in creation.[192] John's description of the throne-room scene parallels in some ways imperial cultic stories of humans reaching an exalted status that allowed for appropriate worship. However, given John's clear commitment to the Jewish tradition and use of OT allusions, it is unwise to assume that he is being overly influenced by imperial cultism. Instead, as Steven Friesen asserts, it is perhaps more suitable to marvel at the fact that "in a [Jewish monotheistic] system that ought not to allow a second deity, Jesus was declared worthy of honors equal to God" in 4:8-5:13, where a rhythm of praise to God (4:8, 11) and the lamb (5:9-10, 12) unite in 5:13.[193] We can also note that Revelation 3:21 appears to be a setup to this passage, given its statement about Jesus sitting on his Father's throne, and also as a counterpart to Satan's throne in 2:13 and the throne of the beast in 16:10.[194]

We should note here the pro-Nicene concepts of oneness and yet distinct personhood. God does not lose his place to the lamb, nor are he and the

---

[191]Laszlo Gallusz, *The Throne Motif in the Book of Revelation*, LNTS 487 (London: Bloomsbury, 2014), 305.

[192]The word μέσῳ could be translated as "in the midst of" (CSB, KJV, NKJV), "between" (ESV, NLT), or "at the center of" (NIV). The NIV might be the closest here, as the worship the Lamb receives seems to mirror that of God. "At the center of" also meshes with 7:17, which uses μέσον, which is "center" or "on."

[193]Steven J. Friesen, *Imperial Cults and the Apocalypse of John* (Oxford: Oxford University Press, 2001), 198-99.

[194]Tabb, *All Things New*, 39. See also G. K. Beale, *The Use of Daniel in Jewish Apocalyptic Literature and the Revelation of St. John* (Eugene, OR: Wipf & Stock, 2010), 180.

lamb the same person. Instead, they appear to share the one throne as two distinct persons. Craig Koester helpfully highlights the striking parallels between God and Christ:

> The four creatures and twenty-four elders who bowed before God's throne (Rev. 4:10) now make a remarkable shift by bowing down before the Lamb (5:8). The harps that were traditionally used to praise God (Ps. 150:3) now sound praises to the Lamb, and the bowls of incense that signified prayer to God (Ps. 141:2) are now placed before the Lamb (Rev. 5:8). If a "new song" was a fitting way to celebrate God's rule over the earth (Ps. 96:1), a "new song" is now sung to the Lamb; and the heavenly chorus that acclaimed God "worthy" (Rev. 4:11) now acclaims Christ "worthy" (5:9).[195]

However, Koester says of Christ's divinity: "Yet despite the shift in focus, the Lamb does not usurp God's place, for all that the Lamb has accomplished ultimately serves God's purposes."[196]

While there is no disagreement fundamentally between my interpretation and Koester's assertion, Koester stops shorter than he needs to. Indeed, Jesus does the will of his Father and accomplishes his Father's purposes in two ways: within the one will of the triune God and also according to his human will as the obedient servant. Yet, John is less circumspect in his assertions than Koester's qualifications. John has already placed Jesus in the opening doxology of the book, recorded titles for Jesus like "the First and the Last" and "Alpha and Omega," and has described him in exact terms used for YHWH in Israel's Scriptures. For John to truly make sense of his vision of the Lamb on the throne, it appears that he cannot simply elevate Jesus to a superhuman or even a mere heavenly mediator status; he instead feels pressured to reinterpret his views of God through the lens of Christ as a divine figure acting in ways inseparable from YHWH's own name, power, and authority. Moreover, the Lamb is not among those "in heaven or on earth or under the earth" unable "to open the scroll or even to look in it" (Rev 5:3-4), but instead he is on the throne and therefore able to open the scroll (Rev 5:5-6). As Bauckham points out, God opens the scroll in a similar scene in Ezekiel 2:9-10.[197] This could indicate that Jesus has the prerogative and power to implement a divine

---

[195] Koester, *Revelation and the End of All Things*, 79.
[196] Koester, *Revelation and the End of All Things*, 79.
[197] Bauckham, *Theology of the Book of Revelation*, 81.

plan contained in the scroll, once again highlighting his worthiness to act in ways normally reserved for God.[198] This would make sense in the context of OT references that contrast God's hidden and sealed-up word with the prophets' inability to see—much less a worthiness to interpret—the words therein (Is 8:8-17; Dan 12:4-9).[199] In sum, John seems compelled to reflect that God and Christ are of the same nature and purpose that are so interlocked that simply saying "Jesus fulfills God's requests" undervalues the glory and splendor of the enthroned lamb that John saw in his vision.

Moreover, looking at ancient texts like Daniel 7:9-14, b. Sanhedrin 38b, and b. Hagigah 14a, Craig Evans notes that the position at a deity's "right hand" could refer to that figure's vice-regency with God, which does not automatically assume inferiority.[200] This scene also resembles a crown prince who is already exercising corule with his father-king. During the Roman period, for example, Caesar Augustus was depicted on a coin sharing the throne with his son-in-law, Marcus Agrippa, which conveyed shared authority.[201] In any event, Alan Hultberg rightly explains that this throne scene is "an astonishing imposition on the worship of God in heaven, though John reports the acclamation with no sense of impropriety . . . [which] is particularly remarkable in a book like Revelation, which is so concerned with true and false worship. . . . Thus is it noteworthy that Christ does not admonish him for his obeisance in 1:17 and more so that such explicit worship can be paid Christ here in chapter 5."[202] Hultberg also notes that this is another recapitulation by John of Daniel 7, so that "what was implied earlier, becomes explicit in Revelation 5: the Lamb is divine, and is to be worshipped alongside the Lord of hosts."[203] This is illuminated by the fact that Christ is not given some sort of coronation or deification in this vision but appears to be already seated and reigning at the throne. As Whitaker argues convincingly: (1) the text never indicates that the Lamb actually takes the throne but

---

[198]Morton, *One Upon the Throne and the Lamb*, 196.
[199]David I. Starling, *Hermeneutics as Apprenticeship: How the Bible Shapes Our Interpretive Habits and Practices* (Grand Rapids, MI: Baker Academic, 2016), 195-96.
[200]Craig A. Evans, *Mark 8:27-16:20*, WBC 34b, rev. ed. (Grand Rapids, MI: Zondervan, 2015), lxxvii.
[201]Craig R. Koester, *Revelation: A New Translation with Introduction and Commentary*, AB 38A (New Haven, CT: Yale University Press, 2014), 341.
[202]Hultberg, "Messianic Exegesis in the Apocalypse," 326-27.
[203]Hultberg, "Messianic Exegesis in the Apocalypse," 327.

is already seated; (2) his status does not change throughout the scene; (3) he does not receive any sort of insignia, crown, or other symbol of new status; and (4) the "son of man" motif from Daniel 7:13-14 is upended here because Christ is not exalted or given kingship, but rather bestows kingship and priesthood upon the people.[204] This might indicate the eternal rule of Christ (the Son) alongside God, given other references to Christ's sovereignty over history (Rev 22:13), but at the very least it comports with the earlier tradition that presented Jesus as already positioned at his Father's right hand (Acts 7:55-56; Rom 8:34; Eph 1:20; Col 3:1; Heb 1:3; 8:1; cf. Ps 110:1).

According to McGrath, however, neither of these points solidifies the assertion that Jesus shares in God's nature.[205] First, he says that it is not abnormal in Revelation for people to bow down to nondeities. In fact, Jesus tells the Philadelphians in 3:9, "I will cause [those of the synagogue of Satan] to come and worship before your feet."[206] This shows, then, that "sharing the throne nor receiving worship was something this author reserved exclusively for God alone, or even exclusively for God and Christ."[207] Second, McGrath explains that when the Lamb shares God's throne in 5:6-14, the elders are not described as offering prayerful worship to the Lamb: "It is thus possible that the author assumed such prayers to be either offered to God in thanksgiving for Christ, or offered to God *through* Christ."[208] Third, he notes that even though angels do not accept worship from humans (Rev 19:10; 22:9), this refusal has less to do with monotheism and Christology than it does with angels simply identifying as fellow servants with humans who also bow down to God and the Lamb (Rev 4-5).[209] Though Dunn again notes the "striking" fact that *"worship is given to the Lamb unreservedly"* in the throne-sharing scenes of Revelation 5 and 7,[210] he ultimately agrees with McGrath that this worship does not necessitate

---

[204]Whitaker, *Ekphrasis*, 142-43. This view contends with perspectives espoused by Aune, *Revelation 1-5*, 329; Beale, *Book of Revelation*, 365; and Elisabeth Schüssler Fiorenza, *Revelation* (Minneapolis: Fortress, 1991), 73.

[205]The following response to McGrath is drawn from portions of Smith, "What Christ Does, God Does," 184-208.

[206]ποιήσω αὐτοὺς, ἵνα ἥξουσιν καὶ προσκυνήσουσιν ἐνώπιον τῶν ποδῶν σου.

[207]James F. McGrath, *The Only True God: Early Christian Monotheism in Its Jewish Context* (Urbana, IL: University of Illinois Press, 2009), 75.

[208]McGrath, *Only True God*, 75; emphasis original.

[209]McGrath, *Only True God*, 79.

[210]James D. G. Dunn, *New Testament Theology* (Nashville: Abingdon, 2009), 65-66, emphasis original.

Jesus' sharing in the divine nature, since *"worship* is quite a broad category" that "can embrace everything from polite acknowledgement of a superior . . . to the full worship appropriate only to God."[211]

Dunn's and McGrath's points are worth considering, but further context in Revelation exposes a flaw in this contention. This relationship between the Lamb and the throne in 7:9-10 is clearer than they assert, as Jesus receives worship alongside God without any sense of restraint or impropriety from those who survived the great tribulation. In other words, Jesus is offered more than mere obeisance of an emperor over a people—it is hymnic worship of a deity offered to both God and Jesus equally. Whereas in Revelation 6 the throne reflects the wrath and judgment of God, the scene in Revelation 7 offers eschatological hope as the overcoming elect celebrate in unison. These positive and negative judgments lend themselves to the Lamb's coequal status with God as the divine eschatological judge,[212] as we have seen previously in the Apocalypse. Dunn's assertion that worship is not a monolithic category is well taken; however, we must balance this conclusion with the point Kovacs and Rowland make:

> In the Jewish apocalypses the dream-vision, with its extravagant symbols and interpretation, is not usually merged with the heavenly ascent vision, as it is in Revelation 4-5. . . . The use of animal imagery resembles *1 Enoch* 89-90, where animals represent humans. The awkwardness created by this combination, and also in the juxtaposition of the Lion and the Lamb in 5:4-5, point to the unique eschatological reality to which John seeks to bear witness. The Lamb has affected the normal apocalyptic conventions, and hitherto accepted patterns of discourse are shattered along with the understanding and course of history.[213]

So, on the one hand, Dunn is correct that there are multiple modes of worship and something of a continuum between obeisance, veneration, and divine worship. But, on the other hand, we must also acknowledge the Lamb

---

[211]Dunn, *New Testament Theology*, 66, emphasis original.
[212]Of course, 1 Cor 5–6 is an instance of Christians being told to "judge" one another and the world. We can recognize quite easily that human responsibility, discipline, and accountability are commanded while also acknowledging the fundamental Judeo-Christian belief that God is the final judge and that vengeance belongs to him (Deut 32:35; Ps 75:7; Is 33:22; Jer 11:20) and, as we have noted, that the throne belongs to him alone and from the throne comes final eschatological judgment.
[213]Judith Kovacs and Christopher Rowland, *Revelation*, Blackwell Bible Commentaries (Oxford: Blackwell, 2004), 69-70.

subverts the expected norms of heavenly activity and angelic liturgy by receiving the worship of creation as ordinarily directed toward its Creator.

As we have noted elsewhere, Hurtado interpreted this Jesus-worship as a "mutation"[214] of Jewish monotheistic worship, and thus elevated above other forms of exaltation in the known Jewish literary world. Indeed, the throne room is a centering place of worship in the Jewish tradition, where YHWH is worshiped and given praise and honor—and in John's Apocalypse, Jesus shares in the worship reserved for the one on the throne. Friesen has convincingly argued that the throne may in fact be "a circumlocution for the One who abides there. God—located specifically beyond the realm of symbolization—is the center."[215] Friesen's reasoning weakens the spatial arguments about the literal "location" of Jesus in relation to God and the throne. Instead, one could conclude that Jesus' centering presence in the "throne room" is itself an indication of his divine nature.[216]

Further, the phrase in 7:17, "the one sitting on the throne will tabernacle over them" (ὁ καθήμενος ἐπὶ τοῦ θρόνου σκηνώσει ἐπ' αὐτούς) brings to mind God's presence in the midst of his people. The word σκηνώσει more directly means that God will spread his tabernacle over them like a tent. So, Jesus is standing next to God in this temple allusion, receiving the same glory and honor while also co-offering grace to the elect. This passage and the accompanying throne scenes leading up to it work against Dunn's and especially McGrath's conclusion. Jesus is certainly depicted as a mediatorial figure (see also Heb 5), but he also receives honor and praise in Revelation 5 and 7 in ways that no other being in the book is allowed. As Fiorenza has noted, the "new song" in 5:9-10 shows that Christ is alone "worthy to assume the eschatological reign over the world" due to his paschal work and his agency in God's redemptive work.[217]

When Jesus, the slaughtered lamb, takes the scroll out of God's hand in 5:7, the word used (εἴληφεν) carries the connotation of authority, because while everyone else bows subserviently around the throne, Jesus takes initiative to

---

[214]Larry W. Hurtado, "The Binitarian Shape of Early Christian Worship," in *The Jewish Roots of Christological Monotheism: Papers from the St. Andrews Conference on the Historical Origins of the Worship of Jesus*, ed. Casey C. Newman, James R. Davila, and Gladys S. Lewis (Waco, TX: Baylor University Press, 2017), 192.
[215]Friesen, *Imperial Cults and the Apocalypse of John*, 163.
[216]This point will also be briefly considered in the following chapter regarding the Holy Spirit.
[217]Fiorenza, *Revelation*, 61.

Son: The Slain Lamb and Risen King 119

grab hold of the scroll. This should also be obvious given that Jesus stands at the throne while everyone else is seated around it.[218] His taking hold of the scroll leads to all those around the throne falling in worship, because his worthiness and authority to open the seal is unmatched. Indeed, an angel announces the need for someone to open the scroll (5:2), but this angel is apparently unworthy to do so, reminding us that the angels are clearly subordinated even to Jesus. To make the point stronger, in 5:12 Jesus receives glory. Though this glory language could indicate no more than a regal type of majesty appropriate for a king,[219] clearly the "glory" (δόξα) attributed to both God and Jesus in this passage denotes the divinity, radiance, and majesty of God himself. Indeed, the terms "glory and dominion" (δόξα καὶ τὸ κράτος) are used in the first doxology (1:6), and this worship language expands to "glory and honor and power" (δόξαν καὶ τὴν τιμὴν καὶ τὴν δύναμιν) in 4:11 and further intensifies the co-worship of God and the Lamb in 5:12-13 and 7:12, using seven different worshipful terms.[220] The shared worship of God and Jesus as the vision progresses offers a consistent picture of Jesus sharing and having pronounced upon him the glory of the Father. Indeed, one Gospel writer proclaims that God the Son has shared this glory with his Father since before the foundation of the world (Jn 17:5). Even if we were to concede that Jesus' authority is derivative from God, Magnus Striet makes the interesting claim that could be applied to John: "Belief in the existence of a Trinitarian God is inevitable because it is the condition for the possibility of God's incarnation.... Ultimately, however, this belief can be confirmed only by the God of Israel himself."[221] Again, we observe John's incipient trinitarianism as he reckons with the tension between worshiping God alone and a pressure from God's own revelation to worship Jesus equally.

Casey concluded that this scene "is *almost* heavenly worship, but it does not have to be perceived as such," and indeed "he is not actually hailed as

---

[218]Rebecca Skaggs and Priscilla Benham, *Revelation*, Pentecostal Commentary Series (Dorset, UK: Deo, 2009), 68-70.
[219]Charles Brütsch, *Die Offenbarung Jesu Christi* (Zürich: Zwingli, 1970), 263-64.
[220]Skaggs and Benham, *Revelation*, 72-73.
[221]Magnus Striet, "Konkreter Monotheismus als trinitarische Fortbestimmung des Gottes Israels," in *Monotheismus Israels und christlicher Trinitätsglaube*, ed. Magnus Striet (Freiburg: Herder, 2004), 193. My translation of "Glaube an das trinitarische Dasein Gottes zwar unaufgebbar, weil er die Bedingung der Möglichkeit für die Menschwerdung Gottes ist ... Endgültig wird dieser Glaube aber nur durch den Gott Israels selbst bestätigt werden können."

divine even in the pictures of him being praised in heaven."²²² For Casey, John's Jewish monotheism restrains the possibility of him describing Jesus as divine, but his Gentile audience nonetheless perceived his exalted status as equivalent to divinity. To the Jewish hearers, monotheism is not threatened by the exalted connotations for Jesus, because "he is not said to be divine." On the other hand, Casey says, "The change required for John's slaughtered lamb to be perceived as divine was the exercise of sympathetic Gentile perception" in the midst of persecution and a non-Christian Gentile context.²²³

Contrary to Casey's assertion, Jesus' divinity is not merely a possibility for those reared in a Hellenistic context; rather, the text itself attempts to deliberately elicit awareness of and allegiance to Jesus as a divine figure like YHWH. Casey is right that John is a Jewish monotheist, but the question goes back to the point we have been contemplating thus far: How did John's vision of Christ pressure him to (re)define monotheism, if he felt the need to at all? Indeed, whatever one says about John's monotheism, it does not seem overly hindered even by the divine worship Christ is receiving. According to Peter Carrell,

> This worship only allows for a fleeting impression that Jesus is the second object of worship. The worship of Jesus is within the bounds of monotheism. The high point of the heavenly worship is the "joint worship of God and Christ, in a formula in which God retains the primacy." As the object of worship in the Apocalypse we may appropriately conclude that Jesus Christ is divine. . . . Given the monotheistic beliefs which shaped John's theology it is not surprising that references to "God and the Lamb" should not be sustained (e.g., in 22.5, 6). But the fact that there are *several* references to "God and the Lamb" in the culmination of the vision of the new Jerusalem, and that they are made in conjunction with "the temple" and "the throne," suggest that . . . within the Apocalypse God and the Lamb are viewed in such a manner that they are understood as a unity.²²⁴

In other words, John seems to find ways to fit Jesus into the divine nature in a way that requires a definition containing multiple persons. The most

---

²²²Maurice Casey, *From Jewish Prophet to Gentile God: The Origins and Development of New Testament Christology* (Louisville, KY: Westminster John Knox, 1992), 142-43, emphasis added.
²²³Casey, *From Jewish Prophet to Gentile God*, 142-43.
²²⁴Peter R. Carrell, *Jesus and the Angels: Angelology and the Christology of the Apocalypse of John*, Society for New Testament Studies Monograph Series 95 (Cambridge: Cambridge University Press, 1997), 114-16, emphasis original.

obvious point is the aforementioned progression of Jesus' status alongside God and his throne, and it is clear that God and Jesus are not the same person. God is Father in relation to Jesus (Πατρὶ αὐτοῦ, Rev 1:6), and Jesus is the Son of God (ὁ Υἱὸς τοῦ Θεοῦ; Rev 2:18) and God's Christ (Χριστοῦ αὐτοῦ; Rev 12:10). Carrell asserts, "These distinctions, however, should not be pressed too far. When Jesus refers to 'my Father' it is in the context of a declaration that he sat with his Father on his throne (Apc. 3:21)."[225] Indeed, Jesus could have just as easily occupied one of the "other" thrones named in 4:4, and yet he is exalted to God's throne as part of the circle of divine sovereignty and is praised in worshipful song.

It is clear, given the vivid descriptions of the throne room, that there are many creatures present in the doxological sequence, but the throne occupies a unique place. As Gallusz summarizes:

> The worship offered the Lamb by the four living creatures, the 24 elders, and the many angels and every creature (5.8-14) implies his divine character....
> This scene "rounds off the vision" and conveys the closing message that "the One sitting on the throne" and the Lamb are divine beings of co-equal status, who act jointly towards the same end. It would be inconceivable if the idea of divine unity was not expressed by sharing the same divine throne in a vision which primarily highlights the elevation of the Lamb.... While [both God and Jesus] are pictured in the throne-room vision as occupants of the heavenly throne, there is no indication of a throne rivalry, since John's view is that the Lamb shares God's throne. The rest of the book of Revelation describes how this shared authority is practiced.[226]

Indeed, we are informed that the general placement and posture of angels, creatures, and elders amount to worship as they face the throne and offer praises toward those sitting on it. John records with detail, not vagueness, the heavenly splendor of worship offered by every tier of creation (heaven, earth, under the earth). Thus it is reasonable to assume that Jesus really is sitting on the throne in the seat of worship reception, not mere deference. God welcomes him to sit on the throne on which no one else is welcome.

Finally, as noted above, the Philadelphian believers were given an abnormally high honor above the false worshipers in 3:9, but we should also

---

[225]Carrell, *Jesus and the Angels*, 116.
[226]Gallusz, *Throne Motif in the Book of Revelation*, 157-58.

remember that they never share a throne with God. Neither do angels, as we have seen. Though McGrath downplays angelic refusal of worship, he still understates the significance of Jesus' acceptance of their worship alongside humans. God only reserves space for Jesus on his worship-worthy throne, and as Gorman contends of Revelation 5, "The slaughtered Lamb is now not only our central and centering vision, but also the interpretive lens through which we read the remainder of the book. Divine judgment and salvation must be understood in light of—indeed defined by—the reality of the slaughtered Lamb who is worthy of divine worship."[227]

Hultberg, in a similar vein of Gallusz above, argues that the shared worship of Jesus and God in the temple stretches all the way to the eschatological finale of Revelation. He notes:

> In 21:22, the Lord God almighty and the Lamb function as the Temple of the New Jerusalem, obviating the need for a physical structure. It is clear that John envisions the eschatological worship to center on both. God and his Christ; the Lamb reigns with God as the objects of the cult in the New Jerusalem. Similarly, in Revelation 21:23, the New Jerusalem requires no sun or moon because the glory of God illumines it, and its lamp is the Lamb. . . . So when John tells us of the single throne of God and of the Lamb in chapter 22, the Lamb has been elevated to a place co-equal with God and he is no longer merely his messianic vice-regent.[228]

In this passage, the crescendo of Revelation offers a clear link between God and Christ in terms of both reign and worship. That a Jewish writer would include anyone but YHWH at the center of the temple in Israel's renewed city raises doubts about subordinationism.

In *De Christo et Antichristo (Treatise on Christ and the Antichrist)*,[229] Hippolytus of Rome draws on this passage and others to describe the myriad ways that Christ's divine work and the Antichrist's satanic work stand in stark contrast to one another. Near the beginning of the work, he says, "Now, as our Lord Jesus Christ, who is also God, was prophesied of

---

[227]Michael Gorman, *Reading Revelation Responsibly: Uncivil Worship and Witness: Following the Lamb into the New Creation* (Eugene, OR: Cascade, 2011), 115. "The remainder of the book" indicates chaps. 6 and following.

[228]Hultberg, "Messianic Exegesis in the Apocalypse," 328-29.

[229]Unless otherwise noted, English translations are from *The Ante-Nicene Fathers*, vol. 5, ed. Alexander Roberts and James Donaldson (New York: Christian Literature, 1885).

Son: The Slain Lamb and Risen King 123

under the figure of a lion, on account of His royalty and glory, in the same way the Scriptures also aforetime spoken of Antichrist as a lion, on account of his tyranny and violence."[230] In his comparison here, Hippolytus takes for granted that Christ is God, using Revelation 5:5's description of Jesus as a lion as an illustration of his "royalty and glory." This illustration serves as a picture of Christ's divine attributes over and against the satanic qualities of the Antichrist ("tyranny and violence"). We see here that Revelation's picture of the enthroned Christ (who is both the Lion who opens the scroll and the Lamb who was slaughtered) helped Hippolytus reinforce his description of Christ's divine glory, stating plainly upfront that he is "also God."

Further along in the treatise, through an extended reflection on the woman, child, and dragon in Revelation 12, he continues his portrayal of the divine Christ in contrast to the satanic Antichrist.[231] For Hippolytus, the woman represents the church, the child represents Jesus, and the dragon represents the Antichrist who will rise up and persecute the church during the great tribulation.[232] Hippolytus does not merely discuss the child in terms of incarnation, resurrection, or even second coming. Instead, he highlights that in Revelation 12:5a ("The child is going to rule the nations") John is referring to "Christ, the perfect man-child of God, who is declared to be God and man, becomes the instructor of all nations." Further, he notes that Revelation 12:5b ("Her child was caught up to God and his throne") signifies that Jesus "is a heavenly king, and not an earthly."[233] These ideas indicate that Revelation helped Hippolytus build a vivid case for the inadequacy of the Antichrist in his persecution of the church over and against the divine rule of Christ.

Toward the end of the letter, Hippolytus encourages the treatise's recipient (Theophilus) not to fear the end of days. He tells Theophilus that the promised resurrection in Revelation 20:6 brings hope and perseverance.[234] Indeed, quoting in part Titus 2:13, Hippolytus says that he should be "looking for that blessed hope and appearing of our God and Savior, when, having

---

[230] *Antichr.* 6.
[231] *Antichr.* 60.
[232] *Antichr.* 61.
[233] *Antichr.* 61.
[234] *Antichr.* 65-66.

raised the saints among us, He will rejoice with them, glorifying the Father."[235] Here Hippolytus weds language in Titus describing Jesus' divinity with a passage in Revelation that offers ultimate eschatological hope.

In the end, Collins, McGrath, and Dunn insist on explaining away or highlighting caveats for any descriptor or grammatical nuance in relation to Jesus' divinity or reception of worship. However, their attempts are finally overshadowed by theological pressures arising from the text that lend themselves toward John's consistent attempts at dealing with Jesus' apparent identification with God in the doxologies and throne-room scenes of his vision. Given the complexity and importance of the throne-room vision(s), this passage as much as any other is aided by *redoublement* because it helps us affirm Jesus' divine nature and mediatorial activity while not conflating him with the Father.

The wrath of the Lord (Rev 6:15-17). The wrath of the Lord is attested to throughout the biblical witness, so the idea of Jesus' inflicting wrath upon the earth raises questions about his nature and activity. The language here (ἔκρυψαν ἑαυτοὺς εἰς τὰ σπήλαια καὶ εἰς τὰς πέτρας τῶν ὀρέων) is similar to Isaiah 2:19: "People will go into caves in the rocks and holes in the ground, away from the terror of the Lord and from his majestic splendor, when he rises to terrify the earth." Indeed, the idea of God's wrath being unendurable is a common refrain in prophetic literature (Joel 2:11, 31; Nahum 1:6; Zeph 1:14; Mal 3:2).[236] However, there is no clear reference to Jesus asserting the same type of wrath until Revelation.

In this passage we see that Jesus is not an antithesis to "the God of Israel" who strikes down individuals and nations; rather, Jesus is described as the codispenser of divine wrath from which the people try to escape. Of course, this fits with several other passages covered in this chapter that depict Jesus as a divine eschatological judge. It also accords with inseparable operations, as we are pressured to note that God—the Father, Son, and Spirit—is wrathful toward sin and has the power and authority to respond in judgment.

Further, Keener notes that John intentionally lists the "entire social order ... emphasizing that no marks of distinction will exempt anyone

---

[235]*Antichr.* 67.
[236]Ford, *Revelation*, 112.

from judgment—from the 'divine' Caesar on down."²³⁷ Aune further explains that

> "the kings of the earth" is a phrase that was taken up into the eschatological vocabulary of Judaism and early Christianity (Ps 2:1-2 quoted in Acts 4:25-26; Isa 24:21; *Sib. Or.* 3.663; 4 Ezra 15:20). The phrases "mighty kings," "powerful kings," and "the kings and the mighty" occur frequently in the so-called Similitudes of Enoch (*1 Enoch* 38:5; 55:4; 62:1, 3, 6, 9; 63:1, 2, 12; 67:8, 12), and though their historical identification is a matter of dispute, they clearly function as enemies of God and his people. The same phrase is found in [Rev] 13:16 and 19:18. This looks like a gloss inserted to democratize those who will be terrified by the imminent day of the wrath of God.²³⁸

These observations lend themselves toward further extrapolation: if John is indeed paralleling Jesus (alongside God) in contrast with Caesar or more generic earthly kings (as he does so often), it stands to reason that John is calling Jesus divine in contrast to their own supposed divinity and sovereignty. He does this in a twofold way: (1) by associating Jesus with the distribution of YHWH's wrath; and (2) by juxtaposing the authority and power of Christ with the cowering of the supposed divine Caesar. This is important to point out here, for pagan kings, angels, locusts, and a host of other agents have been known to carry out the judgments of the Lord; however, as we have noted already and will see in subsequent passages, the judgment carried out by Jesus appears to be both God's and *his own*, and we see later that the heavenly host worships and follows him into war.

The names on their foreheads (Rev 14:1-5). John circles back in this passage to a vision of God and Jesus receiving worship from the saints. In 14:1 the 144,000 have the names of both God and the Lamb on their foreheads in a similar scene of "cultic service" as Revelation 21–22.²³⁹ Further, the scene takes place on Mount Zion, the city of YHWH (Is 60:14) and the seat from which he and his Anointed One inaugurate their eschatological reign (Ps 2:6, 90:2; Is 24:23; Obad 21; Mic 4:7).²⁴⁰

---

²³⁷Craig S. Keener, *Revelation*, NIVAC (Grand Rapids, MI: Zondervan, 2000), 222.
²³⁸David E. Aune, *Revelation 6-16*, WBC 52b (Nashville: Thomas Nelson, 1998), 419.
²³⁹Hultberg, "Messianic Exegesis in the Apocalypse," 330.
²⁴⁰Ford, *Revelation*, 239-40.

McGrath acknowledges the "interesting cultic metaphor in reference to both God and the Lamb, with the Lamb being mentioned alongside God precisely as recipient of this offering."[241] Yet he asserts, "However, precisely because it is a metaphorical usage, its significance should not be pressed too far."[242] This point might be convenient for McGrath's assertions, but it is not expedient for a consistent, thick description of the God-Jesus relationship expressed throughout the book. However, he doubles down on this position: "In all such instances of worship, even if the salvation accomplished by the Lamb is the reason and motivating factor for the worship in question, and thus the worship has the Lamb in view as well, nevertheless God is always either the sole or primary recipient of the worship that is offered."[243]

McGrath's statement that God is "the sole or primary recipient" raises the question as to whether Jesus can be a type of secondary recipient and still be worshiped in a divinely appropriate way. While John was obviously familiar with Jewish cultic scenes that depicted God as the primary recipient of prayer and worship, this does not exclude the possibility that the Lamb is still receiving unparalleled divine worship on par with God. McGrath's theory about the Lamb sharing roles and titles within the context of Christian worship is helpful to a point. He is right to note that in early Judaism "reverence and obeisance before God's agent of salvation could often be appropriate; to show the same reverence to a pagan king who did not honor God or to a god other than the one true God was unacceptable and blasphemous."[244] However, he seems too committed to the idea that Jesus was an exalted figure who was in some ways allowed certain *types* of worship, but that his reception of worship previously reserved for God alone is "an overinterpretation of the evidence."[245] One must wonder, however, how far this argument goes. It is true that receiving divine titles and veneration does not *require* a divine ontology; however, an ontology must be included alongside the functional elements given that Jesus shares in the eternality of the divine plan, is described by John as clearly distinct from creatures, is *already seated* on God's throne (versus being a man elevated to a place near the throne as

---

[241] McGrath, *Only True God*, 73.
[242] McGrath, *Only True God*, 73.
[243] McGrath, *Only True God*, 73.
[244] McGrath, *Only True God*, 77.
[245] McGrath, *Only True God*, 78.

in other comparable literature), and is worthy to open the scroll in a way only YHWH has been previously allowed to.

Not only that, but McGrath begs the question in his assumption that John *must* think a certain way simply because he was Jewish. Indeed, we have shown that whatever might have been considered a "Jewish understanding" of monotheism, John often makes distinct exegetical and theological moves from the tradition and his contemporaries. Certainly the historical background and context for John's writing are helpful aids to consider how we uses similar concepts, but we have already seen the mistake in flatly assuming John's unmitigated reliance on these ideas.

Given this passage alongside others already addressed, it seems that McGrath is too quick to soften the worship of Jesus in Revelation in general and this setting in particular. The evidence of Jesus' divine nature—through scriptural allusions tying him with descriptions and actions of YHWH, obvious throne sharing with God, unparalleled human-angelic worship aimed at both him and God, and an explicit rejection of worship of angelic beings—is continually stacked against McGrath's argument.

In sum, even if we grant the subordination of the Messiah in the OT context of the OT prophets, the preponderance of textual suggestions in Revelation so far support the work that John does not see an exalted Messiah standing next to God in a strictly subordinate position; rather, the Lamb receives worship alongside God. That John repeatedly tethers Jesus to YHWH's nature ultimately eliminates the presumption that Jesus is merely sharing in titles and roles akin to other exalted figures of the day. Put another way, while John is certainly reworking Jewish traditions about heavenly figures who are not divine in nature, he is also working with something new: a unique visionary experience in which the idea of the divine nature is being reshaped before his eyes. As we have mentioned throughout this book, John is not always blandly repeating OT and other Jewish stories; he reworks them in ways that fit his prerogative and interpretation of the vision. Moreover, highlighting the "subordination" elements at the expense of the ontological implications for Jesus' worthiness and willingness to receive worship flattens out the theological depth of this passage, revealing the genius of pro-Nicene that attend to the redoubled vantage point of unity of nature and distinction of person.

Lord of lords and King of kings (Rev 17:14). John continues his Danielic allusions to Jesus' deity as he describes the war between the beast and the lamb.[246] This text is close to the Theodotion and MT versions of Daniel 7:21, and John uses the idea of a horn as a metaphor for a king in battle who overpowers the saints. However, John slightly changes this allusion in the broader context of this passage to indicate that the Lamb's saints are the horned ones who obtain ultimate victory.[247]

A further twist happens here in 17:14. The saints overcome their oppressors because of their association with the lamb. John credits Jesus' victory to his title as "Lord of lords and King of kings" (κύριος κυρίων ἐστὶν καὶ βασιλεὺς βασιλέων). This title has a storied history in YHWH's relationship with Israel, as Deuteronomy 10:17; Psalm 136:3; and Daniel 2:47; 4:37 LXX use different versions of "Lord of Lords," "Lord of kings," and "God of gods." "King of kings" is used as a title for God in other ancient Jewish literature, such as 2 Maccabees 13:4, 3 Maccabees 5:35, 1QM 14:16, and m. Sanhedrin 4:5. "King of kings" and "Lord of kings" were also used to speak of exalted kings in a multitude of ancient Near Eastern contexts.[248] In 1 Enoch 9:4 we see a combination: "And they said to the Lord of the ages: 'Lord of lords, God of gods, King of kings, <and God of the ages>.'" In the New Testament this title is given to God in 1 Timothy 6:15: "He is the blessed and only Sovereign, the King of kings and the Lord of lords," and is likewise given to Jesus in Revelation 19:16.

Beale asserts that, given this extensive OT and Jewish background of the phrase in relation to God/YHWH, John is giving Jesus the designation of a divine king who defeats earthly kings.[249] Leithart takes a similar but different approach, noting that "King of kings, Lord of lords" is not a redundant mishmash of royal epithets but rather

---

[246] As Onesimus Ngundu rightly notes, kingship language here and in Rev 19:19 compares and contrasts the two "kingships" of Christ and the beast. "Revelation," in *Africa Bible Commentary*, ed. Tokunboh Adeyemo (Grand Rapids, MI: Zondervan, 2006), 1597.
[247] Beale, *Book of Revelation*, 880.
[248] David E. Aune, *Revelation 17-22*, WBC 52c (Nashville: Thomas Nelson, 1998), 954-55.
[249] Beale, *Book of Revelation*, 881, argues that Dan 4:37 LXX is the most likely referent for John here. He notes that this passage explicitly uses the title as a reason for YHWH's victory over Nebuchadnezzar and that John is making the same claim that the divine Lamb will defeat the latter-day king of Babylon. He argues that 1 En. 9:4 may also be using Dan 4:37 LXX as its basis. He also surmises that John may also be using Dan 7:21 in either the MT or the Theodotion translation.

two superlatives are drawn from quite different contexts. Yahweh is "Lord of lords" (Deut. 10:17; Ps. 136:3), but only figures described as "king of kings" in the Hebrew Bible are human beings—Gentile emperors like Artaxerxes (Ezra 7:12) and Nebuchadnezzar (Ezek. 26:7; Dan. 2:37). Ancient emperors conquered kings, and so became king over kings. To say that Jesus is Lord of lords is to say that he is Yahweh. To say that he is King of kings is to say that he is the Fifth Monarch, the heir of the empires of Babylon, Persia, Greece, and Rome, the greater Nebuchadnezzar, Cyrus, Alexander, Augustus. He is the Head of all things, an eighth that does *not* go to destruction. To say that he is both Lord of lords and King of kings is to say that he is the divine emperor, the Lord or lords made flesh as King of kings.[250]

Written and delivered in the context of Roman Caesar, Sebastos, and/or Parthian worship, this worship of Jesus as the divine emperor would likely have landed heavily on its audience. Relatedly, Ford argues that John introduces an intentional interplay between the beast and the Lamb:

> The title in Revelation 17:14 is possibly introduced deliberately as a contrast to the title of the emperors proclaimed as "Lord of Lords and King of Kings." The epithets for the companions of the Lamb are "called and elect and faithful" (vs. 14); this forms an antithesis to the predestination to destruction in 17:8. Thus there is a parallel in ch. 17. The beast bears a parody of the name of Yahweh and the dwellers of the earth are predestined to damnation, the Lamb has the title of Yahweh and his followers are predestined to eternal felicity.[251]

For Ford, this title indicates Jesus' identification with YHWH in blatant contrast to the false divinity of the beast. As Hays further asserts about this passage, "Christ's lordship stands in flat antithesis to Caesar's."[252] There is no question, then, that John is describing Jesus in divine terms in ways that both reshape Jewish monotheism and challenge cultural political devotion, pressuring his audience to consider the nature and activity of this Lord.

As a Christian writer, with apparent Jewish heritage, writing in a Greco-Roman context, one can imagine the dizzying worldview clashes between Jews, Christians, Greeks, Romans, and other local ethnic groups. Ancient

---

[250]Leithart, *Revelation 12-22*, 199.
[251]Ford, *Revelation*, 291-92.
[252]Richard B. Hays, *The Moral Vision of the New Testament* (New York: HarperSanFrancisco, 1996), 173.

peoples ordinarily worshiped deities who required devotion. Irenaeus is right, then, to pick up on John's language Revelation 1:8 and 17:12-14: Jesus is "the one who is to come," the conqueror of their kings as the King of kings and Lord of lords—proof that Christ is exalted and will enact divine judgment in the last days.[253]

The rider on the white horse (Rev 19:11-16). This passage describes a rider on a white horse, coming out of the clouds to wage eschatological war on God's enemies. A few questions arise when reading this passage. First, what is the identity of the rider and how do we interpret the descriptions applied to him? Second, what is his nature and purpose?

Aune notes, "In the Greco-Roman world, the image of a celestial rider was widely understood as a savior who could deliver people from various kinds of trouble [and] it would be natural and logical for the reader to construe this rider as Michael."[254] If it were merely Michael riding the horse, it would be easy to dismiss this act of war as God's armies being sent out to battle on his behalf. However, Jesus is clearly the rider. This is obvious given that the white horse is mentioned in Revelation 6:2 with the Messiah as the rider, and elsewhere Revelation uses "faithful" (3:14) and the image of a sword protruding from his mouth (1:16) to speak of Jesus. The title "Word of God" also matches John 1:1-18. With that settled relatively easily, we can explore the significance of this passage with regard to our thesis.

The phrase "he judges in righteousness" (ἐν δικαιοσύνῃ κρίνει) has messianic overtones in Isaiah 11:4 and is also interpreted messianically in Jewish texts such as Targum Isaiah 11:1-6, Psalms of Solomon 17:24-26, and 4 Ezra 3:9-11.[255] There is no doubt that Jesus is the Messiah of Israel both in Revelation and the broader early Christian literature; however, there is more to consider with his description, because numerous biblical passages also attribute YHWH with being a righteous judge or judging with righteousness (Pss 7:11; 9:4-8; 50:6; 72:2; 75:2; 96:13; Jer 11:20; 2 Tim 4:8; 1 Pet 2:23). Though not entirely conclusive on its own, our base knowledge already established shows that John tends to identify Jesus with YHWH in his OT allusions.

---

[253] *Haer.* 4.26.1.
[254] Aune, *Revelation 17-22*, 1053.
[255] Aune, *Revelation 17-22*, 1053.

Son: The Slain Lamb and Risen King

Further, Revelation 19:12 also describes him as wearing "many crowns on his head" (ἐπὶ τὴν κεφαλὴν αὐτοῦ διαδήματα πολλά). As Smalley points out,

> The only other figures wearing "diadems" on their heads in the Apocalypse are false claimants to an authority which is sovereign and universal: namely, the dragon (12.3) and the beast (13.1). . . . Both dragon and beast are adorned with a limited number of crowns (seven and ten); and they are clearly idolatrous opponents of Christ, whose "many" diadems speak of a kingship which is cosmic and eternal.[256]

John's description of Jesus' crowns obviously indicates a kingly authority, but Smalley brings out an important note: the unlimited number of diadems in contrast with the dragon and beast points to a unique and unmitigated worship of Jesus that seems suited for a divine king, not merely an earthly king. Indeed, John seems concerned throughout Revelation with showing that earthly kings assume that their decadence and power are eternal, but God intends to show through Christ that divine kingship is true kingship (e.g., Rev 17–18).

Moreover, the title "Word of God" carries Johannine and related later patristic conceptions of preexistence; however, John the seer is perhaps making a second and complementary point about the divinity of Jesus with this title. In the so-called magical papyri of the ancient world, the names of divine beings were sometimes kept secret and then eventually disclosed.[257] This view is present in various pieces of Greco-Roman mythical literature and even made its way into early Christian literature like Gospel of Philip 54:5-7; Martyrdom and Ascension of Isaiah 9:5; and 1 Enoch 48, which indicate that Jesus has a secret name.[258] Aune suggests, "The very fact that the rider has a secret name suggests that the rider is either a divine being (see Gen 32:29) or an angelic being (Judg 13:17)."[259] Smalley also notes that his name is perhaps revealed on his crowns as an affront to the earlier description of the beast's blasphemous names written on his crowns (Rev 13:1; 17:3-5).[260] If we are left to choose between Jesus as a divine being or an angel,

---

[256] Stephen S. Smalley, *The Revelation to John* (Downers Grove, IL: IVP Academic, 2005), 489.
[257] For a helpful introduction to the possible influence of magic on early Christianity, see Aune, *Apocalypticism, Prophecy and Magic*.
[258] Aune, *Revelation 17-22*, 1055-56. Aune does not note the 1 Enoch reference.
[259] Aune, *Revelation 17-22*, 1055.
[260] Smalley, *Revelation to John*, 489.

this passage alongside others we have covered thus far lends itself toward Jesus' divine nature.

Origen again relied on Revelation in his commentary on John's Gospel, but relevant to our discussion here, Revelation 19 helped him explicate the idea in John 1 of Jesus being λόγος who "was in the beginning with God." Brian Daley deftly notes that Revelation 19:11 ("Faithful and True"), 19:13 ("Word of God"), and 19:16 ("King of kings and Lord of lords")[261] help Origen build "a kind of miniature treatise on the divine Logos" as he comments on John's Gospel.[262] Daley explains Origen's further contention that John the seer drops the definite article ("the") on the "Word of God" title "so as not to suggest a multiplicity of intellectual mediators between the spiritual world and the world of creatures."[263] Additionally, Origen read these texts as an explanation that Jesus is the "sole revealer of divine reality" and the embodiment of God's justice.[264] In all of this, we can see a clear picture of how Revelation portrays the divine nature of Jesus.

Irenaeus also uses a series of quotations from Revelation, drawing on them to highlight the extent to which God made himself visible to humanity. Citing this passage along with Revelation 1:12, 15; 5:6, he turns his attention to the Father's appearances to the OT prophets through visions and manifestations, though noting that he did not appear fully;[265] instead, the prophets only caught glimpses of the Father as the Spirit worked through them. However, the Father finally did visibly reveal himself through the sending of the Son, "the only-begotten God" in a riff on John 1:18.[266] Here, Irenaeus lifts up John's vision of Jesus as the pinnacle disclosure of the heavenly glory not seen by the OT prophets. The vision John experienced is so vivid that

---

[261]*Comm. Jo.* 2.42-63.
[262]Brian E. Daley, "'Faithful and True': Early Christian Apocalyptic and the Person of Christ," in *Apocalyptic Thought in Early Christianity*, ed. Robert J. Daly, Holy Cross Studies in Patristic Theology and History (Grand Rapids, MI: Baker Academic, 2009), 120.
[263]Daley, "'Faithful and True,'" 120; cf. Origen, *Comm. Jo.* 2.13-18.
[264]Daley, "'Faithful and True,'" 121. Of course, a mediator who is merely created and not ontologically equal to the Father can do this type of work and even hold a subordinate title such as "God's Word" or "God's Wisdom." Origen may have meant it this way, at least in some sense. However, given Origen's dabbling with ontological equality and the aforementioned fact that we cannot expect pro-Nicene precision from him, the idea of Jesus as the revealer of a divine reality, the embodiment of God's justice, and the like serves the later trinitarian project well.
[265]*Haer.* 4.20.3-12. If the Father is invisible, then none of the prophets, for example, saw him with their own eyes in a proper sense.
[266]*Haer.* 4.20.11.

he "fell at [Jesus'] feet as though he were dead" (Rev 1:17), which calls to Irenaeus's mind the warning in Exodus 33:20: "No man sees God and lives." For Irenaeus, the glory of Christ in Revelation is akin to the glory of God himself in the OT. With the vision of Jesus as the climax of Revelation, Irenaeus explains in detail the Father's providential work, which culminates in the incarnation, resurrection, and exaltation of his Son.

Since we have established in various places that John explicitly does not equate Jesus with angels, we can make two observations. First, John intentionally places Jesus on the horse with divine titles and descriptions to indicate that God himself—not merely his angelic hosts—will enact the judgment. Jesus' role as a divine judge has been established in Revelation, as we have seen in 3:14 and 14:14. This idea also meshes well with this passage's OT allusions of YHWH as a righteous judge. Second, John perhaps picks up on contemporary usage of the magical "secret name," repurposing it to identify Jesus as a divine being, God's very Word, who brings judgment from heaven. Even though angels carry out God's judgment in certain places (Rev 8–9; 12; 14–17:1), this does not automatically require that Jesus is a type of commissioned agent. As Origen noted, the heavenly host *follows* the Word of God as their leader.[267]

The preponderance of passages we have examined thus far indicate that while Jesus may perform some functions similar to angelic beings, he certainly acts in uniquely divine ways and is portrayed by John and other worshipers as displaying the nature and authority of YHWH. As Carrell says, "The *Logos*-name encapsulates Jesus as the revealer" of God's message, and Logos—coupled with the titles Faithful and True and King of kings and Lord of lords—make clear his divine characteristics and that "he is in himself the personal expression of the *logos* of God."[268] We can reasonably conclude, then, that John viewed Jesus as an eschatological divine judge rather than exalted Michael-like angel. Put another way, John's language pressures readers to interpret Jesus not as a mere angel but in some sense as YHWH himself. Here we continue to see the benefit of pro-Nicene tools that help us see that Jesus, as the divine and eternally begotten Son, can be the economic revealer of God's purposes and yet nonetheless be truly divine in every

---

[267] *Comm. Jo.* 2.62.
[268] Carrell, *Jesus and the Angels*, 216.

meaningful sense. Indeed, because he is divine, he is able to carry out divine judgment as the judge himself, not merely as an angelic intermediary.

Receiving priestly activity (Rev 20:6). The surrounding context of this passage is often used as a crux in the argument about the nature and extent of the "millennium." However, for our purposes in this book, those details are both extrinsic and peripheral. What is more interesting for our present purposes is how Jesus can be included with God as a recipient of priestly activity.

Aune suggests that this passage is a "likely" reference to Exodus 19:6 ("You will be my kingdom of priests and my holy nation") and a "possible" reference to Isaiah 61:6 ("You will be called the LORD's priests; they will speak of you as ministers of our God").[269] In either instance, the reference would relate only to YHWH's relationship with his people as they carry out their cultic and missional duties as "priests" and "ministers." Smalley further concludes that this passage reveals a "unity of nature" between God and Christ, given that the priests throughout Revelation are seen as priestly mediators of God's salvation and judgment.[270] These are complementary, astute observations. Though Jesus is identified with the saints as a co-heir of the kingdom with them with the phrase, "and they will reign with him" (καὶ βασιλεύσουσιν μετ' αὐτοῦ; cf. Rom 8:17), there is a clear distinction between the saints, who are offering the priestly activity, and God and Christ, who are receiving it.

Oscar Cullman rightly calls this passage "the final act of Christ's lordship."[271] One could argue specifically that Revelation 19–22 solidifies John's methodical inclusion of Jesus in the divine nature and activity, given the intensity with which he includes Jesus in divine titles and actions. Indeed, when compared to 1 Peter 2:5, which gives the impression that Christ is the conduit through whom sacrifices can be offered ("You yourselves, as living stones, a spiritual house, are being built to be a holy priesthood to offer spiritual sacrifices acceptable to God through Jesus Christ"), John appears to raise the stakes even among NT writers by asserting that both God and

---

[269] Aune, *Revelation 17-22*, 1093.
[270] Smalley, *Revelation to John*, 510.
[271] Oscar Cullman, *The Christology of the New Testament*, trans. Shirley C. Guthrie and Charles A. M. Hall (Philadelphia: Westminster, 1965), 231.

Christ receive the sacrifices themselves. While ancient emperors often received offerings from their subjects, the context here ties Christ to God, denoting his status as higher than a vicegerent or earthly emperor. While this should not surprise us given the worship Jesus has already received throughout the vision, it is worth noting the connections John is making here between God, Jesus, and OT temple motifs. Again, Jesus' mediatorial activity does not require an ontological subjugation; instead, it is just as valid to claim that being truly divine validates his ability to receive sacrifices.

The first and the last (Rev 22:12-13). Jesus' self-introduction as the Apocalypse concludes contains two noteworthy components. First, he says that "my reward is with me to repay to each one according to his work."[272] This language brings to mind YHWH's declaration of salvific recompense for the faithful in Isaiah 40.[273]

Second, Jesus again refers to himself as "the First and the Last" (ὁ πρῶτος καὶ ὁ ἔσχατος), as he does in 1:17 and 2:8. John may have picked up on Danielic overtones here, as well, given that the word or symbol את (the first and last letters of the Hebrew alphabet) is used thirty-nine times in Daniel to indicate God bringing him into the vision. This, of course, is also reminiscent of the "Alpha and Omega" language, which carries the same denotation of God's eternal nature and sovereignty over history. Indeed, ἐγὼ τὸ ἄλφα καὶ τὸ ὦ (the Alpha and the Omega) and ἡ ἀρχὴ καὶ τὸ τέλος (the Beginning and the End), were also used for God in 1:8 and 21:6 respectively. As Beale comments,

> Now all these titles, which are used in the OT of God, are combined and applied to Christ to highlight his deity. The titles figuratively connote the totality of polarity: Christ's presence at and sovereignty over the beginning of creation and over the end of creation are boldly stated in order to indicate that he is also present at and sovereign over all events in between. The emphasis of the bipolar names here at the end of the book is to underscore Christ's divine ability to conclude history at his coming.[274]

This again highlights the shared nature between the Father and Son, as Jesus is shown to exercise the same power normally reserved for YHWH.

---

[272] ὁ μισθός μου μετ' ἐμοῦ ἀποδοῦναι ἑκάστῳ ὡς τὸ ἔργον ἐστὶν αὐτοῦ.
[273] Smalley, *Revelation to John*, 572.
[274] Beale, *Book of Revelation*, 1138.

For example, it was God himself who held the keys to death and Hades in Jewish literature, such as Wisdom 16:13.[275]

Bede the Venerable takes a similar approach of engaging the implications for Jesus' humanity and divinity by examining the "Alpha and Omega" title. He determines, "Jesus is the Alpha in his eternal divinity and Omega is the humanity assumed."[276] Similarly, Clement of Alexandria's *Stromata* 4.25.156,[277] which has been called "the decisive passage for the doctrine of the trinity in Clement,"[278] alludes to Revelation 1:8; 21:6; and 22:13, saying, "Wherefore the Word is called the Alpha and Omega, of whom alone the end becomes beginning, and ends again at the original beginning without any break."[279] In the end, Clement roots his understanding of God in the incomprehensibility of the Father revealed through the incarnation of the comprehensible Son, in whom all things have their beginning and end.

So, though Jesus' divinity was somewhat implicit leading up to this passage (as we saw in our immediately preceding sections), it rings loud and clear at the final climax of the revelation: Jesus has been with God from creation to new creation, beginning to end. In these interpretations, this pairing of titles lends itself to partitive exegesis and the hypostatic union, as readers are pressured to acknowledge Jesus as the eternal one over and before history (according to his divine nature) and his death and resurrection (according to his human nature).

Conclusion

In this chapter, we saw that a theological-canonical method which draws on pro-Nicene tools helped us work through issues related to the triadic dynamic native to John's writing. Jesus is inextricably linked to God in terms of nature and activity. John's use of the OT to reflect Jesus' unique relationship to the Father is particularly noticeable, as he repeatedly applies OT descriptions of YHWH to Jesus. Further, we have observed that Jesus is

---

[275]Witherington, *Revelation*. 82.
[276]Quoted in Leithart, *Revelation 12-22*, 424.
[277]Unless otherwise noted, English translations are from *The Ante-Nicene Fathers*, vol. 2, ed. Alexander Roberts and James Donaldson (New York: Christian Literature, 1885).
[278]Eric Osborn as quoted in Bucur, *Angelomorphic Pneumatology*, 28.
[279]*Strom.* 4.25.157. Bucur, *Angelomorphic Pneumatology*, 29, explains all of this nicely: "The Son founds the multiplicity of creation, but this multiplicity, being founded by the same one principle, can eventually be reduced to Logos."

depicted in terms similar to the Son of Man in other apocalyptic literature but is clearly exalted above them in descriptions and functions indicative of Israel's God. While some have argued that John uses angelomorphic or polymorphic imagery and angelic tropes to describe Jesus, he makes clear that Jesus is more than an angel by virtue of his sharing God's throne, which enables him to be worshiped alongside God in a way that no other character of the vision is allowed. We see that Jesus is more than an exalted man or angel; he is elevated above all other beings of creation, placed on par with God himself. Indeed, Jesus in John's vision relates to creation, salvation, and judgment in the same way as God the Father, not merely as an agent but also as a divine person. So, Jesus does not merely act on behalf of God; rather, it is clear that he is of the same divine substance by virtue of his reception of worship and his exercise of divine prerogatives.

We also see that Jesus acts inseparably from Father as he carries out his revelation and judgments, while simultaneously claiming the revelation and judgments as his own. Jesus also acts inseparably from the Spirit in a way that reflects the broader pattern in Christian literature of the Father and Jesus as the dispensers of the Spirit. In fact, when Jesus speaks, the Spirit speaks, giving the indication of shared divine power, authority, and will. John's theology presents a trinitarian dynamic—a "web of relations"—that a close reading of the text reveals, and we saw that pro-Nicene tools helped us exegete difficult passages related to Jesus' nature and activity. While a reading of the text could lead to subordinationist conclusions about the angelic or creaturely nature of Jesus, we see via *redoublement* that John depicts the Son's shared nature with the Father. He also describes his ability to enact and embody divine prerogatives of sitting on the throne, receiving worship, ruling over creation, and dispensing the Spirit—to whom we now turn our attention.

FOUR

Holy Spirit

The Revealer to John and Speaker to the Churches

Our vision of the triune God fittingly finds its culmination in the Holy Spirit. He is the marvelous gatekeeper to God's throne room, the one who opens John's eyes to the wonders of heaven, and speaks alongside the Son as the promised comforter.[1] His sevenfold power is evident as he is worshiped in John's doxology and able to effortlessly traverse between heaven and earth, coming to and from the throne at will. His work brings God's work to its final, glorious end. Without him, John's vision is blind, and God's promises are silent.

When discussing the person and agency of the Spirit in Revelation, we encounter several ambiguities. First, there is debate regarding whether the Spirit is an angel, a "person," or simply a means of ecstatic visions and/or heavenly transportation. Further, some have argued that the Spirit is angelic or ontologically subordinate in patristic literature, particularly but not exclusively in the second and third centuries. Our aim in this chapter is to describe the Spirit in Revelation in light of these historical, cultural, and theological issues and then show how pro-Nicene tools aid our understanding of Revelation's pneumatology.

Considering the aim of this book, the most pertinent passages for our discussion below will highlight how the Spirit relates to the Father and Son, and/or how he exhibits a divine nature and activity. We have already

---

[1] I will refer to the Holy Spirit as a "he" primarily to designate his personhood, though one could debatably draw on the masculine pronoun used for the Spirit in Jn 15 as well.

discussed the ways the Father and Son relate to one another, and at times we mentioned the Spirit; however, now we will notice primarily the Spirit's relation to the Father and Son, particularly how he elucidates the vision for John and in some sense moves history toward its final culmination as the visionary revealer and perfecter of the Father and Son's work. We will examine passages in which the Spirit is acting on behalf of or because of the Father and/or the Son. But first we will survey how patristic theologians articulated a trinitarian account of the Spirit's nature and activity.

Patristic Conceptions of the Holy Spirit

The patristic development of pneumatology included the issues we mentioned above: Is the Spirit an angel, perhaps a chief angel? Is the Spirit a subordinated figure? Is he distinct from God and Christ, or somehow a mode or extension of them? Should we read Revelation in a more *binitarian* manner versus a trinitarian reading? We will now discuss how these issues were handled in the patristic era, noting at times where similar issues arise in Revelation.

In pro-Nicene grammar, God the Spirit is fully divine, and thus singular in will, power, and authority with the Father and Son. As the Constantinopolitan Creed (381) says, "We believe in the Holy Spirit, the Lord, the giver of life, who proceeds from the Father. With the Father and the Son he is worshipped and glorified; he has spoken through the prophets."[2] In terms of the eternal relations of origin, the early church eventually spoke of the Spirit's *procession*—the Spirit eternally proceeds or spirates from the unbegotten Father.[3] To reiterate, the pro-Nicenes saw no division in essence or hierarchy; rather, they used "eternal procession" as a way to describe the order (*taxis*) within the Godhead without implying an ontological difference. Further, some of the pro-Nicene theologians noted below further articulated the idea of inseparable operations that we have mentioned throughout this book.[4] For example, prepositional designations such as "Spirit *of* the Lord" or "Spirit *of* Christ" do not infer subordination, but rather highlight his

---

[2] Καὶ εἰς τὸ Πνεῦμα τὸ Ἅγιον, τὸ κύριον, τὸ ζωοποιόν, τὸ ἐκ τοῦ Πατρὸς ἐκπορευόμενον, τὸ σὺν Πατρὶ καὶ Υἱῷ συμπροσκυνούμενον καὶ συνδοξαζόμενον, τὸ λαλῆσαν διὰ τῶν προφητῶν.
[3] See the previous chapter for discussions surrounding the filioque controversy.
[4] Lewis Ayres, *Nicaea and Its Legacy: An Approach to Fourth-Century Trinitarian Theology* (Oxford: Oxford University Press, 2004), 214n85, notes, however, that "the seeds of the doctrine had long been available" in, for example, Origen, *Princ.* 1.2.12.

unique ontological relationship to the Father and Son and his divine power and authority to complete and carry out divine prerogatives.

This creedal conception of the Spirit was further worked out after the earlier christological debates as new disparate teachings arose after Nicaea in particular.[5] Since the Spirit receives only one brief line in the Nicene Creed (AD 325), it is no wonder that more language and logic needed to be addressed. As Hanson notes,

> The early second-century concept of the Incarnation as the taking of a human body by the Holy Spirit had given way to a recognition of the separate existence of the Holy Spirit from the Son in the Apologists and even more clearly in Irenaeus and Tertullian, though the belief that God is spirit continued to trouble theologians in their efforts to create a consistent pneumatology.[6]

Hanson also highlights that the "strong tendency to subordinate the Spirit drastically to the Son evident among some third-century authors" has led some scholars to charge the early church with a type of "binitarian" apathy toward the Spirit.[7] Graham Cole says that it is plausible to assert that the Spirit was "operationally" subordinated even into the later patristic period.[8] He notes that "despite the espoused equality of the Spirit with the Father and the Son in the Trinity," there existed a "somewhat minimal treatment of the Spirit in comparison with the Father and the Son in the great creeds of Christendom, whether Apostles,' Nicene, or Athanasian."[9] While somewhat fair, we will see below that pneumatology received a serious boost in interest and articulation among the pro-Nicenes in response to disparate teachings.

As Barnes has shown most helpfully and succinctly, there was a development of pneumatology over the first four centuries of Christian thought

---

[5] For a helpful survey of pneumatology in the early church, see Kyle R. Hughes, *How the Spirit Became God: The Mosaic of Early Christian Pneumatology* (Eugene, OR: Cascade, 2020).
[6] R. P. C. Hanson, *The Search for the Christian Doctrine of God: The Arian Controversy, 318–381* (Grand Rapids, MI: Baker Academic, 2005), 738.
[7] Hanson, *Search for the Christian Doctrine of God*, 738. Hanson disputes this charge of apathy, however, noting that Novatian, Victorinus, and Origen explicated versions of a divine and separate Spirit during this time. Though they certainly subordinated the Spirit, Hanson argues that the Spirit was still important to their theological projects. Indeed, Origen even uses "Godhead" language when describing the Spirit.
[8] Graham A. Cole, *He Who Gives Life: The Doctrine of the Holy Spirit* (Wheaton, IL: Crossway, 2007), 29.
[9] Cole, *He Who Gives Life*, 29.

that started with Jewish views of the Spirit as Creator and Wisdom; then, the early church transitioned away from these ideas closely associated with rabbinic Judaism in particular, instead describing the Spirit within an "ordered" Godhead; and finally, a retrieval or adaptation of sorts occurred amongst the pro-Nicenes who sought to recover the "higher" pneumatology of earlier periods.[10]

Starting with Origen once again, we will see some ways his pneumatology prefigured pro-Nicene debates. Janet Rutherford rightly says that, for Origen, "the Holy Spirit is associated in dignity and honour with the Father and Son" and clearly not made or created.[11] However, it has been argued that the Spirit was nonetheless "lower" than the Son in Origen's work.[12] Like Irenaeus before him, Origen tended to speak of the Spirit as participating in the divine life and activity, but the stable ontological definition used by the pro-Nicenes was obviously a later development.[13]

In a brief exposition on the Spirit, Origen indicates that the Spirit plays a crucial role in the triune life and the life of the believer: "But the Gospel [of John] shows [the Holy Spirit] to be of such power and majesty that it says the apostles were not able to receive those things that the Saviour wanted to teach them until the Holy Spirit should come, who, pouring himself into their souls, would be able to enlighten them regarding the nature and faith of the Trinity."[14]

Hanson argues that though Origen certainly subordinated the Spirit in some sense, the Spirit was still important to Origen's theological project, as the above quote reveals.[15] That said, Origen is clear that the Spirit is "not, as some think, a mere power of God which, according to them, has no being

---

[10]Michel René Barnes, "The Beginning and End of Early Christian Pneumatology," *AugStud* 39, no. 2 (2008): 169-86.

[11]Janet E. Rutherford, "The Alexandrian Spirit: Clement and Origin in Context," in *The Holy Spirit in the Fathers of the Church: The Proceedings of the Seventh International Patristic Conference, Maynooth, 2008*, ed. D. Vincent Twomey and Janet E. Rutherford (Dublin: Four Courts, 2010), 41-43. Hughes, *How the Spirit Became God*, 96-97, makes a similar point: "As opposed to all created beings, the Spirit exists eternally with the Father and the Son. . . . Origen's subordinationism could be understood not as ontological but rather as describing the origins of the *hypostases* from eternity past."

[12]Hanson, *Search for the Christian Doctrine of God*, 738.

[13]Ayres, *Nicaea and Its Legacy*, 212.

[14]*Princ.* 2.7.3. English translation from Behr.

[15]Hanson, *Search for the Christian Doctrine of God*, 738.

of its own."[16] In some sense, then, Origen sees the Spirit as his own "being" that participates in the triune life and is above all created things.

As the fourth century went along, pneumatology began to take a more concrete shape in between the Councils of Nicaea and Constantinople, but it was a slow and somewhat inconsistent plod.[17] As we explored in the previous chapter, Arius was famously denounced for denying the substance-sharing of the Father and Son, arguing instead that the Son came into existence. Athanasius charged him with similar feelings toward the Spirit: "The substances of Father, Son, and Holy Spirit are separate in nature, alienated and cut off from each other, and having no participation with each other. . . . So, as regards likeness of glory and of substance, the Word, he says, is quite other than Father and the Holy Spirit."[18]

Though Athanasius polemically calls this position "Arian," Eusebius of Caesarea was perhaps the exemplar for the subordination of the Spirit. He insisted that the Spirit is subordinate to the Son and is "one of the things which have come into existence through the Son," which led him to exclude the Spirit from his doctrine of God. His pneumatology—that the Spirit was not to be worshiped alongside the Father and Son—was so influential that it was "faithfully reproduced" by several groups afterward.[19]

As Hanson and Cole noted above, while the pro-Nicenes would eventually denounce subordinationist logic regarding the Spirit, their language was not often as clear and profound as that of the Father and Son. From AD 325 to 360, several statements took a minimal approach. The Creed of Nicaea offered only five words to the Spirit ("and in the Holy Spirit"; καὶ εἰς τὸ Ἅγιον Πνεῦμα). While this brevity does not entail a subordination of the Spirit by any means, we will see below that Constantinople in 381 intentionally added clarifying language about the Spirit. Some of the

---

[16]Origen, *Origen: Spirit & Fire: An Anthology of His Writings*, ed. Hans Urs von Balthasar, trans. Robert J. Daly (Washington, DC: The Catholic University of America Press, 1984), 184. Origen makes this particular claim while refuting Celsus and the Stoics.

[17]See Hanson, *Search for the Christian Doctrine of God*, 738-90, for a helpful overview of this development.

[18]As quoted in Rowan Williams, *Arius: Heresy and Tradition* (Grand Rapids, MI: Eerdmans, 2001), 101.

[19]Hanson, *Search for the Christian Doctrine of God*, 738. Here, Hanson calls this reproduction "Arian," but we have sought to avoid that term when not applied to Arius himself or self-described Arians. Rowan Williams, "R. P. C. Hanson's Search for the Christian Doctrine of God," *SJT* 45 (1992): 101-11, critiques Hanson for being too simplistic with this Arian language, ignoring the diversity of views among non-Nicenes.

creeds drawn up at Antioch in 341 expand on the language, giving "a brief account of the function of the Holy Spirit but say nothing about his status."[20] Creeds written in Serdica (AD 343) and Sirmium (351) include the Spirit, though both still stop short of calling the Spirit "God." The set of anathemas written at the Council of Ancyra (358) does not mention the Spirit, and the creeds drawn up at Nice (359) and Constantinople (360) "have the barest mention of the Spirit."[21] We mentioned in previous chapters that Athanasius's attempt to recover Nicaea as the definitive creed included his polemic against "Arians" and many of these councils; interestingly, though Nicaea's language for the Spirit may appear thin, Athanasius nonetheless declared along with the Council of Alexandria (AD 362) that Nicaea had sufficiently settled the issue of the Spirit's divinity.[22] These assorted creeds dabble in varying descriptions of the Spirit's work— comforter, sanctifier, and unifier of the Father and Son to name a few—but they say little about his divine nature. Two exceptions are worth noting. The first, Cyril of Jerusalem, did not explicitly call the Spirit "God" but tied him into the Father and Son's "status" in worship, baptism, and the plan of redemption. The other, Basil of Ancyra, includes the Spirit in the Godhead with language of *hypostases* and subsistence in one of his letters written around 359.[23] Basil of Ancyra, however, eventually joined Macedonius of Constantinople in being condemned at the Council of Constantinople in 360 because they refused to renounce their *homoiousian* doctrine.[24] Some later credited the Macedonian school for affirming the full divinity of the Son, but not the Spirit. Moreover, the Macedonians' later connection to the Pneumatomachians (πνευματομάχοι; "Spirit-fighters") is debated, but there existed in both groups an overt subordination of the Spirit to the Father and Son.[25]

---

[20]Hanson, *Search for the Christian Doctrine of God*, 741.
[21]Hanson, *Search for the Christian Doctrine of God*, 743.
[22]See, for instance, *Ep. Afr.* 11.1. It is worth noting that creedal statements are summaries of the debates and/or conversations that provoked the councils' meetings, so a five-word pneumatology does not automatically require a thin pneumatology among the actual bishops and churches. That said, the contextual issues pre-381 are no doubt christologically oriented.
[23]Hanson, *Search for the Christian Doctrine of God*, 743.
[24]Hanson, *Search for the Christian Doctrine of God*, 760.
[25]Hanson, *Search for the Christian Doctrine of God*, 760-72. I will use "Pneumatomachians" generally in this chapter, acknowledging that this group may not have been monolithic.

However, Hanson argues that Basil of Caesarea and his Cappadocian colleagues, Gregory of Nazianzus and Gregory of Nyssa, showed a higher interest in the Spirit than their contemporaries, including even Athanasius.[26] We will discuss each of them here. First, Basil of Caesarea's pneumatology historically has been influential, even if there is some debate regarding his definition (or lack thereof) of the Spirit's mode of existence (τρόπος τῆς ὑπάρξεως).[27] However, as Mark Smith observes, Basil was content to uphold the authority of Nicaea; for example, against heterodox formulations of *ousia* and *hypostases*, he says, "The blessed fathers of Nicaea had regarded these two words as entirely distinct—there being three *hypostases* and one *ousia* in the Godhead," while also respectfully recognizing the meager attention to the Spirit.[28] Ayres credits Basil as "an excellent example of the complex process of theological development and intra-ecclesial accommodation that was central to the emergence of fully pro-Nicene theology."[29] For instance, he does not emphasize the unitary action of the divine persons as precisely as Gregory of Nyssa, but rather speaks of the "peculiar" action of the Spirit to complete the work of the Father and Son in a causal sequence.[30]

---

[26] Hanson, *Search for the Christian Doctrine of God*, 772. As we will see below, while Athanasius might have been largely preoccupied with Father-Son debates while also traveling in and out of exile, he did not ignore the Spirit in his works.

[27] Space does not allow a full engagement with Basil's *Contra Eunomium* and his theological trajectory from potentially homoiousian to pro-Nicene, but Ayres, *Nicaea and Its Legacy*, 188-211, and Stephen M. Hildebrand, *The Trinitarian Theology of Basil of Caesarea: A Synthesis of Greek Thought and Biblical Truth* (Washington, DC: The Catholic University of America Press, 2007), 76-82, provide helpful summaries. For more on this debate, see Christopher A. Beeley, "The Holy Spirit in the Cappadocians: Past and Present," *Modern Theology* 26, no. 1 (2010): 90-119. In short, Beeley highlights the tension created by Basil's use of the terms like "communion in nature" with the Father and Son and his relative lack of interest in explaining the Spirit's generation. He ultimately describes Basil's pneumatology as "an unresolved composite of several different elements." For Beeley, Basil was not a homoousian in the vein of Athanasius and other pro-Nicenes, though his work on the Spirit "has several enduring strengths." For an argument that Basil's theology resembled a pro-Nicene method, see Mark DelCogliano, "Basil of Caesarea on John 1:1 as an Affirmation of Pro-Nicene Trinitarian Doctrine," in *The Bible and Early Trinitarian Theology*, ed. Christopher A. Beeley and Mark E. Weedman (Washington, DC: The Catholic University of America Press, 2018), 132-48.

[28] Mark S. Smith, *The Idea of Nicaea in the Early Church and Councils, AD 431–451*, OECS (Oxford: Oxford University Press, 2018), 25; cf. Basil of Caesarea, *Ep.* 125.1. and *Ep.* 258.2. Christopher A. Beeley, *Gregory of Nazianzus on the Trinity and the Knowledge of God: In Your Light We Shall See Light* (Oxford: Oxford University Press, 2008), 300-301, argues instead that by comparison with Gregory of Nazianzus, "Basil's understanding of the Spirit's divinity is not, in the end, all that different from the doctrine of an anti-Nicene figure like Eusebius of Caesarea" and that those who assume Basil's belief in a "full divinity of the Spirit ... give him the benefit of *Gregory's* theology," emphasis original.

[29] Ayres, *Nicaea and Its Legacy*, 187.

[30] Ayres, *Nicaea and Its Legacy*, 216.

Indeed, one could argue then that Basil teaches the doctrine of inseparable operations in pro-Nicene thought.[31]

In *De Spiritu Sancto*,[32] Basil accused those who he considered heretics—many who taught the subordination of the Spirit—of "hair-splitting reasoning . . . concerning syllables and words."[33] For Basil, those who denied the divinity of the Son and Spirit by conflating "different expressions" of the trinitarian persons with "difference in nature" are "malevolently opposed to true religion."[34] For example, Aetius pit two phrases in 1 Corinthians 8:6—"from whom" and "through whom"—against one another to assert that the different words signified a different nature between the Father and Son.[35] Basil's ultimate critique is that these "pagans" were simply bad philosophers who misused language to lead others astray.[36] It is worth remembering, after all, that a large piece of Basil's theological project on the Spirit included contributions from Greek philosophy and church tradition, which he called "general ideas" and "the non-scriptural tradition of the fathers."[37] Primarily, though, Basil's Spirit-doctrine was rooted in scriptural logic and doxological appropriateness. His rebuttal against the "pagans" who mince words was ultimately scriptural in nature, for he used passages such as Matthew 12:28, John 15:26, and Psalm 50:12-14 to assert the Spirit's divine attributes such as an immaterial and indivisible nature, omnipotence, omnipresence, life-giving and sanctifying power, and inspiration.[38] Further, he highlighted multiple passages in John[39] to note that the unity between the Father, Son, and Spirit should be understood as a unity of both nature and mission—even if in a causal sequence; for example, the Spirit is sent by the Father and Son, as

---

[31]See, for instance, Shawn Bawulski and Stephen R. Holmes, *Christian Theology: The Classics* (New York: Routledge, 2014), 41. However, Beeley, *Gregory of Nazianzus on the Trinity and the Knowledge of God*, 300, again sees much greater precision in Gregory of Nazianzus.

[32]While *De Spiritu Sancto* is not the only place Basil writes on the Spirit, it is the closest representation of his fully developed pneumatology.

[33]*D.S.S.* 2.4.

[34]*D.S.S.* 2.4.

[35]*D.S.S.* 2.4.

[36]*D.S.S.* 3.5.

[37]*D.S.S.* 9.22. Hanson, *Search for the Christian Doctrine of God*, 773n180, points out that Basil's influence from Greek philosophy and tradition are not antiscriptural, but rather seen as teachings "consonant with Scripture."

[38]*D.S.S.* 9.22. It is worth noting that Basil, particularly early on, did not use *homoousios* to talk about the shared nature of the persons; cf. Ayres, *Nicaea and Its Legacy*, 188-91.

[39]Including Jn 12:28; 14:16; 16:14; and 17:4.

well as shares titles with them.⁴⁰ Doxologically, Basil introduced the *Gloria Patri* ("Glory be to the Father and to the Son and to the Holy Spirit") as a way of worshiping the Spirit alongside the Father and Son, which was used against Aetius and those who, in Basil's mind, misused grammar.⁴¹ In light of this, Fred Sanders has noted that "Basil gave close attention to those smallest parts of speech because they mark relations, and the doctrine of the Trinity stands or falls with the right understanding of relations in God."⁴²

Though we noted above Basil's attention to the same issues of unity and distinction, some assert that Gregory of Nazianzus's pneumatology was more precise than Basil's.⁴³ As J. Warren Smith has observed, Gregory's *Theological Orations* model a type of pro-Nicene "Rule of Faith that established the theological pattern or grammar" that guided the church's theology and liturgy.⁴⁴ Notably for our purposes, Gregory arguably used stronger language regarding the consubstantiation and generation of the Spirit in relation to the Father and Son, namely with the word "divinity" (θεότης) and as the first to refer to the Spirit's "procession" (ἐκπορεύεσθαι).⁴⁵ For example, in *Or.* 25, he says, "The special characteristic of the Father is his ingenerateness, of the Son his generation, and of the Holy Spirit his procession."⁴⁶ In *Or.* 31, he appears to

---

⁴⁰*D.S.S.* 9.22 and 18.46. As Matthew Levering points out, Basil particularly relied on shared titles that depicted the persons' unity, such as "Paraclete," "Spirit of truth," and "Spirit of wisdom"; cf. Matthew Levering, *Engaging the Doctrine of the Holy Spirit: Love and Gift in the Trinity and the Church* (Grand Rapids, MI: Baker Academic, 2016), 82-85.

⁴¹Michael Horton, *Rediscovering the Holy Spirit: God's Protecting Presence in Creation, Redemption, and Everyday Life* (Grand Rapids, MI: Zondervan, 2017), 23-24. For Basil, the use of prepositions "to," "through," and "with" in this debate indicated deeper theological commitments; cf. Christopher A. Hall, *Learning Theology with the Church Fathers* (Downers Grove, IL: IVP Academic, 2002), 103-4, and Khaled Anatolios, *Retrieving Nicaea: The Development and Meaning of Trinitarian Doctrine* (Grand Rapids, MI: Baker Academic, 2011), 25.

⁴²Fred Sanders, *The Triune God*, NSD (Grand Rapids, MI: Zondervan Academic, 2016), 35.

⁴³Beeley, "Holy Spirit in the Cappadocians," 99, notes: "Gregory asserts the Spirit's divinity in the same terms that he speaks of the Son's. While Basil treats the Son and the Holy Spirit for the most part separately, and, as we have seen, with unequal terms and arguments, Gregory confesses the Spirit's divinity with equally strong terms, and he understands the fundamental issue to be faith in the Trinity as a whole." Though Beeley still makes the case that Gregory is more antimodalist than homoousian (101). Andrew Radde-Gallwitz agrees with Beeley on the antimodalism point in "The Holy Spirit as Agent, not Activity: Origen's Argument with Modalism and its Afterlife in Didymus, Eunomius, and Gregory of Nazianzus," *VC* 65 (2011): 227-48. See also Ayres, *Nicaea and Its Legacy*, 217.

⁴⁴J. Warren Smith, "The Trinity in the Fourth-Century Fathers," in *The Oxford Handbook of the Trinity*, ed. Gilles Emery and Matthew Levering (Oxford: Oxford University Press, 2012), 109.

⁴⁵For instance, see the discussion in Beeley, "Holy Spirit in the Cappadocians," 99-102.

⁴⁶*Or.* 25:16. English translation is from St. Gregory of Nazianzus, *Select Orations*, trans. Martha Vinson (Washington, DC: Catholic University of America Press, 2003), 172.

cite John 15 and lays out a fully-formed pro-Nicene account of eternal relations of origin: "Insofar as he proceeds from the Father, he is no creature; inasmuch as he is not begotten, he is no Son; and to the extent that procession is the mean between ingeneracy and generacy, he is God."[47] Then, he makes a claim even he admits is bold:

> If there was a "when" when the Father did not exist, there was a "when" when the Son did not exist. If there was a "when" when the Son did not exist, there was a "when" when the Holy Spirit did not exist. If one existed from the beginning, so did all three. If you cast one down, I make bold to tell you not to exalt the other two. What use is incomplete deity? Or rather what is deity if it is incomplete? Something is missing if it does not have Holiness, and how could it have Holiness without having the Holy Spirit? Either God's Holiness is independent of the Holy Spirit (and in that case I should like to be told what it is supposed to be) or if it is identical with the Holy Spirit, how, I ask, could it fail to be from the beginning—as if I had at one time been to God's advantage to be incomplete and without his Spirit.[48]

Here, Gregory reasons that the Spirit must be of the same substance as the Father and Son, for one cannot understand the shared eternity or creational power without a shared divine nature. He then makes it more personal: "If he did not exist from the beginning, he has the same rank as I have, though with a slight priority—we are both separated from God by time. If he has the same rank as I have, how can he make me God, how can he link me with deity?"[49]

So, for Gregory, the Spirit is the one who enables humanity's ability to incorporate into the divine life. In sum, we cannot understand the relations of the persons without a shared nature, and further we cannot understand the redemptive activities of each person or salvation itself without a shared nature in the Godhead. Indeed, Gregory was disturbed by groups such as the Eunomians, Homoians, and Pneumatomachians who "made war" against the Spirit's divinity, because denying the Spirit's divinity was an assault on the very nature of God.[50]

---

[47] *Or.* 31.8.
[48] *Or.* 31.4.
[49] *Or.* 31.4.
[50] *Or.* 25.15; 31.5; 42.13.

Gregory of Nyssa's arguments about God's power, surveyed in chapter three, relate to our discussion about the Spirit and inseparable operations, because the Spirit's power to complete and perfect the work of the Father and Son is an indication that he is of the same nature.[51] For Gregory, if the operations of the persons are one, then the divine power which gave rise to them must also be one.[52] Further, in *Letter 38*—which was attributed to Basil of Caesarea for some time but is now widely considered to be from the pen of Gregory[53]—also reveals perhaps the most thoroughgoing pro-Nicene combination of *ousia* and *hypostasis* language. He asserts that while the "consubstantiality" (ὁμοούσιοι) of the Father, Son, and Spirit must be affirmed,[54] the *hypostasis* is "that conception which through the manifest individualities gives stability and circumscription in a certain object to the common and uncircumscribed."[55] He then summarizes: "Whatever your thought suggests to you as the Father's mode of being . . . you will think also of the Son, and likewise of the Holy Spirit. For the principle of the uncreated and of the incomprehensible is one and the same, whether in regard to the Father or the Son or the Holy Spirit. For one is not more incomprehensible and uncreated and another less so."[56]

Put another way, Gregory is arguing that the unity of nature is not threatened by the individual persons and their activity. If one takes note of any of the persons, one is taking note of the divine "mode of being." As we have advanced the idea of *redoublement* in this book, Gregory offers a helpful framing here—what is common (nature) and what is distinct (personhood) are not at odds. Vidu helpfully summarizes: "The Trinity is simple but differentiated. In the same way, the divine activity *ad extra* is one, yet not without personal distinctions."[57]

---

[51] *Ad Ablabium* 3.1.50.
[52] Ayres, *Nicaea and Its Legacy*, 355.
[53] See, for instance, discussions in Reinhard Hübner, "Gregor von Nyssa, als Verfasser der sog. Ep. 38 des Basilius. Zum unterschiedlichen Verständnis der ousia bei den kappadozischen Brüdern," in *Epektasis. Mélanges patristiques offerts au Cardinal Jean Daniélou*, ed. Jacques Fontaine and Charles Kannengiesser (Paris: Beauchesne, 1972), 463, and Johannes Zachhuber, "Nochmals: Der 38. Brief des Basilius von Caesarea als Werk des Gregor von Nyssa," ZAC 7, no. 1 (2003): 73-90.
[54] *Letter 38* 2b. All English translations are from Anna M. Silvas, *Gregory of Nyssa: The Letters: Introduction, Translation and Commentary*, Vigiliae Christianae Supplements 83 (Leiden: Brill, 2007).
[55] *Letter 38* 3b.
[56] *Letter 38* 3e-3f.
[57] Adonis Vidu, *The Same God Who Works All Things: Inseparable Operations in Trinitarian Theology* (Grand Rapids, MI: Eerdmans, 2021), 63.

While it is true that the Cappadocians advanced the pneumatology of pro-Nicene theology in important ways toward the end of the fourth century, we cannot ignore Athanasius's contribution to the pro-Nicene understanding of the Spirit. Kevin Hill has argued that Athanasius's "pneumatological reticence"—particularly in his earlier works—is likely due to his focusing on particular apologetic arguments regarding the cross of Christ, in which he was laser-focused on the task at hand and omitted any extra theological arguments that may distract from his goal.[58] Hill asserts, "Athanasius does not seem to have concluded that the Holy Spirit is truly of the same divine nature and rank as the Father and Son until at least the end of the 350s."[59] Whether or not this assertion is entirely fair due to lack of extant pneumatological writings, Hill admits that Athanasius at least *implies* the shared divine nature and rank with the Father and Son in earlier works, even if it is not as "mature" as later works.[60] However, it is difficult to assess the maturity of any patristic theologian's theology, given that their theologies are not always identical to other theologians', and the development and trajectory of their theological positions or writings sometimes depend merely on occasion or context rather than an explicit linear development. Though Athanasius writes on the Holy Spirit elsewhere, I will focus on these letters since they contain his most sustained arguments.[61]

These letters detail at length Athanasius's polemical battles with the "Figurists" or "Misinterpreters" (τροπικοί; Tropikoi)[62] who he accused of "fighting against the Spirit" (πνευματομαχουντες; Pneumatomachians)[63] by

---

[58] Kevin Douglas Hill, *Athanasius and the Holy Spirit: The Development of His Early Pneumatology* (Minneapolis: Fortress, 2016), 3-34. Perhaps in comparison to the Cappadocians, his work is relatively slim; however, we see a robust doctrine of the Holy Spirit as his career and debates progressed.

[59] Hill, *Athanasius and the Holy Spirit*, 104.

[60] Hill, *Athanasius and the Holy Spirit*, 104. "Mature" is Hill's term.

[61] Along with Hill, *Athanasius and the Holy Spirit*, Charles Kannengiesser, "Athanasius of Alexandria and the Holy Spirit Between Nicea I and Constantinople I," *ITQ Quarterly* 48, no. 3-4 (1981): 166-80, also ably reviews some of his other pneumatological works.

[62] These Tropikoi (or Tropici) appear to have been an Egyptian Christian group who explicitly identified the Spirit with angels; cf. Anatolios, *Retrieving Nicaea*, 24-25. I will refer to the Tropikoi and Pneumatomachians together (but not interchangeably) since their theologies were similar in terms of subordinating the Spirit to a lesser status.

[63] This term appears to have been coined here by Athanasius and, as we noted above, would be at times used interchangeably with the Macedonians, who were problematically named after Macedonius of Constantinople; cf. Ayres, *Nicaea and Its Legacy*, 214-15.

diminishing him to the status of an angel.⁶⁴ In true polemical fashion, he compares these Spirit-fighters to Arian heresy:

> You wrote that certain ones who have withdrawn from the Arians on account of their blasphemy against the Son of God have nonetheless set their minds against the Holy Spirit, claiming not only that he is a creature, but that he is one of the ministering spirits and is different from the angels only in degree. . . . For just as Arians by denying the Son also deny the Father, so too these people by disparaging the Holy Spirit also disparage the Son.⁶⁵

The logic employed by Athanasius seems rather straightforward: just as the "Arians" denied the *homoousios* between the Father and Son, so the Tropikoi and Pneumatomachians similarly deny the divinity of the Holy Spirit by comparing him to angels, who are of a lower rank of nature.

Second, we noted that the Tropikoi and Pneumatomachians did not see an ontological continuity between the Spirit and the Father and Son. At best, depending on who you read, they viewed the Spirit as an angel or ignored him altogether. In this instance, however, Athanasius charged them with blasphemy for denying the full divinity of the Spirit. Ayres points out that "*Letters to Serapion* may well represent the earliest clear statement of the doctrine [of inseparable operations] applied to all three persons."⁶⁶

This brief summary of fourth-century pneumatology is important for our purposes here because a central aspect of understanding the Spirit in Revelation is dealing with the possibility of the Spirit as subordinate to God and Christ either as a distinct agent or as an angel. Just as language for the Spirit's ontology was not always terminologically stable even into the later stages of the pro-Nicene theologies, it is also difficult to handle this issue in Revelation. Given John's use of imagery and concepts from the Jewish tradition, it takes care to parse out his Spirit language from angelic or subordinate

---

⁶⁴*Ep. Serap.* 1.1.2 and 1.32.2. For a brief introduction to this debate, see Athanasius the Great and Didymus the Blind, *Works on the Spirit*, 19-22.

⁶⁵*Ep. Serap.* 1.1.2-3. We cannot forget here that Didymus the Blind makes similar claims about the Spirit and inseparable operations, especially clear in his treatise *On the Holy Spirit*, 81-86.

⁶⁶Ayres, *Nicaea and Its Legacy*, 214. Ayres also notes that Athanasius presented the Spirit as the Son's ἐνέργεια (energy) while trying to defend their unity of nature, which "will soon be problematic" when the Cappadocians debate the Homoiousians, who the Cappadocians perceive to be using "energy . . . to indicate a lack of real existence"; cf. *Or.* 31.5. Ayres illuminates this point by noting that Athanasius appears to be "trying out formulations," which is a stark reminder of theological trajectories during the fourth century.

language. This is why some seemed unable to find consistent or stable language for the Spirit in the first few centuries of the church. However, I will discuss below ways that this distinction can be found, which does not differ significantly from the logic of the later patristics.

Basil's warning about "hair-splitting reasoning" that ultimately conflates the persons of the Trinity is a helpful caution when reading Revelation through a trinitarian lens. On the one hand, we certainly need to approach the text with care; on the other hand, we need not ignore some of John's clearest signs of incipient trinitarianism with respect to the Spirit. That said, we will now address a few select passages from Revelation that highlight John's use of Spirit language. We will see below using a careful reading and employing pro-Nicene tools that John seems able to distinguish between the Spirit and angels in some ontological sense. This will all help support our thesis that a trinitarian reading is not an imposition on the text but rather is drawn from a close reading of the text.

INTERPRETATION OF SELECT PASSAGES

The passages covered in this section were selected because they highlight the ways in which John equates the Spirit with the divine nature of the Father and Jesus and/or describing their relationships. We will see that rather than a nebulous force or a subordinated agent, the Spirit in Revelation is worshiped and regarded similarly to the Father and Jesus, albeit in different ways. A trinitarian reading helps us see the distinct and dynamic ways that John writes about the Spirit's ontological equality with and yet economic distinction from the other persons. We will therefore interact with the best interdisciplinary works and ideas on interpreting these passages both to highlight their strengths and show how our approach might provide alternate or better readings.

The seven spirits (Rev 1:4-5b).[67] While the role of the Holy Spirit in Revelation may appear less robust than Jesus', he is not on the periphery of John's vision. Aside from the doxology, one should note from the outset that the Spirit brings John into the vision (1:10) and guides him through the visionary journey (4:2; 17:3; 21:10). It should not be overlooked that the "seven spirits"

---

[67]This language also appears in 3:1; 4:5; 5:6, which we will discuss in this section.

and the phrase "in the Spirit" occur at these key places in the book. As John Christopher Thomas has said, the Spirit gives John's Apocalypse its structure, "making clear that the work attributed to the Spirit in the Apocalypse is at the same time the work of God" and "the Spirit is the means by which the revelation of Jesus Christ takes place."[68]

The language of "seven spirits" (τῶν ἑπτὰ πνευμάτων) has led to a variety of potential identities of these "spirits." The inclusion of the seven spirits in the salutation causes further confusion, both because they are included in the divine blessing and because they appear to be the conduit through which God sends his blessings.[69] If one wants to compare Revelation to other Jewish apocalyptic works, one might think of the seven angels in 1 Enoch's Watchers who work and speak on God's behalf (1 En. 9:1; 10:4; 23:4; 40:9). Since angelic figures are prominent in Revelation and some argue for the seven spirits as angels, this is a possibility.

Thinking more canonically, the number seven also represents the number of completion throughout Scripture and could denote something of both the perfection of the Spirit and his omnipresent work among the seven churches listed in the book (both divine qualities).[70] The general use of the number seven in the Apocalypse adds another wrinkle—the seven churches and the seven cycles of judgment are two glaring examples wherein John is possibly using the number to describe a single place or event but in a sevenfold fashion. With regard to the churches, seven receive a message, but it is possible that Revelation was a circular letter read to the entire Christian body of Asia Minor. In the same way, God's judgment is poured out over the entire earth, yet John explains the application of judgment in various scenes and particularities.

Witherington has challenged the assertion that the seven spirits represent the Spirit. He argues that the meaning here is more closely associated with the other sevenfold descriptions in Revelation—the blazing lamps, the Lamb's eyes, and the stars. So these seven spirits are "the angels who are the eyes of the great King, keeping watch over the church for the Lamb," which

---

[68] John Christopher Thomas, "Revelation," in *A Biblical Theology of the Holy Spirit*, ed. Trevor J. Burke and Keith Warrington (Eugene, OR: Cascade, 2014), 258.

[69] John Christopher Thomas and Frank D. Macchia, *Revelation*, THNTC (Grand Rapids, MI: Eerdmans, 2016), 76, assert this point as well.

[70] Richard Bauckham, *The Theology of the Book of Revelation* (Cambridge: Cambridge University Press, 1993), 109-10, asserts this point.

is corroborated by Scripture (Heb 1:14) and early Jewish texts (Tob 12:15; 1 En. 20:1-8, to name a few).[71] Bucur agrees, also noting that "the angelic traits of the seven spirits are quite obvious" because of their association with the symbolism of the seven stars and seven angels.[72] He concludes that because they offer up prayers in a subordinated role "before the divine throne" (1:20), they represent "standard elements in the depiction of angelic intercession, contemplation, and service."[73]

According to Jonathan Knight, the language of "seven spirits" in Revelation 1:4 likely parallels "the Spirit" in Revelation 22:17. However, he is perplexed by the Spirit's lack of appearance in the heavenly court in Revelation 4–5, "where if anywhere he might have been included."[74] In light of this confusion, he concludes, "This passage has a trinitarian air but it certainly does not use the language of later trinitarian orthodoxy," and "it lies beyond the author's purpose to offer a developed trinitarianism within the context of the revealed mysteries."[75] Two responses are in order. First, it is a valid point to assert that John was not using later trinitarian terms, nor was he offering a creedal trinitarianism; he could not have properly done so. However, it is too abrupt to conclude that because the Spirit is not placed at the throne in the same way as the Lamb, then he must be treated differently. Instead, we can acknowledge that John might have different ways of associating the Spirit with God's identity and power. Second and relatedly, the Spirit *is* arguably present in the throne-room scene of Revelation 4–5. In 4:2 John explicitly claims to be "in the Spirit" when he sees the vision, as though the Spirit acts as a guardian of the throne-room entrance. And since John recognizes the divine worship that the Spirit deserves in the 1:4 doxology, it would seem odd to forget the Spirit shortly afterward in 1:10-11 and in 4:2. Likewise, as we have noted elsewhere, angels are not worshiped in Revelation, whereas the seven spirits are included in doxological language.

It is also worth noting that John's "in the Spirit" vision is different from other Christian apocalyptic works, such as Martyrdom and Ascension of

---

[71] Ben Witherington III, *Revelation* (Cambridge: Cambridge University Press, 2003), 75.
[72] Bogdan G. Bucur, "Hierarchy, Prophecy, and the Angelomorphic Spirit: A Contribution to the Study of the Book of Revelation's *Wirkungsgeschichte*," *JBL* 127, no. 1 (2008): 177.
[73] Bucur, "Hierarchy, Prophecy, and the Angelomorphic Spirit," 177.
[74] Jonathan Knight, *Revelation*, Readings: A New Biblical Commentary (Sheffield: Sheffield Academic Press, 1998), 34.
[75] Knight, *Revelation*, 34.

Isaiah 6–7, wherein the Spirit also brings a heavenly vision but traverses between speaking from heaven and bringing Isaiah into his vision. John's experience seems more concretely rooted in a prophetic and embodied revelation rather than a mere conversation with the Spirit. It seems more akin to prophetic visions such as Ezekiel 37. First, Ezekiel notes that God's Spirit brought him into a valley full of bones and led him around it. Similarly, John says that he was "in the Spirit" during his vision(s) (1:10; 4:2). Second, Ezekiel notes that during his vision the Lord commands him to speak to the bones in his name (37:4) and to write down his words as a message to Israel (37:16). John receives a similar command to write down Jesus' words for the churches (1:10; 19). Finally, God promises in Ezekiel's vision to bring life and land to Israel and to dwell with them through his Spirit and sanctuary (37:12-28). John uses similar language in Revelation 22, when the Spirit testifies that God's people can come and drink from the water of life, right after God comes to dwell with his people in the new Jerusalem.[76]

Moreover, Whitaker provides helpful language for describing the imagery of the seven spirits as the eyes of God and Jesus, though she does not explicitly tie their identity to the Spirit:

> Despite having a distinct identity of their own (1:4), the seven spirits are also associated with God's throne (4:5), and belong to the Lamb (5:6). . . . John's fluid and complex imagery thus associates the seven spirits with the enthroned God and Lamb, as well as giving them autonomy to roam the earth. In doing so, he attributes an omniscient and omnispective gaze to God in his various guises.[77]

This language of God's eyes having an "omnispective gaze" can be compared to passages such as Proverbs 15:3: "The eyes of the LORD are everywhere, observing the wicked and the good." Whitaker's perspective offers somewhat of a bridge between a complete denial that the seven spirits are the Spirit while also acknowledging both a closeness and distinction between the seven spirits and God and the Lamb.

Charles challenges the placement of the seven spirits in 1:4 altogether, asserting that the addition of this language must have come from a "later

---

[76]The Spirit's role in wisdom, revelation, and renewal has a long history in Jewish literature. See, for example, 1 En. 49:3; 1QS 4:26; *Gig.* 5:23; *Virt.* 203; Wis 1–2, 7–8, 15–16.

[77]Robyn J. Whitaker, *Ekphrasis, Vision, and Persuasion in the Book of Revelation*, WUNT 2, no. 410 (Tübingen: Mohr Siebeck, 2015), 115.

hand (probably early in the 2nd cent.)" because John "cannot have put forward such a grotesque Trinity" by including the Holy Spirit in a grace-and-peace salutation.[78] He comes to this conclusion by arguing that the seven spirits represent some sort of angels, which John would not include in a worship setting. While other references to the seven spirits may be from John's hand (3:1), he does not believe the first reference in 1:4 is original. Some scholars, however, have been willing to take the seven spirits language a step further.

Bauckham concludes that Zechariah 4:1-14 "seems to have been the key Old Testament passage for John's understanding of the role of the Spirit in the divine activity in the world," especially the language of Zechariah 4:6 about the Spirit establishing God's rule on earth.[79] Soulen similarly advocates that, in a clear allusion to Zechariah 4:10, John is equating the "eyes of the Lord" in the Zechariah passage with the seven spirits in Revelation 1:4 and those in 5:6, where the "sevens spirits of God" are sent to be his eyes on earth.[80] He then contends that these seven spirits or eyes are indeed representative of the Spirit: "Like other New Testament writers, John understands the first person of the Trinity to be the ultimate source of the Spirit, even as Jesus Christ is its proximate source as the Spirit is poured out on the earth in the end times (cf. Acts 2:33; Jn 20:22). John's language is equivalent to the teaching that 'the Holy Spirit proceeds from the Father through the Son.'"[81]

As we have mentioned before, John has a habit of distinct recapitulations of familiar texts and traditions. Not only does he use Isaiah 11 as a structural key in Revelation 5, as we have seen, but he also combines a messianic text such as Genesis 49:9 with a seven-spirits text like Zechariah 4:10 to create a complex new interpretation of the texts.[82]

Paul further highlights that the seven spirits' placement *between* God and Jesus in the doxology's order could denote a purposeful inclusion in the divine name or nature.[83] He also says elsewhere,

---

[78]R. H. Charles, *A Critical and Exegetical Commentary on the Revelation of St. John*, vol. 1 (Edinburgh: T&T Clark, 1920), 9.
[79]Bauckham, *Theology of the Book of Revelation*, 110.
[80]R. Kendall Soulen, *The Divine Name(s) and the Holy Trinity*, 2 vols. (Louisville: Westminster John Knox, 2011), 1:180.
[81]Soulen, *Divine Names and the Holy Trinity*, 1:180.
[82]Garrick V. Allen, *The Book of Revelation and Early Jewish Textual Culture*, SNTS 168 (Cambridge: Cambridge University Press, 2017), 131-32.
[83]Ian Paul, *Revelation* (Downers Grove, IL: IVP Academic, 2018), 62.

This conjunction has two effects: firstly to identify in some sense the lamb and Yahweh, since the "eyes of Yahweh" have now become the "eyes of the lamb"; and secondly to place the Spirit in a subordinate position in relation to both God and the lamb. The situation of the seven lamps "before the throne" is one that is shared by the various members of the assembled throng (including elders, living creatures, and angels) and which signifies worship and obedience. The fact that the throne itself belongs to God, but the lamb then occupies it, and the (seven) Spirit(s) being the eyes of both Yahweh and the lamb offers a narrative portrayal which might be later expressed in a different register as the Spirit "proceeding from the Father and the Son."[84]

In the context of other NT writings, John may be thinking of Jesus' sending of the Spirit to fulfill the Great Commission (Mt 28:18-20; Jn 14:26), paired with Zechariah's description of the power of the Spirit rebuilding the temple (Zech 4:6), which John also describes as God building his temple through the Spirit (Rev 3:12; 11:1) and finds its eschatological culmination in the New Jerusalem (21:3, 16, 22).[85] Beale and McDonough agree, adding that this designation of the Holy Spirit expresses "the diversity of God's work in the church and the world."[86] The number seven as a sign of the Spirit's divine fullness might also be an allusion to the LXX translation of Isaiah 11:2-3, with its sevenfold description of the gifts and activities of the Lord's spirit.[87]

Further, the "seven stars" in Jesus' hand in 2:1 coupled with the number seven attached to πνευμάτων could be seen as symbolic and therefore point back to the idea of a singular, omnipresent Spirit. Apringius of Beja, who wrote his *Tractate on the Apocalypse* in the sixth century, commented that the Spirit "is one in name, sevenfold in power, invisible and incorporeal, and

---

[84]Ian Paul, "The Trinitarian Dynamic in the Book of Revelation," in *Trinity Without Hierarchy: Reclaiming Nicene Orthodoxy in Evangelical Theology*, ed. Michael F. Bird and Scott Harrower (Grand Rapids, MI: Kregel Academic, 2019), 90.

[85]Peter S. Williamson, *Revelation*, Catholic Commentary on Sacred Scripture (Grand Rapids, MI: Baker Academic, 2015), 44.

[86]G. K. Beale and Sean M. McDonough, "Revelation," in *Commentary on the New Testament Use of the Old Testament*, ed. G. K. Beale and D. A. Carson (Grand Rapids, MI: Baker Academic, 2007), 1089. See also Michael Gilbertson, *God and History in the Book of Revelation* (Cambridge: Cambridge University Press, 2003), 89: "[There is] is a complex of ideas relating to the Spirit of God, in which God's activity and the church's witness are interconnected."

[87]Bruce Metzger, *Breaking the Code: Understanding the Book of Revelation* (Nashville: Abingdon, 1993), 23-24. The seven designations being wisdom, understanding, counsel, might, knowledge, godliness, and the fear of God. Williamson and Apringius both allude to the same Isaiah text to support their arguments mentioned in this section.

[his] form is impossible to comprehend."[88] During the medieval period, Richard of Saint Victor noted the "sevenfold grace of the Holy Spirit," with its seven prophecies manifested to the seven churches—"more generally [addressing] the present and future states of the holy catholic church"— reveal a sevenfold structure that "points to the perfection of the doctrine contained in the prophecy."[89] This idea of the Spirit's sevenfold perfection and fullness can also be applied to Revelation 4:5 (seven lamps) and 5:6 (seven eyes of the Lamb).[90] It is also possible that the seven angels are sent into the world under the direction of the Spirit,[91] which is feasible so long as the spirits and angels are not too closely tied ontologically. However, John's reading of Zechariah 4 seems to dispel this notion entirely. The angels might be under the divine instruction of the Spirit, but it is reasonable in any case to deny that the seven angels and seven spirits are in some way interchangeable designations or that the spirits are higher-ranking angels.

Bucur acknowledges strengths on both sides. On the one hand,

> The structure of the phrase (καί . . . καί . . . καί) suggests that "the seven spirits before his [God's] throne" are one among three coordinated entities. The blessing with "grace and peace" is suggestive of divine origin. The three must, then, some way stand for the divinity. . . . It seems most likely, therefore, that the mentioning of the "seven spirits" corresponds to the expected reference to the Holy Spirit.[92]

This parallels many of the arguments above. Bucur continues: "On the other hand, the angelic traits of the seven spirits are quite obvious,"[93] which others contended above. He notes that there appears to be conflation between the seven "stars" and "spirits" and "angels" (Rev 1:4, 20; 3:1; 8:2). Further, ancient readers often understood "star" language not in an astronomical sense but rather in terms of an angel or holy power "in the form of a star," so it is likely that early Christians would have assumed John's language as a reference to angels. However, he also points out that in

---

[88]As quoted in *Ancient Christian Texts: Latin Commentaries on Revelation*, ed. and trans. William C. Weinrich (Downers Grove, IL: IVP Academic, 2011), 4.

[89]Quoted in *The Book of Revelation*, trans. and ed. David Burr, The Bible in Medieval Tradition (Grand Rapids, MI: Eerdmans, 2019), 76.

[90]James L. Resseguie, *The Revelation of John* (Grand Rapids, MI: Baker Academic, 2009), 66.

[91]This idea was given to me by Edith Humphrey in private correspondence.

[92]Bogdan G. Bucur, *Angelomorphic Pneumatology: Clement of Alexandria and Other Christian Witnesses*, VCS 95 (Leiden: Brill, 2009), 91-92.

[93]Bucur, *Angelomorphic Pneumatology*, 93.

Isaiah 63:9-10 LXX, "angel" and God's "holy spirit" are used interchangeably. Bucur ultimately promotes the angelic view due to (1) the interchangeable terms used by John and (2) the clear subordination of these groups to Christ.[94]

We have continually discussed the ways John separates Jesus from the angels. However, Malcolm Yarnell has summarized well numerous rebuttals for the idea that the seven spirits represent "chief" angels: (1) John never joins the tradition found in the Dead Sea Scrolls, for example, in equating "spirit" with angels; (2) he "use[s] apocalyptic imagery in his own way," and including Hebrew angelology would have been odd; (3) the seven angels found in Revelation do not function the same as the seven spirits; (4) angelic hierarchies seem out of place in the Apocalypse; and (5) the spirits curiously are never described as worshiping God in Revelation 4 and 5, but rather the reader must consider whether John "subtly included them with God and the Lamb in the objective center of the worship directed toward the throne."[95] While it would pose no real threat to our argument here of the seven spirits being the Spirit, it is not out of the realm of possibility that John did in fact borrow from Hebrew angelology or other contemporary works. Perhaps he uses such imagery only as a foil to make the case in Yarnell's fifth rebuttal—that, ultimately, God's Spirit is on the divine side of the Creator-creature divide. In other words, if angelology is at play in relation to the Spirit, it is to draw the audience into language they would understand so as to reorder their thinking about what an angel is and who God's Spirit is. John makes a point to show how the Spirit is not just another messenger of God but is of the same nature as the Father and Son in his worthiness to receive worship and the power to perform revelatory functions.[96]

The doxological inclusion of the seven spirits should cause the most pause when trying to explain the seven spirits as merely angels. Indeed, Jewish literature describes angels offering up sacrifices, praying, and singing toward God—sometimes alongside humans—but benedictions and reception of praise belong to YHWH.[97] Further, as Paul notes,

---

[94]Bucur, *Angelomorphic Pneumatology*, 93-94.
[95]Malcolm B. Yarnell, *God the Trinity* (Nashville: B&H Academic, 2016), 212-13. He mentions that even Robert Mounce, who actually agrees with the chief-angel suggestion, concedes Yarnell's point here.
[96]Thomas and Macchia, *Revelation*, 73, contend that the inclusion of the Spirit in the salutation "suggests that all that follows is closely connected to the work of the Spirit."
[97]Shaye J. D. Cohen, *From the Maccabees to the Mishnah*, 2nd ed. (Louisville, KY: Westminster John Knox, 2006), 60-62.

There is a large and varied cast of angels throughout the text (most notably in the six arriving as two sets of three in ch. 14) so there is no reason to think that John would slip a further seven in here "in disguise" as it were. And the insertion of this reference between the titular introductions of God and Jesus, who (as we shall see) converge in title, function, and authority, has the effect of removing any ambiguity, since "grace and peace" as divine blessing flow from all three.[98]

Again, given the extensive attention John gives to the object of true and false worship, it seems out of character for him to have included a nondivine creature in the opening refrain of praise. As we discussed in the previous chapter, angels in Revelation routinely and without equivocation stress the importance of John *not* worshiping them.

Later, in 3:1, Jesus explains that he "has the seven spirits of God" (ἔχων τὰ ἑπτὰ Πνεύματα τοῦ Θεοῦ). This repeated connection of Jesus and the seven spirits to God's throne might be a clear indication that John wants his audience to notice how intimately connected their identities and activities are.[99] If we consider all of the ways we have discussed the connection between the identities and activities of God, Christ, and the Spirit throughout this book, this only becomes more obvious.

However, one could also contend that while this phrase may simply mean that Jesus has authority over some group of spirits or even the Holy Spirit, the usage might be intentionally applied to the church at Sardis based on their situation. Sardis is on the brink of death and is warned against being erased from the book of life. Given the seemingly dire spiritual state of the church in Sardis, Jesus' sending of the Spirit may be a way of showing his intense concern for their ability to discern and apply his commands.[100] In 3:5 Jesus informs them that those who are not in the book will not be acknowledged in front of the Father and the angels. If, as we have noted, the seven stars represent God's angels, then 3:1 and 3:5 are connected (seven stars = angels at the judgment). It would make sense, then, that John connects the seven spirits or Spirit too. In the scope of biblical history, God's Spirit is one who gives life (Ezek 11:19-20; 37:13-14; Jn 6:63; 2 Cor 3:4-6) and is

---

[98] Paul, "Trinitarian Dynamic in the Book of Revelation," 89.
[99] Thomas, "Revelation," 259-60.
[100] Rebecca Skaggs and Priscilla Benham, *Revelation*, Pentecostal Commentary Series (Dorset, UK: Deo, 2009), 45.

involved in judgment or removal of God's blessing (Judg 3:10; 1 Sam 16:14; Ps 51:11; Mt 12:31-33). The mention of the seven spirits or Spirit here, then, might indicate that he has come with Jesus to give life to Sardis—indeed, the eternal life that comes with having one's name listed in the book. This life-giving role of the Spirit is parallel with the life-giving nature of the Father and Jesus throughout Scripture (Gen 2:7; Neh 9:6; Jn 1:3-4; 14:6). As Andrew of Caesarea pointed out, if the seven spirits are indeed indicative of "the life-giving Spirit," then Christ is shown as "the supplier of the Spirit."[101] Further, John 4:10-24 identifies "the water of life" with the Spirit, and John 7:38 and 19:34-35 identify the Spirit as water flowing from the new temple. So, this language of Christ supplying the Spirit and the Spirit giving life might also be present in Revelation 22:1, with the Spirit symbolized as the "river of life" (ποταμὸν ὕδατος ζωῆς) in God's new temple-city.[102] Interestingly enough, "giver of life" is a title for the Spirit in the Constantinopolitan Creed (AD 381).

Bucur points out that "Revelation never uses the expression 'holy spirit,'" concluding that attributing a speaking role to the Spirit is a way to "evade the difficulty" by resorting to "convenient dogmatic 'shortcuts.'"[103] However, some portions of the NT depict the Spirit as the one who reminds believers of God's message by continually convicting them and applying it to their hearts (Jn 14:26; 16:13; Rom 8:26; 1 Cor 2:13). Peter proclaims that the Spirit even spoke through the OT prophets without qualifying that he was only a conduit of Christ's words (2 Pet 1:20-21). So, every time Jesus authoritatively speaks to the churches, he bookends the message by tying his authority to the Spirit (and vice versa, tying the Spirit's authority to himself).

Bucur, however, favors the explanation that "what seems to be a trinitarian opening" instead "remains determined by a binitarian framework."[104] However, this binitarian explanation seems too reductionistic. We have already argued that the Spirit could be offering "grace and peace" along with the Father (1:4) and the Son (1:5), similar to the structure of 1 Peter 1:2. Assuming Revelation was read as a circular letter to churches in Asia Minor,

---

[101] Andrew of Caesarea, *Commentary on the Apocalypse* 3.1., as quoted in *Revelation*, ed. William C. Weinrich, Ancient Christian Commentary on Scripture (Downers Grove, IL: IVP Academic, 2005), 40.
[102] Paul, "Trinitarian Dynamic in the Book of Revelation," 104-5.
[103] Bucur, "Hierarchy, Prophecy, and the Angelomorphic Spirit," 185-86.
[104] Bucur, "Hierarchy, Prophecy, and the Angelomorphic Spirit," 183.

the one-two punch of "Jesus-Spirit says" would be hard to overlook, given that they would have heard the phrase numerous times throughout the letter. In turn, the audience (then and now) must deal with the tension John creates doxologically and linguistically.

Bucur's conclusion regarding the seven spirits not only defends the angelic view but further says that "the patristic exegetes" also admitted that the "stars" and "spirits" were likely the same reference to angelic beings worshiping around God's throne, even if they tried to avoid downplaying orthodox trinitarianism.[105] One of his footnotes references Andrew of Caesarea's commentary on Revelation 3. Andrew summarized that the "seven stars" are "divine angels" and that the "seven spirits are either the angels themselves or the acts of the Life-giving Spirit."[106] In commenting on 1:4-5, Andrew noted the possibility of the seven spirits being angels but in the same paragraph says that it could also be "the activities of the Life-giving Spirit. . . . For in many places each divine Person is indifferently placed and arranged" by John.[107] Later, commenting on Revelation 4:5-6, he once again takes the middle ground by saying the seven spirits are *either* chief angels or the Holy Spirit.[108] So in one sense Bucur is right—there is patristic precedent for equating the stars and spirits with each other and/or with angels and Andrew also offers an alternative trinitarian interpretation. But regardless of Andrew's unknown motivations about protecting orthodoxy—Bucur raises the question but does not prove the point—it is noteworthy that a patristic commentator highlighted the possibility of a trinitarian reading of the seven-spirits language.

We have seen that it might be reasonable to conclude that John employs a similar pneumatology in which the Spirit is both an angel and worthy of worship. However, for Athanasius, equating the Spirit with angels was a

---

[105] Bucur, *Angelomorphic Pneumatology*, 94.

[106] Andrew of Caesarea, *Commentary on the Apocalypse*, trans. Eugenia Scarvelis Constantinou (Washington, DC: The Catholic University of America Press, 2011), 73.

[107] Andrew of Caesarea, *Commentary on the Apocalypse*, 57.

[108] Andrew of Caesarea, *Commentary on the Apocalypse*, 83. Interestingly, Andrew refers to Irenaeus's position that the spirits are "chief angels." The edition of the commentary quoted here footnotes *Epideixis*. In Armitage Robinson's translation, he concludes in a footnote that the connection between the Holy Spirit and angels led a later editor to remove the phrase, "thee the Paraclete worshippeth"; cf. St. Irenaeus of Lyons, *The Demonstration of the Apostolic Preaching*, trans. Armitage Robinson (New York: Macmillan, 1920), 23.

blasphemy on par with Arianism, though one could imagine how the Tropikoi or Pneumatomachians could conceivably utilize Revelation's language for their own angelic-Spirit arguments. Though the Tropikoi or Pneumatomachian logic might argue that the spirits are angels who surround God's throne and do his ministerial bidding, Athanasius was clear (using Revelation 22:9 as his reasoning) that angels could not be worshiped due to their subordinate nature. Instead, the Son could receive worship because he is "the Father's own Son by essence."[109] If the prohibition of worshiping angels is married to the inclusion of the Spirit in doxological summaries, Athanasius has the better argument, even if we grant some angelic attributes associated with the Spirit. The supposed resemblances between the Spirit and angels are not surprising—both are technically "spirit"—but are ultimately superficial given the context of John's descriptions.[110]

Though Basil was not commenting directly on the debate over angels and the Spirit in Revelation, he also made an important distinction between angels and the Holy Spirit: "The angelic powers are not by their own nature holy; otherwise there would be no difference between them and the Holy Spirit."[111] Extending this logic, he asserted:

> Holiness is not part of their essence it is accomplished in them through communion with the Spirit. . . . If we agree that the Spirit is subordinate, then the choirs of angels are destroyed, the ranks of archangels are abolished, and everything is thrown into confusion, since their life loses all law, order, and boundary. How can the angels cry, "Glory to God in the highest," unless the Spirit enables them to do so? "No one speaking by the Spirit of God ever says, 'Jesus be cursed!' and no one can say 'Jesus is Lord' except by the Holy Spirit [1 Cor 12:3]."[112]

This ontological claim is fitting of pro-Nicene logic and provides an avenue for seeing the divinity of the Spirit. John at some level grasped the idea that angels were not to be worshiped—much like Paul in Basil's example—and so the explanation for the seven spirits as merely angels in

---

[109]*C. Ar.* 2.23.
[110]This insight is owed to John R. Gilhooly in personal correspondence (March 2, 2020).
[111]As quoted in St. Basil the Great, *On the Holy Spirit*, 63. This edition in the Popular Patristics Series differs from the edition translated by Stephen Hildebrand, which is the primary English source used elsewhere in this book.
[112]Basil, *On the Holy Spirit* 63. See note above.

his doxology seems unusual. Further, as we will see, the Spirit's activity elsewhere highlights the Cappadocians' insistence that he displays divine power in perfecting the work of the Father and Son. Again, in a book like Revelation, which is so concerned with true and false worship, we must continue to remember the ways the Son and Spirit are included in worship language and scenes.

As we briefly mentioned above, Origen leans on Revelation 1:4-6 in his Leviticus commentary to create a trinitarian model for how the sacrifices of the OT point to the sacrifice of Christ. When explaining the need for a sevenfold sprinkling of the blood of the sacrifice on the altar (Lev 4:16-17), Origen sees this as an allusion to the Spirit being described as "the seven spirits" in Revelation 1:4 and the necessary step toward casting out the "seven demons" (Lk 11:26) in the hearts of sinners.[113] He makes this point again regarding the sevenfold sprinkling of oil, offering a more triadic shape to the allusion:

> The gift of the grace of the Spirit is designated through the image of "oil" that this one who is converted from sin, not only can attain cleansing but also be filled with the Holy Spirit by whom he can receive the best "robe and ring" and, having been reconciled to the Father, can be restored to the place of a son, through our Lord Jesus Christ himself, "to whom is the glory and power forever and ever. Amen."[114]

He uses this same doxological formula of Revelation 1:6 to end almost all of his homilies on Leviticus. He sometimes uses phrases like "illuminated by the law of the Holy Spirit, we may be worthy to obtain the spiritual grace in Christ Jesus our Lord 'to whom is the glory and power forever and ever. Amen.'"[115] Other times he words it as, "May we also be found pure and clean through Christ our Lord through whom is to God the Father with the Holy

---

[113] *Hom. Lev.* 3.5.1; 8.11.15.

[114] *Hom. Lev.* 8.11.15.

[115] *Hom. Lev.* 6.6.6. His doxologies also resemble 1 Pet 4:11 at times. However, based on Origen's repeated reference to the Spirit as "sevenfold" and the way he uses Revelation broadly in this commentary and other works, there is reason to assume that he is thinking of Rev 1:6 throughout these doxologies. At the very least, it could be said that he sometimes uses combinations of Scriptures. In his homilies on Genesis, Exodus, and Joshua, for example, he also uses doxological wording that resembles Gal 1:5 as well as Rev 1:6; 5:13; and 7:12. Again, there can be no doubt, given his extensive use of Revelation in general, that his doxologies have the book in mind.

Spirit 'glory and power forever. Amen.'"[116] Preceding another doxology, he refers to John's description of the gospel as "eternal" in Revelation 14:6 and then ends the homily saying, "For heaven and earth will pass away, but his words will not pass away," but they will always remain as he himself always remains. Through whom to God the Father with the Holy Spirit "is glory and power forever and ever. Amen!"[117] In sum, Origen clearly sees the doxology as a representation of the divine grace offered by the sacrifice of Christ through the Spirit in praise of the Father.

We have thus far considered arguments that the "seven spirits" might be an angelic host. We have also considered that the seven spirits could alternatively represent the Spirit because they are named with God and Jesus in a doxology, and we remember that angels denied John's attempts at worshiping them. I. Howard Marshall proposes that the description of the seven spirits in 1:4 and 3:1 indicates the doctrine of the Spirit's development by the time of Revelation's writing.[118] Indeed, if Revelation was written near the end of the first century, John may have obtained a more developed kerygma related to the nature and activity of the Spirit. As we saw earlier, his language resembles the way the early Christians spoke of the Spirit's relation to the work of the Father and Son and furthers the assertion that the early church's understanding of the Trinity was not yet developed but was also not absent.[119] However, a divine pneumatology seems to pervade all of the NT, from earlier writings (e.g., Paul's epistles) to later writings (e.g., John's Gospel and Revelation).

In comparison with the Jewish, Greco-Roman, and Christian concepts of the divine spirit, John seems to elevate the Spirit as a distinct agent or person who is both unique in some sense and also concretely related to YHWH's nature. We can conclude, then, that the seven-spirits language here may inhabit the language and concepts of chief angels, but angels are explicitly not worshiped in Revelation, and so John has clearly reimagined and reinterpreted any other seven-spirits tradition he *may have* interacted with, filtering it through a triadic doxology that pressures readers to consider the

---

[116]*Hom. Lev.* 7.7.3.
[117]*Hom. Lev.* 4.10.6.
[118]I. Howard Marshall, *New Testament Theology* (Downers Grove, IL: IVP Academic, 2004), 550.
[119]Bauckham, *Theology of the Book of Revelation*, 113.

nature and activity of the seven spirits. Following the logic of Gregory of Nyssa, if the Spirit is the perfection or completion of God's work, this comports with the idea of the perfect, complete sevenfold Spirit exercising divine power along with the Father and Son to bring all of creation to its perfected culmination. To worship God is to worship the Father, Son, and Spirit who are of the same substance, have the same will and power, and who act inseparably in the redemption of humanity.

In the Spirit (Rev 1:10-11).[120] It was mentioned above that Knight questions the presence of the Spirit in the heavenly court scene in 4:2. Commenting on 1:10-11, he says, "When John says he was 'in the Spirit,' he means that he entered a trance."[121] He defends this claim by rooting his language and experience in "trance-like" states found in Ezekiel 11:1, Martyrdom and Ascension of Isaiah 6, and the Jewish text *Hekholath Rabbati*. In these visions the seer describes being carried into a sort of out-of-body experience and even at some level prepares himself for going into a trance. One possibility offered by Knight is, "This section draws extensively on the Jewish theophanic tradition. Meditation on the biblical theophanies possibly even helped *induce* a mystical experience of this kind. It would be foolish to discount this possibility even if the practice cannot be proved."[122] This claim will be examined in a moment, but Knight also explains that this type of vision is found in 1 Enoch 14, Mark 1:10, and Acts 7:55. These parallels are worth a response, as Knight skips over the trinitarian connections within these texts.

First, Knight mentions 1 Enoch 14. Here, Enoch intimates that his vision of heaven is unexplainable due to its absolute splendor, and he goes on to *try* and describe what he sees in the vision. This certainly parallels John's account, as Knight notes. However, Enoch is more mechanical than John: "the vision was shown to me" and "shooting stars and lightning flashes were hastening me and speeding me along" (1 En. 14:8). Enoch was summoned into God's presence almost by being reeled in like a fish on a lure. To Knight's point, John explicitly uses "in the Spirit" language without much description of an actual journey. One might say that this is merely semantics, because Enoch also understood that God himself gave him the vision (1 En. 1:2).

---

[120]This language also appears in 4:2, 17:3, and 21:10, which we will cover here as well.
[121]Knight, *Revelation*, 38.
[122]Knight, *Revelation*, 58, emphasis original.

However, the reason for John's "in the Spirit" has a more direct theological resonance with the Jewish and Christian traditions we discussed above, in which the Spirit enables a distinct revelatory function. So, whether a trance or something else, this does not erase the fact that John uses a traditional theological phrase to describe the genesis and mode of his vision.

Second, Knight offers that in Mark 1:10 the Gospel writer explains a heavenly vision that occurs in conjunction with Jesus' baptism. The heavens opened, the Father spoke from the heavens, and the Holy Spirit came upon Jesus. We must acknowledge, however, that this familiar story offers up three clear trinitarian observations: (1) the Father sends the Spirit down to the Son as an act of approval; (2) all three persons work inseparably in the triune God's redemption mission; and (3) Jesus' mission does not truly begin until this moment, which can only indicate that the Spirit is posed as an important piece in revealing God's purposes in Jesus. In light of this, it stands to reason that John's (and therefore his audience's) ability to understand the work of God through the ministry of Jesus is by revelation from the Spirit. The Spirit descending on Jesus *from* heaven and John the seer's ascension *to* heaven by the Spirit are essentially the same act—the glory and power of God and Jesus revealed by way of heavenly unveiling. Moreover, the baptism of Jesus serves as a trinitarian prefiguring of the trinitarian baptismal formula in Matthew 28:18-20.

Finally, Knight also mentions Acts 7:55, in which Stephen is able to see into heaven while "full of the Holy Spirit." Yet, what did Stephen see? "The glory of God and Jesus standing at the right hand of God." The same Spirit, whom the Father sent from heaven to Jesus in Mark 1:10, allows Stephen to look back up at heaven to see the Father and Son at the throne. This is perhaps the most striking parallel with John's "in the Spirit" vision of God and the Lamb at the throne. Knight seems to downplay the role of the Spirit here too.

In summary, Knight's discussion on Revelation 1:10-11 and 4:1-2 goes like this: First, he says that the Spirit is not present in the throne-room scene. Then, he asserts that John is in some sort of trance that could possibly be self-induced. And to round it out—on the same page as his assertion that the vision may have been self-induced—he refers to passages showing the types of visions similar to John's but never mentions the Spirit, even though the biblical passages he cites center on the Spirit's work in revealing heaven to the seer. He notes Enoch, whose vision is similar but who uses different language than John; he notes Ezekiel, who uses the same "in the Spirit" language; he mentions Mark, who offers one of the most obvious trinitarian formulas in the NT; and he notes Stephen, who explicitly mentions the Spirit's role in his unveiling. Finally, he gives no discussion to the potential of the "seven spirits" language of 4:5 and 5:6.

Knight does not attend to the fact that God has revealed himself to his people through the Spirit throughout Israel's sacred literature and John's vision corresponds with this scriptural thread. Perhaps John knew he was "in the Spirit" because the tradition he inherited had consistently used this language, so John used the same vernacular. So, then, his only way of making sense of his journey into the heavenly realm was to reckon that he must have been "in the Spirit." Though Knight says the Spirit is not present, we see that the Spirit is the very vehicle through which John approaches or sees the throne. Sweet is right in saying that John's vision is "an ecstatic experience" that we cannot ultimately understand but that scriptural writers attributed to the Spirit "the immediacy of their experience of God in Christ."[123] In any event, John's focus is immediately on the heavenly throne, not on the coordinates or sights of his journey. Boring affirms our earlier note: "In contrast to other apocalyptic literature, he spends not a syllable on curiosity-titillating descriptions of the heavenly journey itself. . . . All attention is focused on the throne."[124] So, then, one should take note of the one bit of data we have—that John claimed to be "in the Spirit," a statement in continuity with the biblical accounts of the Spirit's work in revelation. And though Knight might rather believe something he admits "cannot be proved," the biblical narrative reveals that a trinitarian lens makes better sense of this passage given the Spirit's agency in revealing divine oracles to John.

Furthermore, as we have noted in a previous chapter, the spatial component of the throne must also be considered. If the throne is a symbol of the centrality of God in Revelation's worship rather than a literal "place,"[125] the fact that the Spirit is enabling the vision of this center of worship

---

[123] John Sweet, *Revelation* (London: SCM Press, 1979), 58.
[124] M. Eugene Boring, *Revelation*, Interpretation (Louisville, KY: John Knox, 1989), 102.
[125] Steven J. Friesen, *Imperial Cults and the Apocalypse of John* (Oxford: Oxford University Press, 2001), 163.

indicates the Spirit's divine power and authority to bring John into the "throne room" where God dwells and where worship is received. Put another way, John's emphasis is not about the Spirit as the *means* of a trance or heavenly transportation but the Spirit's *mediation* into the divine presence, which, in combination with the Son's place on the throne, lends itself towards a trinitarian understanding of the Spirit. In pro-Nicene terms, we can say that the divine prerogative of revelation is fitting of the Spirit as he brings John into the vision, signaling his inseparable operations with the Father and Son, from whom the Spirit proceeds.

One could also consider the political underpinnings of Revelation, wherein God's purposes are set against Satan's and/or the Roman imperial power. Indeed, John's language "presents his provocative prophetic witness to the sovereignty of God and his co-regent Jesus Christ in a world that Rome thinks it rules."[126] In this light, it seems John's "in the Spirit" language is explicitly theological, not merely psychological; he is concerned with establishing his vision as divine revelation.[127] Leithart further notes, "Revelation is organized in four sections by references to the Spirit. . . . The Spirit is the agent of the unveiling; he searches the deep things of God in order to communicate them to the church. Through the Spirit, John unmasks the powers to expose their bestiality."[128]

This becoming "in the Spirit" (ἐν πνεύματι) and "carried away by the Spirit" (ἀπήνεγκέν) actually seems to be how John receives this prophetic revelation of God in the same way as Jewish prophets and seers, noting that he is commanded by God to "write down everything" he sees (1:11). Similar prophetic inspiration is found, for example, in Ezekiel 3:12 and 11:24.[129] Peter's statement that God spoke through the prophets by way of the Spirit to confess the knowledge of Christ also comes to mind here (2 Pet 1:21). Seen in this light, John may explicitly describe the Spirit as giving him direct revelation from God as an underhanded critique of Caesar's supposed access to divine authority.

---

[126]John T. Carroll, *The Holy Spirit in the New Testament* (Nashville: Abingdon, 2018), 131.
[127]Carroll, *Holy Spirit in the New Testament*, 132. Jack Levison, *Inspired: The Holy Spirit and the Mind of Faith* (Grand Rapids, MI: Eerdmans, 2013), 86-87, is more willing to see an ambiguity in the exact mode and intent of John's psychological state.
[128]Peter Leithart, *Revelation 1–11*, The International Theological Commentary on the Holy Scripture of the Old and New Testaments (New York: T&T Clark, 2018), 70.
[129]Dennis E. Johnson, *Triumph of the Lamb* (Phillipsburg, NJ: P&R, 2001), 34.

John's pneumatology bears a family resemblance to the Jewish traditions of the OT, Qumran texts, Philo, Josephus, Enoch, Ezra, and even the Greek poet Hesiod that speak of God's Spirit or the spirit as an inculcator of divine wisdom, visions, and oracles.[130] Further, the activity of the Spirit bringing John into the divine presence reminds us in particular of the Cappadocians' explication of inseparable operations, wherein the Spirit's work brings the Father and Son's work to completion and perfection. We might also mention Cyril of Alexandria, who defined the Holy Spirit as consubstantial with the Father and Son, with the divine mission of inspiring biblical writers to both receive and communicate God's commands.[131] For John, being "in the Spirit" during his visionary journey meant he was receiving divine revelation and being brought into divine presence in the same way as his cultural and spiritual ancestors; however, the placement of the Spirit in the location of the throne and not merely *around* the throne with other creatures is a notable distinction that pressures us to consider the divine nature and activity of the Spirit.

The Spirit speaks (Rev 2–3). Building off our previous passage, Koester makes the case that "in the Spirit" and "the Spirit speaks" are intertwined concepts for John:

> Although this message began as a word from Christ, it concludes by saying that "the Spirit" speaks to the assemblies (2:7). The Spirit mediates the word of the risen Christ Jesus in two ways. First, the Spirit enables *John* to receive the words of the risen Christ through his vision. John said that he received the vision "while in the Spirit" (1:9). This expression likens him to the biblical prophets, who were moved by the Spirit to convey a word from God. Second, the Spirit enables *the readers* to receive the risen Christ's words through John's text. Communication is complete when the word given to John in visionary form is received by the readers in written form. In this process the Spirit shares Christ's authority: both speak as one (2:1, 7).[132]

---

[130] See e.g., Gen 41:39; Ex 31:1-5; 35:31; Num 27:18; 1 Sam 10:10, 16:12-13; Ezek 37; Dan 4:8-18; 5:11-12; 6:3; 2 Pet 1:21; 1QS 3:13-4:16; Wis 1-2; 7-8; 15-16; *Gig.* 5.23; *Her.* 249, 265; *Virt.* 203; *Spec.* 4.123; *Det.* 86; *A.J.* 4.118; *Theog.* 29-33.

[131] See Matthew R. Crawford, *Cyril of Alexandria's Trinitarian Theology of Scripture*, OECS (Oxford: Oxford University Press, 2014), for an overview of Cyril's work and how it is consistent with the rest of the patristic tradition.

[132] Craig R. Koester, *Revelation: A New Translation with Introduction and Commentary*, AB 38A (New Haven, CT: Yale University Press, 2014), 270; emphasis original.

In Revelation 2–3 one is undoubtedly struck with the way in which the Spirit acts as a collaborative messenger to the seven churches alongside Jesus. Jesus speaks to each church, yet the message always ends with some variation of "this is what the Spirit says to the churches." A somewhat plain reading seems to indicate that the Spirit is not merely carrying Jesus' message; rather, they both speak to the churches with one voice, bringing to mind Jesus' claim in John's Gospel that the Spirit will say what he hears from Jesus and will glorify Jesus accordingly (Jn 16:13-14). In patristic terminology, this reveals the persons' inseparable operations: if the churches are hearing Jesus, they should be hearing the Spirit, and if they are hearing the Spirit, they will hear the Father and Son. The Spirit gives the illumination or filling of divine virtue—a virtue these churches evidently need, given their almost-universal rebuke from Jesus. Hans-Goerg Gradl put it this way: "The reference to the Spirit (τί τὸ πνεῦμα λέγει) highlights the revealing character and transcendent self-understanding of the letters. The presentation of the individual addresses as messages initiated or triggered by the Spirit once again calls for a changed perspective and perception of the community's reality."[133]

Put another way, the Spirit speaking to the churches reminds the churches to heed the warnings of Jesus as though Jesus' words themselves are divine oracles. As Thomas says,

> The Spirit who is speaking now, in the prophetically spoken words of Jesus, is the same Spirit who is before the One who sits on the throne (1.4) and is the Spirit who makes possible John's revelatory experience (1.10). The former idea may even suggest that these words of Jesus are not only coterminous with the Spirit's words, but are also directly connected with the One who sits on the throne.[134]

In a sense, then, the Spirit is functioning as Lord over the churches through inspired utterances and prophetic words of direction, rebuke, and

---

[133]Hans-Goerg Gradl, *Buch und Offenbarung: Medien und Medialität der Johannesapokalypse*, Herders Biblische Studien (Wein: Herder, 2014), 201. My translation of "der Hinweis auf den Geist (τί τὸ πνεῦμα λέγει) den offenbarenden Charakter und das transzendente Selbstverständis der Sendschreiben. Die Präsentation der Einzeladressen als vom Geist veranlasste oder gewirkte Mitteilungen fordert abermals zu einer veränderten Perspektive und Wahrnehmung der gemeindlichen Wirklichkeit auf."
[134]Thomas, "Revelation," 259.

encouragement. Further, though perhaps angels are involved in the delivery at some level, there is no angel declaring, "Thus sayeth the Lord"; instead, the text pressures us to see how God himself is speaking directly through Jesus and Spirit. As Carroll puts it, "Since the voice of Jesus-and-Spirit is conveyed by the (Spirit-inspired) prophet, John is laying claim to a divine source for his prophetic teaching."[135]

These passages reflect similar frameworks for both the cultural-theological backgrounds to Revelation and patristic conceptions of the Spirit. For example, the Father speaks through his Spirit in the Jewish tradition and the NT, and the Spirit reveals the words of Christ to his people (Jn 14:26; 16:13-14; Acts 1:2; Gal 4:6). Here Christ is declaring the message of God to the seven churches along with the Spirit. This also comports with the way the Spirit produces or begets wisdom and oracles in the prophets of the Second Temple period. From a patristic perspective, there is a similar assumption that the Spirit works alongside the Father and Son in order to impart upon believers the words and work of Christ, and through *redoublement* we can see how the Spirit's activity must also be tied to his divine nature, given his codelivering of Jesus' words, which in the beginning of Revelation in some sense come from the Father. This idea of receiving and sharing the vision reminds us again of Cyril's trinitarian framework of Scripture.

Conclusion

This chapter has aided our thesis that a trinitarian reading of Revelation is not an imposition on the text but rather is drawn from a close reading of the text. We saw that a theological-canonical method that draws on pro-Nicene tools helped us work through issues related to the triadic dynamic native to John's writing. For example, we were able to make sense of the "seven spirits" language in comparison to an assortment of Second Temple Jewish literature. While this language resembles that of 1 Enoch and Tobit, wherein seven angels are "watchers" over God's creation, we see that John shockingly places them in the middle of a doxology. In John's vision, the seven spirits

---

[135]Carroll, *Holy Spirit in the New Testament*, 131. Charles, *Revelation*, 53, also concludes that "the Spirit here is the Holy Spirit," though he also clarifies that this reference "has nothing to do with the seven spirits" named in 3:1. Unfortunately, he gives no explanation for this conclusion.

are not only around or proceeding from the throne; they appear to be acting distinctly from angels mentioned elsewhere in the vision by unreservedly receiving worship alongside the Father and Son. The Spirit, then, is not depicted as an angel (or seven of them) but as a person who exercises divine power and receives worship fitting of God.

Moreover, we have seen that the revelatory and doxological language regarding the Spirit lent itself to patristic interpretation of the Spirit's role in the doctrine of the Trinity. In particular, as we mentioned above, Origen, Andrew of Caesarea, and Apringius of Beja all saw Revelation's language as a reference to the Spirit. Moreover, the doxological language and refusal of worship by various angels in Revelation fit with the ontological distinctions made by the Cappadocians and Athanasius over and against Tropikoi or Pneumatomachian tendencies. Indeed, the Spirit's continued role in John's vision(s) reveal what was later called inseparable operations—he is of the same divine nature and therefore exercises the same divine power, authority, and will as the Father and Son. This is clear in his worthiness to be worshiped, his ability to usher John to the throne, his activity flowing from the throne itself, and his authoritative speaking to the churches alongside Jesus.

In sum, it seems reasonable to infer that in Revelation the description of the Spirit contributes to a trinitarian reading. John's language about the Spirit is influenced by, but not beholden to, his contemporaries' tendencies. On the one hand, the Spirit appears to be distinct from and in service to God and Jesus, which explains why some would understand the Spirit in a type of subordinationist relationship. On the other hand, if the seven spirits represent the Holy Spirit, then we see the Spirit being worshiped in ways God and Jesus are and the angels are not. The pro-Nicenes again resolved the tension by noting that the Spirit can be of the same nature as the Father and Son, yet with a distinct economic mission. John, of course, would not have used such language, though he appears to be creating the same sort of tension while trying to explain a vivid and unique apocalyptic vision of heaven. With all of these factors together, we see that a trinitarian reading of Revelation is bolstered by its portrayal of the nature and activity of the Holy Spirit.

FIVE

A Constructive Account of the Trinity in Revelation

THUS FAR, MY PRIMARY TASK has been to demonstrate that a trinitarian reading of Revelation is not an imposition on the text but rather is drawn from a close reading of the text. The task of this chapter is to provide a constructive account of how a trinitarian reading of Revelation ultimately contributes to trinitarian theology and exegesis today. First, however, I will summarize our chapters as a reminder of our conclusions, showing in particular how we described the unity and distinction of each person of the Trinity. Then, we will discuss several ways our trinitarian reading contributes to trinitarian theology, exegesis, and practice.

Reflecting on a Trinitarian Reading of Revelation

Through a theological-canonical approach that implements patristic retrieval and theological exegesis, we have shown that John's doctrine of God is best described within a trinitarian framework. In her discussion on the relationship between the Trinity and the NT, Frances Young argues,

> The debates which generated the discourse of Trinitarian theology certainly show that different edifices could be built on the foundation of the New Testament. Deductive processes actually produced (and as some of my asides indicated, still produce) a variety of models: as different issues were raised and different considerations came into play, we can trace oscillation from one point to another on a kind of spectrum of thought. But the "orthodox" voices consistently appeal to a unitive narrative or "mind" of scripture, recognizing

that the overall thrust is more important than discrete proof-texts.... I would argue that the New Testament consistently presents the activity of Christ and the Spirit as the work of the one true God of the Law and the Prophets, Psalms and Wisdom. Under pressure that relationship had to be articulated in ways that the New Testament writers themselves had not envisaged, but it was always there, at least in narrative form.[1]

Young is right in noting that the NT's own narrative presentation of the Father, Son, and Spirit provides not only the ingredients for but pressure toward the affirmation of trinitarian theology. Nevertheless, as we noted at throughout this book, many scholars are skeptical of such a statement; for them, any sort of "trinitarian reading" of the text necessarily requires anachronism or eisegesis. This is a fair warning; however, at one level, all readings are partly eisegetical in that readers never completely escape their own subjectivity and often read texts in light of their own knowledge and experience. What matters, then, is explanatory power, the ability to explain the world behind the text (Jewish monotheism and Christian origins), the world inside the text (its assertions, narratives, rhetoric, and intertextuality), and the world in front of the text (the history of its reception). A reading is meaningful and persuasive the more it can coherently and clearly connect all three worlds that the text interfaces with. As we have seen, theological interpreters have long since been convinced that trinitarian doctrine is a hermeneutically compelling reading of the NT and OT, and the pro-Nicenes in particular offer valuable interpretive and conceptual tools.

That said, John's incipient trinitarianism emerges from John's reworking of his Jewish heritage, apocalyptic tradition, cultural context, Christian hermeneutics, and religious experience in such a way as to construct a symbolic world that, when explored and exegeted by early interpreters, compelled them to envisage God as triune. This trinitarian dynamic was partly a theological judgment about John's writing and a complex presentation of the Father, Christ, and the Spirit. The reception history of the text shows that the pro-Nicenes were faithful readers of Scripture, and that they understood

---

[1] Frances Young, "The Trinity and the New Testament," in *The Nature of New Testament Theology*, ed. Christopher Rowland and Christopher Tuckett (Oxford: Blackwell, 2006), 299. Of course, Young would not agree with every conclusion or methodological move that I have made in this book.

the trinitarian dynamic already present in the biblical writings. Moreover, it is readily acknowledged and obvious that Paul's letters and the fourth Gospel provided copious materials for patristic theology; however, we can infer from Revelation's reception history, especially with figures such as Origen and Athanasius, that the contribution of Revelation was not peripheral and was at times integral to particular arguments and rhetoric. In that sense, the reception history itself would suggest that a trinitarian reading of Revelation was internally coherent and hermeneutically compelling to early readers. So, we demonstrated our claim in the following ways.

In chapter one we set a trajectory for the legitimacy of a trinitarian reading of Revelation by clarifying terms and evaluating potential pitfalls. In particular, we sought to show that a close reading of Revelation reveals the trinitarian dynamic already present in the text. Over and against rebuttals suggesting that Jesus and the Spirit are subordinated agents to God the Father, we set out to show that a close reading of the text reveals a native trinitarian dynamic. So, we suggested that John's trinitarianism is incipient rather than technically pro-Nicene, explaining that although later creedal terminology was distinct from John's, this did not require a denial of John's own contribution to trinitarian theology or a charge of anachronistic eisegesis. We demonstrated this point through explaining the potential of a multifaceted theological exegesis and set of pro-Nicene tools to bring clarity to otherwise confusing or contested passages.

In chapter two we discussed God the Father's portrayal in Revelation. We noted that Revelation resonates with early Christian devotional practices that related to God as Father in prayer and in christological discourse which affirmed Jesus' unique filial relationship to God as Father. Further, we saw that the patristic period's tendency to treat the Father as the source of divine nature and activity was not monolithic and was honed over time, but that this general tendency comports well with Revelation's depiction of the enthroned and glorified Father sitting on the throne and acting as a source of revelation, authority, and life. Ultimately, theological exegesis of the text revealed that the Father is presented as the fountainhead of divine nature and activity. For example, he gave the revelation to Jesus, sits on the throne and has the prerogative to share this throne with Jesus (and in some sense the Spirit), and enacts and receives the mediatorial work of Jesus and the

Spirit. However, we also sought to show through pro-Nicene tools—such as eternal relations of origin and inseparable operations—that this primacy in the divine nature and activity did not require ontological subordination on the parts of the Son and Spirit.

In chapter three we looked extensively at the portrayal of Jesus in Revelation, noting that his place as the centering figure in the text requires significantly more attention. First, we surveyed Jewish, Greco-Roman, and early Christian conceptions of monotheism, divine agents, and cultic worship. We also saw that divinity in the first-century Greco-Roman world was by no means monolithic among either Jews or Hellenists, with varying levels of divine agency and deification present in these sources. We saw in particular that various scholars who reflected on this first-century cultural milieu differed on how and why early Christians included—or did not include—Jesus in the divine identity or their cultic worship patterns. Second, we surveyed the complex development of Christology during the patristic period, noting particularly the ways in which various patristic writers sought to make sense of Jesus in light of his relationship to the Father. Many of the questions asked by the early readers are the same questions raised in the text of Revelation, namely questions surrounding his reception of worship and his ability to carry out divine prerogatives alongside and in the same way as the Father. Third and finally, we concluded through theological exegesis of the text that John portrays Jesus as able to sit on God's throne, receive worship, and claim various divine titles for himself. Observing these textual clues pressures readers to acknowledge his divine nature as seen in his unique power, authority, and privileges normally reserved God; moreover, pro-Nicene tools such as *redoublement* helped us see how Jesus' economic mission was carried out distinctly, yet always operating inseparably with the Father and Spirit.

Finally, chapter four sought to explain John's portrayal of the Spirit. First, we saw that the patristic understanding of the Spirit's identity was a complicated and plodding process and that the early church's theology traveled a trajectory from a tendency to place the Spirit on the lower tier of a divine hierarchy in some writers, to the pro-Nicene idea of considering him ontologically equal with the Father and Son. Third and finally, theological exegesis allowed us to see that describing the Spirit in Revelation requires careful attention to the imagery and narratival cues given by John. Namely, we saw that the "seven spirits" are included in his doxology and that the Spirit is integral to John's and the churches' ability to receive the revelation, pressuring readers to conclude that he has the same divine power, authority, and will of the Father and Son.

These chapters have served as the scaffolding for our claim. In this chapter, however, we ultimately hope to show the fruit of a theological and exegetical method that takes seriously both the text itself and the conceptual tools offered by the pro-Nicenes. Rather than placing various scholarly disciplines at odds with one another, we have sought to demonstrate tangibly that biblical studies, systematic theology, church history, and patristics should exist in methodological reciprocity. This connection of the disciplines should not be surprising, given that they had not been siloed from one another until recently, as was made evident particularly in our survey of patristic theology and exegesis.[2] As such, I hope that others take up the task of deepening an appreciation for a robust theological-canonical approach that takes seriously both God and the text God has providentially inspired and ordered. As we conclude this book, then, I want to ask how this work contributes constructively to trinitarian theology and exegesis.

In light of our conclusions throughout this book, I hope to drive home the conviction that our study is fruitful for trinitarian theology and exegesis today. First, I will consider how this trinitarian reading models the benefits of patristic retrieval over and against other contemporary accounts of Revelation's theology, most notably various forms of high/low Christology and binitarianism. Then, I will highlight Revelation's particular contribution to trinitarian theology and exegesis, noting the ways in which Revelation adds vivid color to Scripture's portrait of the Trinity. Finally, I will consider how a trinitarian reading benefits the church.

Moving Beyond High/Low Christology and Binitarianism

Pro-Nicene theologians saw the biblical text and their own theological deductions as existing in a reciprocal relationship, and we saw that this is a

---

[2]This is not to denigrate specific disciplines. While the bifurcation of systematic theology and biblical studies has unfortunately caused an ever-evolving set of subdisciplines and methodological nuances, it has also provided fruitful avenues for discipline-specific expertise. Movements such as TIS will hopefully act as umbrellas underneath which varying disciplines rely on one another to serve the church with different gifts and contributions.

useful strategy for working through some of the difficulties of understanding Revelation's doctrine of God. In particular, we returned to a "pro-Nicene toolkit" that provides a wide range of conceptual resources such as *homoousios*, eternal relations of origin, inseparable operations, hypostatic union, and so forth.

Overly modernistic readings fall into various errors, some of which we drew out in previous chapters. Most notably, an overwrought focus on the time-locked historical situatedness of the text and its human author leaves out—implicitly or explicitly—the divine providence involved in Scripture's content and telos. The premodern impulse to view Scripture as fundamentally a book about God and God's history can be lost, replaced by petri-dish analysis of every jot and tittle of John's vision for the historical-contextual influences "behind" the text. Now, we do not want to throw all facets of the historical-grammatical method out the window; indeed, our trinitarian reading is aided by literary criticism, historical context, and comparative studies that are hallmarks of modern biblical studies. These modern approaches can be helpful as tools, but not as hard-and-fast constraints. Patristic retrieval, however, helps us enhance our exegetical work by keeping our attention on the primary character—the triune God—and then allows us to make sense of the thorny issues related to Revelation's doctrine of God. As Vidu has rightly remarked, "Trinitarian theology is best understood as mining the semantic depth of the Scriptures."[3] In particular, we saw that a firm grasp on pro-Nicene tools allowed us to work through the relational aspects of Revelation's depiction of the Father, Son, and Holy Spirit in a way that is faithful both to the text and to two millennia of orthodox theological reflection.

So, while helpful in many ways, the more historically driven methods from scholars like Bauckham (divine identity) and Hurtado (early Christian worship patterns) still do not satisfy the need for clear categories of unity and distinction among the persons. We surveyed at length the progress made by these members of the "early high Christology club" for discussing Jesus' divinity while biblical scholarship was in the mire of historical-critical fixation. I chose "moving beyond" as part of this section's title intentionally,

---

[3] Adonis Vidu, *The Same God Who Works All Things: Inseparable Operations in Trinitarian Theology* (Grand Rapids, MI: Eerdmans, 2021), 62.

instead of something like "forgetting about" these debates. Their arguments can and *should* continue to be utilized by pastors, scholars, and laypeople alike as historical evidence and theological underpinnings for the Bible's theological claims. Advocates for an "early high Christology" set forth a trajectory in the mid-to-late twentieth century that changed the landscape and enables a book like this to be written. No doubt, this book's previous chapters were helped tremendously by their work and is in many ways built on their foundation, so the gentle critique that follows is offered with deep reverence and appreciation for their enduring benefit to the church.

As Hill has rightly noted, centering this conversation on how high or low Jesus sits on a vertical axis below God introduces conflict between monotheism and Christology, rather than resolving tensions that arise in the biblical text.[4] While there are benefits to discussing the NT's portrayal of Jesus' seemingly surprising identification with YHWH, it also creates a new tension about how far "below" God or "above" creation Jesus actually is. Is he above creation but below God, part of creation but greater than all other creatures, or something else? This high/low bifurcation has become so ingrained in Revelation studies that many of our interlocutors in this book—some with whom we agree, others not so much—start from this premise; they either seek to show how high Christology has reached by the time John wrote the Apocalypse, or they continue to assert various forms of low Christology in which Jesus is a chief angel, mediatory figure, or exalted human. It is worth noting that most scholars in this conversation today fall on the high side of the ledger, yet this taxonomy still is not enough to carry all the weight of trinitarian readings. Indeed, the categories that lead to an implicit or explicit binitarian model should be left behind, in my view, or else reworked in such a way that the result is trinitarian. This study has tried to move beyond models like Hurtado's that imply a binitarianism by showing that the Spirit is also included in doxological settings.

As Hill shows, these "high/low" categories "threaten to obscure the way in which . . . the identities of God, Jesus, and the Spirit are constituted by

---

[4]Wesley Hill, *Paul and the Trinity: Persons, Relations, and the Pauline Letters* (Grand Rapids, MI: Eerdmans, 2015), 24. Hill has also noted the influence of Jürgen Moltmann's trinitarianism on Bauckham's divine identity paradigm, which ends up running against more classically trinitarian language and logic; cf. Wesley Hill, "In Defense of 'Doctrinal Exegesis': A Proposal, with Reference to Trinitarian Theology and the Fourth Gospel," *JTI* 14, no. 1 (2020): 22.

their relations with one another."⁵ The pro-Nicene toolkit, however, helps us overcome these added tensions by offering more precise categories to talk about unity and distinction among the persons. *Redoublement*, for example, offers a way to observe different and yet complementary theological, textual, and linguistic functions to explain, for example, how to make sense of the Father and Son's shared titles, throne, and worship reception. So, since we affirm that the Father and Son are both truly God, *redoublement* offers precise categories for what it means to say each person is truly God, and yet also say that each person acts in a distinct mode of operation within the singular divine power and will. In short, *redoublement* helps us "double back" and speak about their distinct relations and operations or missions even within this singular divine nature and its entailments. The doctrine of inseparable operations helps us clarify the Son's ontological equality with the Father even as we acknowledge that this divine Son put on flesh and dwelt among us as truly, ontologically human. The distinction between inseparable operations and *mode* of operation is key here. Though all three persons act inseparably to bring about salvation, for example, the Son's mode of operation is as the incarnate one; the Father does not put on flesh and die for our sins. Again: persons act, not natures. The ability to parse between inseparable operations and personal modes of operation offers a thicker account of the Father, Son, and Spirit's unity and distinction than the "divine identity" category can offer (as helpful as this category has been).

Further, by examining the relationships between the persons in Revelation, we saw that related patristic christological principles such as the hypostatic union also allow us to more constructively exegete a book like Revelation filled with apocalyptic imagery and language. For example, whereas divine identity language can flatten out language related to shared nature and distinct personhood by focusing primarily on *the degree to which* the human Jesus might be considered divine, patristic concepts offer categories that allow us to talk distinctly about the divine nature and incarnation without separating or conflating the Son's divine and human natures. When we describe Jesus in Revelation, then, we are not merely attempting to ascertain the degree to which he is divine given that he also appears creaturely;

---

⁵Hill, *Paul and the Trinity*, 25. Of course, again, Hill is speaking about Paul's theology, but we find the same type of patterns in Revelation.

rather, we are able to take note of the mystery of the incarnation and consider the Chalcedonian Definition (AD 451):

> We, then, following the holy Fathers, all with one consent, teach men to confess one and the same Son, our Lord Jesus Christ, *the same perfect in Godhead and also perfect in manhood; truly God and truly man*, of a reasonable soul and body; consubstantial with us according to the manhood; in all things like unto us, without sin; begotten before all ages of the Father according to the Godhead, and in these latter days, for us and for our salvation, born of the virgin Mary, the mother of God, according to the manhood; one and the same Christ, Son, Lord, Only-begotten, to be acknowledged in two natures, inconfusedly, unchangeably, indivisibly, inseparably; *the distinction of natures being by no means taken away by the union, but rather the property of each nature being preserved, and concurring in one Person and one Subsistence, not parted or divided into two persons*, but one and the same Son, and only begotten, God the Word, the Lord Jesus Christ, as the prophets from the beginning have declared concerning him, and the Lord Jesus Christ himself taught us, and the Creed of the holy Fathers has handed down to us.[6]

Bauckham, however, has been critical of the type of methodology used in this book. He asserts that "the Platonic definition of divine nature which the Fathers took for granted proved serious impediments to anything more than a formal inclusion of human humiliation, suffering and death in the identity of God."[7] Rather than retrieving patristic sources, then, Bauckham created his own category ("divine identity") to attempt to describe the historical-theological phenomenon of early Christians elevating Jesus to a unique identification with the one God of Israel.[8] We have seen in our brief surveys of patristic theologians that, far from lack of real concern for the humiliation or suffering of Christ in the flesh, they fought against heresies ranging from Gnosticism to Nestorianism with a concerted effort at preserving Christ's humanity and defending the reality of his sufferings as a true human.

We must remember that the creeds are contextual documents, so their summaries are just that—*summaries* of larger conversations and debates. In

---

[6]Emphasis added.
[7]Richard Bauckham, *Jesus and the God of Israel: God Crucified and Other Studies on the New Testament's Christology of Divine Identity* (Grand Rapids, MI: Eerdmans, 2008), 59.
[8]Bauckham, *Jesus and the God of Israel*, 6-7.

reality, the Fathers responded to heresies as they gained traction in the church, and not all heresies were the same. If we consider the first few ecumenical creeds, creedal trinitarianism was built over time. At Nicaea in AD 325, the divinity of Christ was the key issue; at Constantinople in AD 381, Nicaea was relitigated in response to other christological heresies and the rise of Pneumatomachianism; at Ephesus in AD 431 and then Chalcedon in AD 451, a fuller explication of Christ's two natures and singular personhood was hashed out as a culmination of the seeds already planted in the earlier creeds. Chalcedon was in some ways the fully blossomed articulation of the importance of Christ's suffering and death as the incarnate Son, over and against Nestorius' attempt to divide the person of Christ and Eutyches's attempt to blend the two natures. In Revelation, for instance, pro-Nicene tools do not require that we overlook the slaughtered Lamb and minimize his sufferings in order to privilege his divinity; the hypostatic union allows us to speak meaningfully about both natures as they are united in one person, Jesus Christ.

Moreover, Hurtado's view, in which he distinguished his work from the conclusions of later creedal confessions by identifying primarily as an historian of early Christianity,[9] led him to assert a type of binitarian understanding of early Christian worship patterns. For Hurtado, Jesus was included in biblical worship patterns normally reserved for YHWH, but the Spirit was not. In this case, the high/low Christology debates bred a type of high/low pneumatology, if not directly, at least by methodological necessity. The more meticulous we become with respect to the degree of divinity that might be applied to Jesus, we are urged methodologically to ask the same questions about the Spirit. So, again, while historically useful, this paradigm leaves us theologically wanting. From a different angle, Bucur furthers a binitarian reading by ultimately identifying the Spirit with angels, because he does not see a trinitarian path forward in his reading of Revelation.

We saw, however, that the pro-Nicene toolkit allowed us to examine the Spirit's relationship to the Father and Son, showing his nature and activity as both unified with and yet distinguished from the other persons. We saw first

---

[9]Larry W. Hurtado, *One God, One Lord: Early Christian Devotion and Ancient Jewish Monotheism*, 3rd ed. (New York: T&T Clark, 2015), viii.

that he is included in doxological language—which was an important facet for Hurtado's understanding of Jesus' "early high" status. Indeed, he is included in this doxological worship language, whereas angels repeatedly deflect worship language away from themselves. Further, his heavenly activity is centered in the throne room similarly to the Father and Son. This unified power and place in the heavenly throne room indicates that he is certainly placed above the angels and all of those who surround the throne. Whereas they circle around the throne and face toward it in worship, the Spirit has direct access to the throne, proceeds from the throne, and has the authority to bring others to the throne. Finally, his divine authority is evident as he speaks alongside Jesus to the churches—they are told to "listen" to him at the same time they listen to Jesus. So, then, patristic conceptual categories allow us to answer the historical question by Hurtado—the Spirit appears to be included in early Christian worship patterns—and the theological-exegetical question by Bucur—the Spirit is separated from angels by virtue of his nature and activity as presented in the text.

Not only that, but the high/low and binitarian categories are largely dependent on the self-consciousness of early Christians, including biblical authors. On the one hand, as I have already mentioned above, I affirm that this historical element is important for understanding the first-century phenomena of Christianity's distinction from its Jewish monotheistic counterparts. On the other hand, however, a pro-Nicene and more generally premodern posture offers a more thoroughgoing account of the triune God's providential ordering of creation, history, Scripture, and so forth. So our approach bolsters the claim that Scripture is a unified witness to the nature and activity of the triune God, and we are not therefore forced to rely on mere historical reconstruction to build a trinitarian doctrine from Scripture.

The methodological approaches of Yeago, Childs, and Rowe mentioned in our first chapter offer various corpus-level trinitarian and/or theological readings of Scripture. Each example in its own way contributes to our trinitarian reading. Yeago's concept or judgment paradigm opens the door for applying pro-Nicene terms like *homoousios* to biblical texts; Childs contributes the idea of "pressures" or "coercions" readers might feel from a close reading of the texts; and Rowe continues the pressures idea with specific focus on the NT's use of the OT to equate Jesus with YHWH. However, our method ultimately relies more directly on pro-Nicene tools used in patristic readings of Scripture, which is more similar to Hill's approach. Revelation's apocalyptic elements can take more diligent exegetical work than other NT texts at times, so Revelation is arguably the best case study for whether these patristic concepts work. We have seen that these tools offer fruitful theological-exegetical promise. A few examples beyond those mentioned above must suffice.

First, concepts such as the eternal relations of origin and inseparable operations helped us discern that the unbegotten Father's mission as the fountainhead of divine life and activity is on display in Revelation, even as he shares his throne, power, and reception of worship with the Son and Spirit. The Father's apparent primacy does not entail a subordination on the part of the Son and Spirit, as is assumed by many that we interacted with throughout this book; instead, we clarified that the three persons are of the same divine nature, and yet have real relations in *the* taxis and, by extension, in their economic operations and missions. Indeed, as we noted, Revelation's throne-room scene in particular allowed some patristic theologians to defend their view of the Father and Son as unified in essence yet distinct in personhood. It is certainly jarring to see the Lamb "on the throne" when it would appear that a throne is a single seat, and we rightly surmise that the Father is already sitting there. However, this method allowed us to (1) remember that Revelation is an apocalyptic work that chastens our assumed understanding of spatial realties in the heavenly realm, and (2) that this throne ultimately represents divine power and glory, and yet it is able to be shared by Jesus since he is fully divine and therefore able to do what only God can do. We see ultimately a shared power between the persons (which also includes the Spirit bringing John to the throne and proceeding from the throne) that *redoublement* clarifies—they are all God, but they are not each other, of the same nature and yet distinct in personhood.

Second, we saw that Jesus' nature and activity in Revelation has created the most stir among modern interpreters, which is unsurprising given that the question about his divinity and humanity was a live issue as early as the first century. As we surveyed the extensive depictions of Jesus in Revelation, we were able to see that he is shown to be both divine and human. The patristic concept of partitive exegesis helped us note more clearly the times when John describes Jesus according to his divine nature, and other times where his true humanity is in view. For example, Jesus' inclusion in doxological and throne-sharing scenes, his sharing of titles and divine names, and his integral role in salvation and judgment are related to his divinity as *homoousios* with the Father. Athanasius, for instance, found Revelation's portrayal of Jesus as sharing titles with the Father and being worshiped by angels as clear signs of his divinity. His humanity is shown especially with respect to his sacrificial death and exaltation as the "Lamb." Far from his humanity insinuating an ontological subordination, this patristic retrieval offers a way to understand and parse the depth and beauty of the hypostatic union and its implications for God's purposes in eternity. We saw ultimately that applying patristic conceptual tools to explain Jesus' divine and human natures in John's vision is more satisfying than hierarchical paradigms that place Jesus below the Father as either a vicegerent or angelic mediatory figure.

Third, while Jesus may draw the most attention in studies on Revelation, the Holy Spirit is perhaps the most overlooked main character in the book. As we saw, some have accused the Spirit of being nothing more than an angel or representative of John's ecstatic experience. However, we saw how inseparable operations and the Spirit's spiration helped us work through perhaps the most challenging assertion of all—that the Holy Spirit is not only present in Revelation but working clearly and distinctly as the third person of the Trinity. When we see the Spirit included in a doxology or separate from other heavenly agents in his ability to bring John into the throne room while also proceeding from the throne (whereas all other beings are facing the throne in worship) we are able to say with the patristic theologians that the Holy Spirit's divinity must be affirmed on the basis that he has truly divine power and that his work is necessary for the completion of God's revelatory and salvific work.

Further, John's language about "being in the Spirit" is often passed over to get to the sensational details of his vivid visions, but the doctrine of inseparable operations allows us to highlight the importance of the Spirit's inclusion in the very ability for John to witness the heavenly throne room in the first place. So, patristic retrieval is beneficial for seeing the Spirit's divinity and personhood in Revelation, where he may be an overlooked figure otherwise. As Gregory of Nyssa noted, the Spirit's mission in completing God's work in history is a clear indication that he is of the same divine nature and activity. Thus, in sum, we cannot speak of God's works in Revelation without including the Spirit's work due to the structure of John's vision, in which the Spirit exercises divine attributes and activity in concert with the Father and Son.

In sum, then, I want to acknowledge the benefit of discussing the Jewish and Greco-Roman backgrounds and context for early Christian writers, including John. It is beneficial to the historical and theological development of our faith to understand how these contextual elements influenced the early Christian communities from which the Scriptures were birthed. So, whatever trinitarian work we do can be enhanced by the high/low conversation's historical claims and its illumination of biblical-theological themes. However, the pro-Nicenes developed helpful tools to understand the nature and activity of the Father, Son, and Spirit in Revelation and other biblical books out of contextual necessity themselves. Their emphasis on the literary and historical elements of the text grounded their methods, such that we can reach into their toolkit some 1,500 years later and describe the incipient trinitarianism in the Bible. We saw throughout this book that the pro-Nicene toolkit illuminated and clarified difficult theological-exegetical issues without bare anachronism or eisegesis.

Revelation's Contribution to Trinitarian Theology and Exegesis

We have concluded in this book that a trinitarian reading of Revelation offers distinct insights into John's doctrine of God. In particular, the patristic retrieval in this book helps us work through Revelation as trinitarians, helping us see that Revelation offers a distinct contribution to the field of trinitarian theology and exegesis with its own literary and theological depictions. Although rich trinitarian theology and exegesis is certainly possible without Revelation given the contributions of other biblical texts, Revelation's distinct apocalyptic elements help add color to Scripture's portrait of the Trinity.

Prophetic witness. We have noted that the throne-room scene (or set of scenes) closely resembles some of the OT prophetic visions. For example, there is a clear echo of visions like that of Isaiah 6 in John's throne-room scenes:

> In the year that King Uzziah died, I saw the Lord seated on a high and lofty throne, and the hem of his robe filled the temple. Seraphim were standing above him; they each had six wings: with two they covered their faces, with two they covered their feet, and with two they flew. And one called to another: Holy, holy, holy is the Lord of Armies; his glory fills the whole earth. The foundations of the doorways shook at the sound of their voices, and the temple was filled with smoke. Then I said: Woe is me for I am ruined because I am a man of unclean lips and live among a people of unclean lips, and because my eyes have seen the King, the Lord of Armies. Then one of the seraphim flew to me, and in his hand was a glowing coal that he had taken from the altar with tongs.

As we have discussed throughout this book, John sees himself as a prophet who witnessed and recorded the fulfillment of God's promises through the prophets, as Jesus himself told him to do. However, we do not see these types of detailed visions in the NT. Whereas Stephen gets a glimpse of Jesus at the Father's right hand in Acts 7:55 and Paul is knocked off his horse by Jesus' heavenly glory in Acts 9, nowhere in the NT do we see a vivid description of the heavenly activity of God's throne with such detail. As such, Revelation's portrayal is a distinct contribution to trinitarian theology by giving the clearest glimpse of the Father, Son, and Holy Spirit on and around the throne, receiving worship and carrying out divine activity. Whereas other passages describe the Son and Spirit's divine power and activity, it is Revelation that offers the most colorful portrait of what the triune God's heavenly activity "looks like," so to speak.

The Lamb. Nowhere else is the divine lamb motif so central to Jesus' identity. The idea of Jesus as the sacrificial lamb is mentioned in various ways throughout the NT. For example, John the Baptist sets up this idea in John 1:29-36:

> The next day John saw Jesus coming toward him and said, "Look, the Lamb of God, who takes away the sin of the world! This is the one I told you about: 'After me comes a man who ranks ahead of me, because he existed before me.' I didn't know him, but I came baptizing with water so that he might be revealed to Israel." And John testified, "I saw the Spirit descending from heaven

like a dove, and he rested on him. I didn't know him, but he who sent me to baptize with water told me, 'The one you see the Spirit descending and resting on—he is the one who baptizes with the Holy Spirit.' I have seen and testified that this is the Son of God." The next day, John was standing with two of his disciples. When he saw Jesus passing by, he said, "Look, the Lamb of God!"

Moreover, all four Gospels allude to the slain lamb prophecy in Isaiah 53:7: "He was oppressed and afflicted, yet he did not open his mouth. Like a lamb led to the slaughter and like a sheep silent before her shearers, he did not open his mouth." However, it is in Revelation where the picture of Jesus as the slain lamb reaches a fuller sense, because here we are able to see not only his connection with this OT theme, but his heavenly exaltation as the lamb who conquered sin and death and has now returned to his heavenly glory. Jesus is not merely *called* a lamb in Revelation in some general sacrificial sense (which is powerful enough given its canonical weight); rather, this moniker becomes a type of title and identity for the work he did and still does. He is always slain and yet always alive. The eternal Son of God who stepped into creation and redeemed it from the inside out will himself usher in the New Jerusalem, as God promised long ago (Is 52:9-10; Zech 8:3). Further, again, we get a glimpse into what Jesus is and will be "doing" in his work as the ascended high priest as he is shown to intercede for us, speak to the churches along with the Spirit, and enact salvation and judgment with the Father. Put another way, if we want a tangible portrait of hypostatic union or inseparable operations, we need to look no further than Revelation.

The Holy Spirit. The Holy Spirit's mission as the revealer of God's purposes is bolstered by Revelation's representation of him. Throughout the NT, we are told that the Holy Spirit indwells us (1 Cor 3:16), reminds us of Jesus' words (Jn 14:26), and gives us insight into the very mind of God (1 Cor 2). However, through the Spirit's work in John's vision, we are given a sneak peek at the Spirit within this vision of heaven's topography. While we should not expect similar throne-room visits ourselves, John's vision allows us to see divine illumination in full color through John's eyes. In Revelation 2-3, we see Jesus and the Spirit's unity in illumination as both persons of the Trinity speak to the churches in Asia Minor, noting that the Spirit reinforces or reminds the churches of

Jesus' words at the end of each message. Paul describes this dynamic similarly in 1 Corinthians 2:10-16:

> Now God has revealed these things to us by the Spirit, since the Spirit searches everything, even the depths of God. For who knows a person's thoughts except his spirit within him? In the same way, no one knows the thoughts of God except the Spirit of God. Now we have not received the spirit of the world, but the Spirit who comes from God, so that we may understand what has been freely given to us by God. We also speak these things, not in words taught by human wisdom, but in those taught by the Spirit, explaining spiritual things to spiritual people. But the person without the Spirit does not receive what comes from God's Spirit, because it is foolishness to him; he is not able to understand it since it is evaluated spiritually. The spiritual person, however, can evaluate everything, and yet he himself cannot be evaluated by anyone. "For who has known the Lord's mind, that he may instruct him?" But we have the mind of Christ.

Do Christians have the mind of God, the mind of the Spirit, or the mind of Christ? The answer is yes. The doctrine of inseparable operations shows us that the one triune God always acts indivisibly. A related idea is Jesus' promise to his disciples in John 14:15-26 that the Spirit would be sent to indwell his disciples and remind them of his words:

> If you love me, you will keep my commands. And I will ask the Father, and he will give you another Counselor to be with you forever. He is the Spirit of truth. The world is unable to receive him because it doesn't see him or know him. But you do know him, because he remains with you and will be in you. "I will not leave you as orphans; I am coming to you. In a little while the world will no longer see me, but you will see me. Because I live, you will live too. On that day you will know that I am in my Father, you are in me, and I am in you. The one who has my commands and keeps them is the one who loves me. And the one who loves me will be loved by my Father. I also will love him and will reveal myself to him." Judas (not Iscariot) said to him, "Lord, how is it you're going to reveal yourself to us and not to the world?" Jesus answered, "If anyone loves me, he will keep my word. My Father will love him, and we will come to him and make our home with him. The one who doesn't love me will not keep my words. The word that you hear is not mine but is from the Father who sent me. "I have spoken these things to you while I remain with you. But the Counselor, the Holy Spirit, whom the Father will

send in my name, will teach you all things and remind you of everything I have told you.

The three persons of the Trinity are unified in salvation, sanctification, and illumination, but the distinct mission of the Holy Spirit is his procession as the postresurrection completion of God's work in believers. So, when Jesus and the Spirit speak to the churches in Asia Minor in unison, they model these inseparable operations. Revelation's depiction of the Spirit speaking alongside Jesus acting with equal authority shows their unity and distinction, and is a palpable fulfillment of the promise Jesus made to his disciples.

Additionally, the "seven spirits" language about the Holy Spirit is unique to Revelation in comparison with other NT texts. While we can rely on other NT texts to assert the Spirit's divinity and personhood, the doxological inclusion of the Spirit's perfect, sevenfold divine power in Revelation offers a fuller understanding of his divine nature and eternal procession/mission. John unsurprisingly draws on the OT to describe the Spirit's work as the third person of the Trinity. We also noted in an earlier chapter the helpful insights of especially Hengel, Bauckham, and Hurtado with respect to "early high Christology." Our work, however, seeks to also expand on their work with a more pro-Nicene, trinitarian-focused interpretive method. Most notably, Hurtado's work regarding the historical phenomenon of early Christian worship patterns in particular highlights a binitarianism among the earliest Christians, whereas we sought to show that Revelation places the Spirit in the doxological patterning at the beginning of the book, challenging the underlying notion that Spirit-worship may have been a later addition to their worship practices.

Trinitarian Readings for the Church

In more general terms, I hope this work serves as an impetus for trinitarian theology and particularly trinitarian readings in the church's preaching, teaching, and discipleship. Whatever our method of biblical exegesis, theological construction, or preaching and teaching, the Trinity should never be taken for granted in how we read Scripture and teach others to read Scripture. The triune God's self-revelation to humanity is the cornerstone of creation and our relationship with him and the bedrock content of Scripture. Indeed, he did not have to communicate with us—before or after the fall—and he certainly did not have to leave us Scripture. Yet he did. So we should be careful not to forget the God who speaks through its pages in both the OT and NT. Below, then, we will briefly make the case for a trinitarian reading of Scripture as the primary hermeneutic that undergirds all others as we seek to read Scripture as the unified revelation of our unified triune God in our churches.

Christian confession. As Augustine beautifully reflected, the chief end of Bible reading is to see not merely words and paragraphs but the face of the God who makes himself known.[10] Few places in Scripture display such a beatific vision than John's own vision, in which he promises that we will see God face-to-face in the new creation (Rev 22:4). Knowing God as he has revealed himself through Scripture is crucial to Christian living, and so a trinitarian reading shapes Christian worship.[11] Additionally, God has revealed himself in Scripture as triune, and God has been affirmed as triune throughout the Christian tradition. Creedal Christianity is built on affirmations from Scripture, not in contradiction to them. This leads to the next point.

Ecclesial reception. Since Scripture is God's Word to his people, it is to be read and received within the community of faith.[12] Following the appeal of Francis Watson, Scripture belongs to the church, "demarcating it from other writings that may or may not perform analogous normative functions in other communities."[13] While tradition is not infallible, the theological reception history of Scripture surveyed throughout this book should not be undervalued. Indeed, the rule of faith has been crucial in preserving theological integrity and preventing heretics from making headway against Scripture's teaching. As J. Todd Billings rightly reminds us: "The word of God is not an abstract word, but word with us, a word for us. The word of

---

[10] See, for example, Augustine, *Exp. Ps.* 10.11.

[11] Heath A. Thomas, "The Telos (Goal) of Theological Interpretation," in *A Manifesto for Theological Interpretation*, ed. Craig G. Bartholomew and Heath A. Thomas (Grand Rapids, MI: Baker Academic, 2016), 198, notes beautifully, "Attending to 'God's address' affirms the church's understanding of the Triune God. Scripture's potency derives from its source: God, who is the Author and Creator of all things. What *God* has said in Scripture remains central for those who read his Word."

[12] Craig G. Bartholomew, *Introducing Biblical Hermeneutics: A Comprehensive Framework for Hearing God in Scripture* (Grand Rapids, MI: Baker Academic, 2015), 9-10.

[13] Francis Watson, "Authors, Readers, Hermeneutics," in *Reading Scripture with the Church: Toward a Hermeneutic for Theological Interpretation*, ed. A. K. M. Adam et al. (Grand Rapids, MI: Baker Academic, 2006), 119.

the triune God is not the word of a generic God, but the word of a God who has shown himself gracious and forgiving in the person of Jesus Christ, and who desires and creates fellowship with those who are in Christ by the Holy Spirit."[14]

One should also avoid the temptation to ignore the Holy Spirit's continued work in preserving and applying Scripture to the church. As Matthew Emerson and Luke Stamps put it, "As we retrieve the past, we seek to renew the present and to ready ourselves for the future, when all of God's people will at last be one even as our great triune God is one (Jn 17:11)."[15]

Eschatology. The God who speaks and acts is the God who guides history to its culmination in the redemption of all things (Rev 21–22). One cannot ignore the Trinity when reading Scripture, and one cannot speak of an eschatological hope without speaking of Father, Son, and Spirit. The God who "was, is, and is coming" (Rev 1) is the God who we worship in Scripture, from beginning to end. The Bible shows us that God is not done with us because of our sin—and that sin will be dealt with by him alone. Scripture then is one unified witness about an infallible God redeeming fallible people. This type of reading is far more satisfying and God-honoring than some modern obsessions with end-times predictions, for example.

Canonical shape. As Scripture clearly shows, the OT is foundational to understanding the NT. Although the OT is commonly called the Hebrew Bible, it remains nonetheless part of the Christian canon and provides context for the NT. The OT does not belong solely to the Jewish community from which it originated; it is one side of the same coin in the two-Testament canon. Rather than imposing a foreign hermeneutic on the OT, a trinitarian reading "alerts us to the historical unfolding of God's revelation in the economy of his world," revealing that "the Father is particularly associated with creation and Israel, the Son with the fulfillment of redemption, and the Spirit with mission."[16] The book of Revelation, for example, does not merely give us another code to unlock—it fills in the outlines already drawn by the canon. It uses OT

---

[14] J. Todd Billings, *The Word of God for the People of God: An Entryway to the Theological Interpretation of Scripture* (Grand Rapids, MI: Eerdmans, 2010), 89.
[15] Matthew Y. Emerson and R. Lucas Stamps, "Conclusion: Toward an Evangelical Baptist Catholicity," in *Baptists and the Christian Tradition: Towards an Evangelical Baptist Catholicity*, ed. Matthew Y. Emerson, Christopher W. Morgan, and R. Lucas Stamps (Nashville: B&H Academic, 2020), 355.
[16] Bartholomew, *Introducing Biblical Hermeneutics*, 10.

language to point to God's ontological reality as it is revealed in the NT. A trinitarian reading draws the Bible reader into a fully developed, theologically rich, canonically shaped hermeneutic. With the entire canon in view, the Trinity is front and center. One cannot concretely know much of what is debated in eschatology or other -ologies, and this is largely why there are so many interpretations. Conversely, and similar to our first point, the truth of the Trinity is not debatable within orthodox Christianity. This is not to say that a trinitarian reading is the easy way out, as though hermeneutics need to be "safe." However, one should not spend more time in conjecture about tertiary matters than in the solid truth of God's nature and activity.

With these considerations in mind, we assert that a trinitarian reading of Scripture aligns the church's preaching, teaching, and discipleship with right theology and in continuity with the identity and mission of God's church. In preaching and teaching, a trinitarian reading of Scripture lifts our congregations' gaze to the beauty and majesty of the triune God who has revealed himself and continues to reveal himself in Scripture. Indeed, preaching and teaching models for the audience how to read Scripture, and so a trinitarian impulse helps them center their interpretation on him and his glory. By extension, people are discipled by the knowledge and wisdom of the triune God and are therefore shaped into the kind of people who tell others about this glorious God who has made himself known to us.

Conclusion

While the bulk of this book is an interdisciplinary look at the legitimacy of a trinitarian reading of Revelation, we hope that this chapter has offered a concluding word about why this book exists and how it might help shape trinitarian theology and exegesis today. Patterned after the premodern assumption that we need not separate Scripture and confession, we hope the reader is able to see how Revelation contributes to trinitarian theology and exegesis, the benefit of patristic retrieval for reading Scripture as a trinitarian, and the broader importance for the church centering its hermeneutic on a trinitarian reading of Scripture. Regardless of one's eschatological view, hermeneutical paradigm, or ecclesiological presuppositions, I hope that a trinitarian reading of Revelation serves as the foundational reading beneath all others.

May we look to Revelation to see a vision of our triune God.

Bibliography

Allen, Garrick V. *The Book of Revelation and Early Jewish Textual Culture.* Society for New Testament Studies Monograph Series 168. Cambridge: Cambridge University Press, 2017.

Anatolios, Khaled. *Athanasius.* The Early Church Fathers. New York: Routledge, 2004.

———. *Retrieving Nicaea: The Development and Meaning of Trinitarian Doctrine.* Grand Rapids, MI: Baker Academic, 2011.

Andrew of Caesarea. *Commentary on the Apocalypse.* Translated by Eugenia Scarvelis Constantinou. Washington, DC: The Catholic University of America Press, 2011.

Athanasius the Great and Didymus the Blind. *Works on the Spirit.* Translated by Mark DelCogliano, Andrew Radde-Gallwitz, and Lewis Ayres. Yonkers, NY: St Vladimir's Seminary Press, 2011.

Aune, David E. *Apocalypticism, Prophecy, and Magic in Early Christianity: Collected Essays.* Grand Rapids, MI: Baker Academic, 2008.

———. *Revelation 1-5.* Word Biblical Commentary 52a. Nashville: Thomas Nelson, 1997.

———. *Revelation 6-16.* Word Biblical Commentary 52b. Nashville: Thomas Nelson, 1998.

———. *Revelation 17-22.* Word Biblical Commentary 52c. Nashville: Thomas Nelson, 1998.

Ayres, Lewis. *Augustine and the Trinity.* Cambridge: Cambridge University Press, 2010.

———. "Introduction." Pages 1-8 in *Christian Origins: Theology, Rhetoric and Community.* Edited by Lewis Ayres and Gareth Jones. New York: Routledge, 1998.

———. "Irenaeus vs. the Valentinians: Toward a Rethinking of Patristic Exegetical Origins." *Journal of Early Christian Studies* 23, no. 2 (2015): 153-87.

———. *Nicaea and Its Legacy: An Approach to Fourth-Century Trinitarian Theology*. Oxford: Oxford University Press, 2004.

———. "At the Origins of Eternal Generation: Scriptural Foundations and Theological Purpose in Origen of Alexandria." Pages 149-62 in *Retrieving Eternal Generation*. Edited by Fred Sanders and Scott R. Swain. Grand Rapids, MI: Zondervan Academic, 2017.

———. "Scripture in Trinitarian Controversies." Pages 439-54 in *The Oxford Handbook of Early Christian Biblical Interpretation*. Edited by Paul M. Blowers and Peter W. Martens. Oxford: Oxford University Press, 2019.

Bandy, Alan S. *The Prophetic Lawsuit in the Book of Revelation*. Sheffield, UK: Sheffield Phoenix, 2010.

Barnes, Michel René. "The Beginning and End of Early Christian Pneumatology." *Augustinian Studies* 39, no. 2 (2008): 169-86.

———. "The Fourth Century as Trinitarian Canon." Pages 47-67 in *Christian Origins: Theology, Rhetoric and Community*. Edited by Lewis Ayres and Gareth Jones. New York: Routledge, 1998.

———. *The Power of God: Dunamis in Gregory of Nyssa's Trinitarian Theology*. Washington, DC: The Catholic University of America Press, 2001.

Bartholomew, Craig G. *Introducing Biblical Hermeneutics: A Comprehensive Framework for Hearing God in Scripture*. Grand Rapids, MI: Baker Academic, 2015.

Basil the Great. *On the Holy Spirit*. Translated by David Anderson. Crestwood, NY: St Vladimir's Seminary Press, 1980.

Bates, Matthew W. *The Birth of the Trinity: Jesus, God, and Spirit in the New Testament and Early Christian Interpretations of the Old Testament*. Oxford: Oxford University Press, 2015.

Bauckham, Richard. "Devotion to Jesus Christ in Earliest Christianity: An Appraisal and Discussion of the Work of Larry Hurtado." Pages 176-200 in *Mark, Manuscripts, and Monotheism: Essays in Honor of Larry W. Hurtado*. Edited by Chris Keith and Dieter T. Roth. Library of New Testament Studies 528. London: T&T Clark, 2015.

———. *Jesus and the God of Israel: God Crucified and Other Studies on the New Testament's Christology of Divine Identity*. Grand Rapids, MI: Eerdmans, 2008.

———. *The Theology of the Book of Revelation*. Cambridge: Cambridge University Press, 1993.

———. "The Worship of Jesus in Apocalyptic Christianity." *New Testament Studies* 27, no. 3 (1981): 322-41.

Bawulski, Shawn, and Stephen R. Holmes. *Christian Theology: The Classics*. New York: Routledge, 2014.

Beal, Timothy. *The Book of Revelation: A Biography*. Princeton, NJ: Princeton University Press, 2018.

Beale, G. K. *The Book of Revelation*. New International Greek Testament Commentary. Grand Rapids, MI: Eerdmans, 1999.

———. *John's Use of the Old Testament in Revelation*. Sheffield, UK: Sheffield Academic Press, 1998.

———. *The Use of Daniel in Jewish Apocalyptic Literature and the Revelation of St. John*. Eugene, OR: Wipf & Stock, 2010.

Beale, G. K., and Sean M. McDonough. "Revelation." Pages 1081-1162 in *Commentary on the New Testament Use of the Old Testament*. Edited by G. K. Beale and D. A. Carson. Grand Rapids, MI: Baker Academic, 2007.

Beeley, Christopher A. *Gregory of Nazianzus on the Trinity and the Knowledge of God: In Your Light We Shall See Light*. Oxford: Oxford University Press, 2008.

———. "The Holy Spirit in the Cappadocians: Past and Present." *Modern Theology* 26, no. 1 (2010): 90-119.

Beckwith, Isbon T. *The Apocalypse of John*. New York: Macmillan, 1919.

Behr, John. *The Nicene Faith*, part 1. Crestwood, NY: St Vladimir's Seminary Press, 2004.

———. "One God Father Almighty." *Modern Theology* 34, no. 3 (2018): 320-30.

———. *The Way to Nicaea*. Crestwood, NY: St Vladimir's Seminary Press, 2001.

Billings, J. Todd. *The Word of God for the People of God: An Entryway to the Theological Interpretation of Scripture*. Grand Rapids, MI: Eerdmans, 2010.

Bird, Michael F. *Are You the One Who Is to Come? The Historical Jesus and the Messianic Question*. Grand Rapids, MI: Baker Academic, 2009.

———. *Jesus the Eternal Son: Answering Adoptionist Christology*. Grand Rapids, MI: Eerdmans, 2017.

———. *What Christians Ought to Believe: An Introduction to Christian Doctrine Through the Apostles' Creed*. Grand Rapids, MI: Zondervan, 2016.

Boring, M. Eugene. *Revelation*. Interpretation. Louisville: John Knox, 1989.

Bousset, Wilhelm. *Kyrios Christos*. Nashville: Abingdon, 1970.

Boyarin, Daniel. "How Enoch Can Teach Us About Jesus." *Early Christianity* 2, no. 1 (2011): 51-76.

Briggman, Anthony. *Irenaeus of Lyons and the Theology of the Holy Spirit*. Oxford: Oxford University Press, 2012.

Briggs, Robert A. *Jewish Temple Imagery in the Book of Revelation*. New York: Peter Lang, 1999.

Brütsch, Charles. *Die Offenbarung Jesu Christi*. Zürich: Zwingli, 1970.

Bucur, Bogdan G. *Angelomorphic Pneumatology: Clement of Alexandria and Other Christian Witnesses*. Vigiliae Christianae Supplements 95. Leiden: Brill, 2009.

———. "Hierarchy, Prophecy, and the Angelomorphic Spirit: A Contribution to the Study of the Book of Revelation's *Wirkungsgeschichte*." *Journal of Biblical Literature* 127, no. 1 (2008): 173-94.

Bultmann, Rudolf. *Primitive Christianity in Its Contemporary Setting*. Meridian, NY: Living Age, 1958.

———. *Theology of the New Testament*. Translated by Kendrick Grobel. Waco, TX: Baylor University Press, 2007.

Burr, David E., ed. and trans. *The Book of Revelation*. The Bible in Medieval Tradition. Grand Rapids, MI: Eerdmans, 2019.

Callahan, Allen Dwight. "The Language of the Apocalypse." *Harvard Theological Review* 88, no. 4 (1995): 453-70.

Carey, Greg. "Early Christianity and the Early Empire." Pages 9-34 in *The State of New Testament Studies*. Edited by Scot McKnight and Nijay K. Gupta. Grand Rapids, MI: Baker Academic, 2019.

Carrell, Peter R. *Jesus and the Angels: Angelology and the Christology of the Apocalypse of John*. Society for New Testament Studies Monograph Series 95. Cambridge: Cambridge University Press, 1997.

Carroll, John T. *The Holy Spirit in the New Testament*. Nashville: Abingdon, 2018.

Carter, Craig A. *Interpreting Scripture with the Great Tradition: Recovering the Genius of Premodern Exegesis*. Grand Rapids, MI: Baker Academic, 2018.

Casey, Maurice. *From Jewish Prophet to Gentile God: The Origins and Development of New Testament Christology*. Louisville, KY: Westminster John Knox, 1992.

Charles, R. H. *A Critical and Exegetical Commentary on the Revelation of St. John*, vol. 1. Edinburgh: T&T Clark, 1920.

Chester, Andrew. "High Christology—Whence, When and Why?" *Early Christianity* 2 (2011): 22-50.

Childs, Brevard S. *Biblical Theology of the Old and New Testaments: Theological Reflection on the Christian Bible*. Minneapolis: Fortress, 1992.

———. "Interpreting the Bible Amid Cultural Change." *Theology Today* 54 (1997): 200-211.

———. *The New Testament as Canon: An Introduction*. Valley Forge, PA: Trinity Press International, 1984.

———. "The 'Sensus Literalis' of Scripture: An Ancient and Modern Problem." Pages 80-94 in *Beiträge zur Alttestamentlichen Theologie: Festschrift für Walter Zimmerli*. Edited by Herbert Donner. Göttingen: Vandenhoeck and Ruprecht, 1977.

———. "Toward Recovering Theological Exegesis." *Pro Ecclesia* 6, no. 1 (1997): 16-26.

Cohen, Shaye J. D. *From the Maccabees to the Mishnah*. 2nd ed. Louisville, KY: Westminster John Knox, 2006.

Cole, Graham A. *He Who Gives Life: The Doctrine of the Holy Spirit*. Wheaton, IL: Crossway, 2007.

Collett, Don C. *Figural Reading and the Old Testament: Theology and Practice*. Grand Rapids, MI: Baker Academic, 2020.

———. "Reading Forward: The Old Testament and Retrospective Stance." *Pro Ecclesia* 24, no. 2 (2015): 178-96.

Collins, Adela Yarbro. "The Origin of the Designation of Jesus as 'Son of Man.'" *Harvard Theological Review* 80, no. 4 (1987): 391-407.

———. "The Use of Scripture in the Book of Revelation." Pages 11-32 in *New Perspectives on the Book of Revelation*. Edited by Adela Yarbro Collins. Bristol, CT: Peeters, 2017.

———. "The Worship of Jesus and the Imperial Cult." Pages 234-57 in *The Jewish Roots of Christological Monotheism: Papers from the St. Andrews Conference on the Historical Origins of the Worship of Jesus*. Edited by Casey C. Newman, James R. Davila, and Gladys S. Lewis. Waco, TX: Baylor University Press, 2017.

Collins, Adela Yarbro, and John J. Collins. *King and Messiah as Son of God: Divine, Human, and Angelic Messianic Figures in Biblical and Related Literature*. Grand Rapids, MI: Eerdmans, 2008.

Crawford, Matthew R. *Cyril of Alexandria's Trinitarian Theology of Scripture*. Oxford Early Christian Studies. Oxford: Oxford University Press, 2014.

———. "The Triumph of Pro-Nicene Theology over Anti-Monarchian Exegesis: Cyril of Alexandria and Theodore of Heraclea on John 14.10-11." *Journal of Early Christian Studies* 21, no. 4 (2013): 537-64.

Crouzel, Henri. *Origen: The Life and Thought of the First Great Theologian*. Translated by A. S. Worrall. San Francisco: Harper & Row, 1989.

Cullmann, Oscar. *The Christology of the New Testament*. Translated by Shirley C. Guthrie and Charles A. M. Hall. Philadelphia: Westminster, 1965.

———. *The New Testament: An Introduction for the General Reader*. Translated by Dennis Pardee. Philadelphia: Westminster, 1968.

Daley, Brian E. "'Faithful and True': Early Christian Apocalyptic and the Person of Christ." Pages 106-26 in *Apocalyptic Thought in Early Christianity*. Edited by Robert J. Daly. Holy Cross Studies in Patristic Theology and History. Grand Rapids, MI: Baker Academic, 2009.

DelCogliano, Mark. "Basil of Caesarea on John 1:1 as an Affirmation of Pro-Nicene Trinitarian Doctrine." Pages 132-50 in *The Bible and Early Trinitarian Theology*. Edited by Christopher A. Beeley and Mark E. Weedman. Washington, DC: The Catholic University of America Press, 2018.

deSilva, David A. "The Testament of Levi and Revelation 4:1-11." Pages 52-58 in *Reading Revelation in Context: John's Apocalypse and Second Temple Judaism*. Edited by Ben C. Blackwell, John K. Goodrich, and Jason Maston. Grand Rapids, MI: Zondervan Academic, 2019.

Dixon, Sarah Underwood. "The Apocalypse of Zephaniah and Revelation 22:6-21: Angel Worship and Monotheistic Devotion." Pages 175-82 in *Reading Revelation in Context: John's Apocalypse and Second Temple Judaism*. Edited by Ben C. Blackwell, John K. Goodrich, and Jason Maston. Grand Rapids, MI: Zondervan Academic, 2019.

Duby, Stephen J. *Divine Simplicity: A Dogmatic Account*. T&T Clark Studies in Systematic Theology 30. New York: T&T Clark, 2016.

———. *God in Himself: Scripture, Metaphysics, and the Task of Christian Theology*. Studies in Christian Doctrine and Scripture. Downers Grove, IL: IVP Academic, 2019.

Dunn, James D. G. *Did the First Christians Worship Jesus?: The New Testament Evidence*. Louisville: Westminster John Knox, 2010.

———. *New Testament Theology*. Nashville: Abingdon, 2009.

Ehrman, Bart D. *How Jesus Became God: The Exaltation of a Jewish Preacher from Galilee*. San Francisco: HarperOne, 2014.

Emerson, Matthew Y. *Christ and the New Creation: A Canonical Approach to the Theology of the New Testament*. Eugene, OR: Wipf & Stock, 2013.

———, and R. Lucas Stamps. "Conclusion: Toward an Evangelical Baptist Catholicity." Pages 351-55 in *Baptists and the Christian Tradition: Towards an Evangelical Baptist Catholicity*. Edited by Matthew Y. Emerson, Christopher W. Morgan, and R. Lucas Stamps. Nashville: B&H Academic, 2020.

Emery, Gilles. *The Trinity: An Introduction to Catholic Doctrine on the Triune God*. Translated by Matthew Levering. Washington, DC: The Catholic University of America Press, 2011.

Erickson, Millard J. *Who's Tampering with the Trinity?: An Assessment of the Subordination Debate*. Grand Rapids, MI: Kregel Academic, 2009.

Evans, Craig A. *Mark 8:27-16:20*. Word Biblical Commentary 34b. Rev. ed. Grand Rapids, MI: Zondervan, 2015.

Fairbairn, Donald, and Ryan M. Reeves. *The Story of Creeds and Confessions: Tracing the Development of the Christian Faith*. Grand Rapids, MI: Baker Academic, 2019.

Fee, Gordon D. "Paul and the Trinity: The Experience of Christ and the Spirit for Paul's Understanding of God." Pages 49-72 in *The Trinity: An Interdisciplinary Symposium*. Edited by Stephen T. Davis, Daniel Kendall, and Gerald O'Collins. Oxford: Oxford University Press, 1999.

Fekkes, Jan. *Isaiah and Prophetic Traditions in the Book of Revelation*. Sheffield, UK: Sheffield Academic Press, 1994.

Fletcher-Louis, Crispin. *Jesus Monotheism, Volume 1: Christological Origins: The Emerging Consensus and Beyond*. Eugene, OR: Cascade, 2015.

Ford, J. Massyngberde. *Revelation*. Anchor Bible 38. Garden City, NY: Doubleday, 1975.

Foster, Paul. "Polymorphic Christology: Its Origins and Development in Early Christianity." *Journal of Theological Studies* 58, no. 1 (2007): 66-99.

Foulkes, Ricardo. *El Apocalipsis de San Juan*. Buenos Aires: Nueva Creación, 1989.

Fowl, Stephen E. *Theological Interpretation of Scripture*. Eugene, OR: Cascade, 2009.

Friesen, Steven J. *Imperial Cults and the Apocalypse of John*. Oxford: Oxford University Press, 2001.

Gallusz, Laszlo. *The Throne Motif in the Book of Revelation*. Library of New Testament Studies 487. London: Bloomsbury, 2014.

Gieschen, Charles A. *Angelomorphic Christology: Antecedents and Early Evidence*. Arbeiten zur Geschichte des antiken Judentums und des Urchristentums 42. Leiden: Brill, 1998.

Gignilliat, Mark S. *Reading Scripture Canonically*. Grand Rapids, MI: Baker Academic, 2019.

Gilbertson, Michael. *God and History in the Book of Revelation*. Cambridge: Cambridge University Press, 2003.

Gilhooly, John R. *40 Questions About Angels, Demons, and Spiritual Warfare*. Grand Rapids, MI: Kregel Academic, 2018.

Goldsworthy, Graeme. *The Son of God and the New Creation*. Wheaton, IL: Crossway, 2015.

Gorman, Michael J. *Reading Revelation Responsibly: Uncivil Worship and Witness: Following the Lamb into the New Creation*. Eugene, OR: Cascade, 2011.

Gradl, Hans-Georg. *Buch und Offenbarung: Medien und Medialität der Johannesapokalypse*. Herders Biblische Studien. Wein: Herder, 2014.

Grant, Robert M. *Irenaeus of Lyons*. New York: Routledge, 1997.

Gregory of Nazianzus. *On God and Christ: The Five Theological Orations and Two Letters to Cledonius*. Translated by Frederick Williams and Lionel Wickham. Crestwood, NY: St Vladimir's Seminary Press, 2002.

———. *Select Orations*. Translated by Martha Vinson. Washington, DC: Catholic University of America Press, 2003.

Gregory of Nyssa. *Contra Eunomium III: An English Translation with Commentary and Supporting Studies*. Edited by Johan Leemans and Matthieu Cassin. Vigiliae Christianae Supplements 124. Leiden: Brill, 2014.

Gundry, Robert H. *The Old Is Better: New Testament Essays in Support of Traditional Interpretations*. Eugene, OR: Wipf & Stock, 2010.

Hall, Christopher A. *Learning Theology with the Church Fathers*. Downers Grove, IL: IVP Academic, 2002.

Hanson, R. P. C. *The Search for the Christian Doctrine of God: The Arian Controversy, 318–381*. Grand Rapids, MI: Baker Academic, 2005.

Harrington, Wilfred J. *Revelation*. Sacra Pagina 16. Collegeville, MN: Liturgical, 1993.

Harrower, Scott. "Bruce Ware's Trinitarian Methodology." Pages 307-29 in *Trinity Without Hierarchy: Reclaiming Nicene Orthodoxy in Evangelical Theology*. Edited by Michael F. Bird and Scott Harrower. Grand Rapids, MI: Kregel Academic, 2019.

Hays, Richard B. "Faithful Witness, Alpha and Omega: The Identity of Jesus in the Apocalypse of John." Pages 69-84 in *Revelation and the Politics of Apocalyptic Interpretation*. Edited by Richard B. Hays and Stefan Alkier. Waco, TX: Baylor University Press, 2012.

———. *The Moral Vision of the New Testament*. New York: HarperSanFrancisco, 1996.

Heine, Ronald E. "God." Pages 106-13 in *The Westminster Handbook to Origen*. Edited by John Anthony McGuckin. Louisville: Westminster John Knox, 2004.

Hengel, Martin. *Judaism and Hellenism: Studies in Their Encounter in Palestine During the Early Hellenistic Period*. London: SCM, 1974.

———. *Son of God: The Origin of Early Christology and the Jewish-Hellenistic Religion*. Philadelphia: Fortress, 1976.

———. *Studies in Early Christology.* New York: T&T Clark, 1995.

Hieke, Thomas. "The Reception of Daniel 7 in the Revelation of John." Pages 47-68 in *Revelation and the Politics of Apocalyptic Interpretation.* Edited by Richard B. Hays and Stefan Alkier. Waco, TX: Baylor University Press, 2012.

Hildebrand, Stephen M. *The Trinitarian Theology of Basil of Caesarea: A Synthesis of Greek Thought and Biblical Truth.* Washington, DC: The Catholic University of America Press, 2007.

Hill, Kevin Douglas. *Athanasius and the Holy Spirit: The Development of His Early Pneumatology.* Minneapolis: Fortress, 2016.

Hill, Wesley. "In Defense of 'Doctrinal Exegesis': A Proposal, with Reference to Trinitarian Theology and the Fourth Gospel." *Journal of Theological Interpretation* 14, no. 1 (2020): 20-35.

———. *Paul and the Trinity: Persons, Relations, and the Pauline Letters.* Grand Rapids, MI: Eerdmans, 2015.

Holmes, Michael W., ed. and trans. *The Apostolic Fathers: Greek Texts and English Translations.* 3rd ed. Grand Rapids, MI: Baker Academic, 2007.

Holmes, Stephen R. *The Quest for the Trinity: The Doctrine of God in Scripture, History and Modernity.* Downers Grove, IL: IVP Academic, 2012.

Holtz, Traugott. *Die Christologie der Apokalypse des Johannes.* Berlin: Akademie-Verlag, 1962.

Horton, Michael. *Rediscovering the Holy Spirit: God's Protecting Presence in Creation, Redemption, and Everyday Life.* Grand Rapids, MI: Zondervan, 2017.

Hübner, Reinhard. "Gregor von Nyssa, als Verfasser der sog. Ep. 38 des Basilius. Zum unterschiedlichen Verständnis der ousia bei den kappadozischen Brüdern." Pages 463-90 in *Epektasis. Mélanges patristiques offerts au Cardinal Jean Daniélou.* Edited by Jacques Fontaine and Charles Kannengiesser. Paris: Beauchesne, 1972.

Hughes, Kyle R. *How the Spirit Became God: The Mosaic of Early Christian Pneumatology.* Eugene, OR: Cascade, 2020.

Hultberg, Alan David. "Messianic Exegesis in the Apocalypse: The Significance of the Old Testament for the Christology of Revelation." PhD diss., Trinity Evangelical Divinity School, 2001.

Hurtado, Larry W. "'Ancient Jewish Monotheism' in the Hellenistic and Roman Periods." *Journal of Ancient Judaism* 4 (2013): 379-400.

———. "The Binitarian Shape of Early Christian Worship." Pages 187-213 in *The Jewish Roots of Christological Monotheism: Papers from the St. Andrews*

Conference on the Historical Origins of the Worship of Jesus. Edited by Casey C. Newman, James R. Davila, and Gladys S. Lewis. Waco, TX: Baylor University Press, 2017.

———. "Early Christian Monotheism." *Expository Times* 122, no. 8 (2011): 383-86.

———. *God in New Testament Theology*. Nashville: Abingdon, 2010.

———. *Lord Jesus Christ: Devotion to Jesus in Earliest Christianity*. Grand Rapids, MI: Eerdmans, 2003.

———. "New Testament Christology: A Critique of Bousset's Influence." *Theological Studies* 40 (1979): 306-17.

———. "Observations on the 'Monotheism' Affirmed in the New Testament." Pages 50-70 in *The Bible and Early Trinitarian Theology*. Edited by Christopher A. Beeley and Mark E. Weedman. Washington, DC: The Catholic University of America Press, 2018.

———. *One God, One Lord: Early Christian Devotion and Ancient Jewish Monotheism*. 3rd ed. New York: T&T Clark, 2015.

———. "Revelation 4-5 in the Light of Jewish Apocalyptic Analogies." *Journal for the Study of the New Testament* 25 (1985): 105-24.

Ip, Pui Him. "Re-imagining Divine Simplicity in Trinitarian Theology." *International Journal of Systematic Theology* 18, no. 3 (2016): 274-89.

Irenaeus of Lyons. *The Demonstration of the Apostolic Preaching*. Translated by Armitage Robinson. New York: Macmillan, 1920.

———. *On the Apostolic Preaching*. Translated by John Behr. Crestwood, NY: St Vladimir's Seminary Press, 1997.

Jamieson, R. B., and Tyler R. Wittman. *Biblical Reasoning: Christological and Trinitarian Rules for Exegesis*. Grand Rapids, MI: Baker Academic, 2022.

Johnson, Dennis E. *Triumph of the Lamb*. Phillipsburg, NJ: P&R, 2001.

Josephus. *Flavius Josephus: Against Apion*. Translated by John M. G. Barclay. Flavius Josephus: Translation and Commentary 10. Leiden: Brill, 2013.

Jowett, Benjamin. "On the Interpretation of Scripture." Pages 330-443 in *Essays and Reviews*. 7th ed. London: Longman, Green, Longman, and Roberts, 1861.

Kannengiesser, Charles. "Athanasius of Alexandria and the Holy Spirit Between Nicea I and Constantinople I." *Irish Theological Quarterly* 48, no. 3-4 (1981): 166-80.

Keener, Craig S. *Revelation*. NIV Application Commentary. Grand Rapids, MI: Zondervan, 2000.

Kimble, Jeremy M., and Ched Spellman. *Invitation to Biblical Theology: Exploring the Shape, Storyline, and Themes of Scripture*. Grand Rapids, MI: Kregel Academic, 2020.

Knight, Jonathan. *Revelation*. Readings: A New Biblical Commentary. Sheffield: Sheffield Academic Press, 1998.
Koester, Craig R. *Revelation and the End of All Things*. Grand Rapids, MI: Eerdmans, 2001.
———. *Revelation: A New Translation with Introduction and Commentary*. Anchor Bible 38A. New Haven, CT: Yale University Press, 2014.
Kovacs, Judith, and Christopher Rowland. *Revelation*. Blackwell Bible Commentaries. Oxford: Blackwell, 2004.
Krautheimer, Richard. *Three Christian Capitals: Topography and Politics*. Berkeley, CA: University of California Press, 1983.
Ladd, George Eldon. *A Commentary on the Revelation of John*. Grand Rapids, MI: Eerdmans, 1972.
Lafont, Ghislain. *Peut-on Connaître Dieu en Jésus-Christ?* Paris: Cerf, 1969.
Lang, Bernhard. "No God but Yahweh! The Origin and Character of Biblical Monotheism." Pages 41-49 in *Monotheism*. Edited by Claude Geffré and Jean-Pierre Jossua. Edinburgh: T&T Clark, 1985.
Leithart, Peter J. *Deep Exegesis: The Mystery of Reading Scripture*. Waco, TX: Baylor University Press, 2009.
———. *Revelation 1-11*. The International Theological Commentary on the Holy Scripture of the Old and New Testaments. New York: T&T Clark, 2018.
———. *Revelation 12-22*. The International Theological Commentary on the Holy Scripture of the Old and New Testaments. New York: T&T Clark, 2018.
Levering, Matthew. *Engaging the Doctrine of the Holy Spirit: Love and Gift in the Trinity and the Church*. Grand Rapids, MI: Baker Academic, 2016.
———. *Participatory Biblical Exegesis: A Theology of Biblical Interpretation*. Notre Dame, IN: University of Notre Dame Press, 2008.
Levison, Jack. *Inspired: The Holy Spirit and the Mind of Faith*. Grand Rapids, MI: Eerdmans, 2013.
Litwa, David M. *Iesus Deus: The Early Christian Depiction of Jesus as a Mediterranean God*. Minneapolis: Fortress, 2014.
Lyman, J. Rebecca. *Christology and Cosmology: Models of Divine Activity in Origen, Eusebius, and Athanasius*. Oxford: Clarendon, 1993.
MacDonald, Nathan. *Deuteronomy and the Meaning of 'Monotheism.'* 2nd ed. Forschungen zum Alten Testament 2, no. 1. Tübingen: Mohr Siebeck, 2012.
Mangina, Joseph L. *Revelation*. Brazos Theological Commentary on the Bible. Grand Rapids, MI: Brazos, 2010.
Marsh, William M. *Martin Luther on Reading the Bible as Christian Scripture: The Messiah in Luther's Biblical Hermeneutic and Theology*. Eugene, OR: Pickwick, 2017.

Marshall, I. Howard. *New Testament Theology*. Downers Grove, IL: IVP Academic, 2004.

Mateo-Seco, Lucas Francisco. "Christology." Pages 139-52 in *The Brill Dictionary of Gregory of Nyssa*. Edited by Lucas Francisco Mateo-Seco and Giulio Maspero. Translated by Seth Cherney. Vigiliae Christianae Supplements 99. Leiden: Brill, 2010.

Matera, Frank J. *New Testament Theology*. Louisville: Westminster John Knox, 2007.

Mauser, Ulrich. "One God and Trinitarian Language in the Letters of Paul." *Horizons in Biblical Theology* 20, no. 2 (1998): 99-108.

Maximus the Confessor. *Two Hundred Chapters on Theology*. Translated by Luis Joshua Salés. Yonkers, NY: St Vladimir's Press, 2015.

Mayordomo, Moisés. "Gewalt in der Johannesoffenbarung als theologisches Problem." Pages 107-36 in *Die Offenbarung des Joannes: Kommunikation im Konflikt*. Edited by Thomas Schmeller, Martin Ebner, and Rudolf Hoppe. Freiburg im Breisgau: Herder, 2013.

Mburu, Elizabeth. *African Hermeneutics*. Carlisle, UK: Langham, 2019.

McCall, Thomas H. *Which Trinity? Whose Monotheism?: Philosophical and Systematic Theologians on the Metaphysics of Trinitarian Theology*. Grand Rapids, MI: Eerdmans, 2010.

McDonough, Sean M. *YHWH at Patmos: Rev. 1:4 in Its Hellenistic and Jewish Setting*. Eugene, OR: Wipf & Stock, 2011.

McGrath, James F. *The Only True God: Early Christian Monotheism in Its Jewish Context*. Urbana, IL: University of Illinois Press, 2012.

Metzger, Bruce. *Breaking the Code: Understanding the Book of Revelation*. Nashville: Abingdon, 1993.

Morris, Leon. *Revelation*. Tyndale New Testament Commentaries. Downers Grove, IL: IVP Academic, 1987.

Morton, Russell S. *One Upon the Throne and the Lamb: A Tradition Historical/Theological Analysis of Revelation 4-5*. New York: Peter Lang, 2007.

Müller, Ulrich B. *Die Offenbarung des Johannes*. Gütersloh: Gütersloher Verlagshaus Gerd Mohn, 1984.

Muse, Robert L. "Revelation 2-3: A Critical Analysis of Seven Prophetic Messages." *Journal of the Evangelical Theological Society* 29, no. 2 (1986): 147-61.

Newman, John Henry. *An Essay on the Development of Christian Doctrine*. London: Pickering, 1878.

Newsom, Carol A., and Brennan W. Breed. *Daniel: A Commentary*. Louisville: Westminster John Knox, 2014.

Ngundu, Onesimus. "Revelation." Pages 1569-1605 in *Africa Bible Commentary*. Edited by Tokunboh Adeyemo. Grand Rapids, MI: Zondervan, 2006.

Oehler, Klaus. "Der Consensus als Kriterium der Wahrheit in der antiken Philosphie und der Patristic." *Antike und Abenland* 10 (1961): 103-17.

Origen. *On First Principles*. 2 vols. Edited and translated by John Behr. Oxford Early Christian Texts. Oxford: Oxford University Press, 2017.

———. *Origen: Spirit and Fire: An Anthology of His Writings*. Edited by Hans Urs von Balthasar. Translated by Robert J. Daly. Washington, DC: The Catholic University of America Press, 1984.

Osborn, Eric. *Irenaeus of Lyons*. Cambridge: Cambridge University Press, 2001.

Osborne, Grant R. *Revelation*. Grand Rapids, MI: Baker Academic, 2002.

Parvis, Sarah. *Marcellus of Ancyra and the Lost Years of the Arian Controversy, 325–345*. Oxford: Oxford University Press, 2006.

Paul, Ian. *Revelation*. Downers Grove, IL: IVP Academic, 2018.

———. "The Trinitarian Dynamic in the Book of Revelation." Pages 85-108 in *Trinity Without Hierarchy: Reclaiming Nicene Orthodoxy in Evangelical Theology*. Edited by Michael F. Bird and Scott Harrower. Grand Rapids, MI: Kregel Academic, 2019.

Paulien, Jon. "Criteria and Assessment of Allusions to the Old Testament in the Book of Revelation." Pages 113-29 in *Studies in the Book of Revelation*. Edited by Steve Moyise. New York: T&T Clark, 2001.

———. "Dreading the Whirlwind Intertextuality and the Use of the Old Testament in Revelation." *Andrews University Seminary Studies* 39, no. 1 (2001): 5-22.

Peppard, Michael. *The Son of God in the Roman World: Divine Sonship in Its Social and Political Context*. Oxford; Oxford University Press, 2011.

Pierce, Madison N. *Divine Discourse in the Epistle to the Hebrews: The Recontextualization of Spoken Quotations of Scripture*. Society for New Testament Studies Monograph Series 178. Cambridge: Cambridge University Press, 2020.

———. "Trinity without *Taxis*?: A Reconsideration of I Corinthians 11." Pages 39-56 in *Trinity Without Hierarchy: Reclaiming Nicene Orthodoxy in Evangelical Theology*. Edited by Michael F. Bird and Scott Harrower. Grand Rapids, MI: Kregel Academic, 2019.

Presley, Stephen O. "Biblical Theology and the Unity of Scripture in Irenaeus of Lyons." *Criswell Theological Review* 16, no. 2 (2019): 3-24.

———. "The *Demonstration* of Intertextuality in Irenaeus of Lyons." Pages 195-214 in *Intertextuality in the Second Century*. Edited by D. Jeffrey Bingham and Clayton N. Jefford. The Bible in Ancient Christianity. Leiden: Brill, 2016.

Prestige, G. L. *God in Patristic Thought*. Eugene, OR: Wipf & Stock, 2008.
Prigent, Pierre. *Apocalypse et Liturgie*. Neuchâtel: Delachaux et Niestlé, 1964.
———. *Commentary on the Apocalypse of St. John*. Translated by Wendy Pradels. Tübingen: Mohr Siebeck, 2001.
Putman, Rhyne R. *The Method of Christian Theology: A Basic Introduction*. Nashville: B&H Academic, 2021.
Radde-Gallwitz, Andrew. "The Holy Spirit as Agent, not Activity: Origen's Argument with Modalism and Its Afterlife in Didymus, Eunomius, and Gregory of Nazianzus." *Vigiliae Christianae* 65 (2011): 227-48.
Radner, Ephraim. *Time and the Word: Figural Reading of the Christian Scriptures*. Grand Rapids, MI: Eerdmans, 2016.
Resseguie, James L. *The Revelation of John*. Grand Rapids, MI: Baker Academic, 2009.
Reynolds, Benjamin E. "The Parables of Enoch and Revelation 1:1-20: Daniel's Son of Man." Pages 37-44 in *Reading Revelation in Context: John's Apocalypse and Second Temple Judaism*. Edited by Ben C. Blackwell, John K. Goodrich, and Jason Maston. Grand Rapids, MI: Zondervan Academic, 2019.
Rowe, J. Nigel. *Origen's Doctrine of Subordination: A Study in Origen's Christology*. Berne, Switzerland: Peter Lang, 1987.
Rowe, Kavin C. "Biblical Pressure and Trinitarian Hermeneutics." *Pro Ecclesia* 11, no. 3 (2002): 295-312.
———. *Early Narrative Christology: The Lord in the Gospel of Luke*. Grand Rapids, MI: Baker Academic, 2009.
Rutherford, Janet E. "The Alexandrian Spirit: Clement and Origin in Context." Pages 32-56 in *The Holy Spirit in the Fathers of the Church: The Proceedings of the Seventh International Patristic Conference, Maynooth, 2008*. Edited by D. Vincent Twomey and Janet E. Rutherford. Dublin: Four Courts, 2010.
Sanders, Fred. "Biblical Grounding for the Christology of the Councils." *Criswell Theological Review* 13, no. 1 (2015): 93-104.
———. "Introduction to Christology: Chalcedonian Categories for the Gospel Narrative." Pages 1-41 in *Jesus in Trinitarian Perspective: An Intermediate Christology*. Edited by Fred Sanders and Klaus Issler. Nashville: B&H Academic, 2007.
———. *The Triune God*. New Studies in Dogmatics. Grand Rapids, MI: Zondervan Academic, 2016.
Sarisky, Darren. *Reading the Bible Theologically*. Current Issues in Theology. Cambridge: Cambridge University Press, 2019.

Schnelle, Udo. *Theology of the New Testament*. Translated by M. Eugene Boring. Grand Rapids, MI: Baker Academic, 2009.

Schrage, Wolfgang. *Unterwegs Zur Einzigkeit Und Einheit Gottes: Zum 'Monotheismus' Des Paulus Und Seiner Alttestamentlich-Judischen Tradition*. Biblisch-Theologische Studien 48. Neukirchen-Vluyn: Vandenhoeck & Ruprecht, 2002.

Schüssler Fiorenza, Elisabeth. *Revelation*. Minneapolis: Fortress, 1991.

Scott, J. Julius, Jr. *Customs and Controversies: Intertestamental Backgrounds of the New Testament*. Grand Rapids, MI: Baker Academic, 1995.

Seitz, Christopher R. *The Character of Christian Scripture: The Significance of a Two-Testament Bible*. Grand Rapids, MI: Baker Academic, 2011.

———. *The Elder Testament: Canon, Theology, Trinity*. Waco, TX: Baylor University Press, 2018.

———. *Figured Out: Typology and Providence in Christian Scripture*. Louisville, KY: Westminster John Knox Press, 2001.

Shepherd, Massey H., Jr. *The Paschal Liturgy and the Apocalypse*. Richmond, VA: John Knox, 1960.

Shepherd, Michael B. "Daniel 7:13 and the New Testament Son of Man." *Westminster Theological Journal* 68 (2006): 99-111.

Sheridan, Mark. *Language for God in the Patristic Tradition*. Downers Grove, IL: IVP Academic, 2015.

Silvas, Anna M. *Gregory of Nyssa: The Letters: Introduction, Translation and Commentary*. Vigiliae Christianae Supplements 83. Leiden: Brill, 2007.

Skaggs, Rebecca, and Priscilla Benham. *Revelation*. Pentecostal Commentary Series. Dorset, UK: Deo, 2009.

Slater, Thomas B. *Revelation as Civil Disobedience: Witnesses not Warriors in John's Apocalypse*. Nashville: Abingdon, 2019.

Smalley, Stephen S. *The Revelation to John*. Downers Grove, IL: IVP Academic, 2005.

Smith, Brandon D. "What Christ Does, God Does: Surveying Recent Scholarship on Christological Monotheism." *CBR* 17, no. 2 (2019): 184-208.

Smith, J. Warren. "The Trinity in the Fourth-Century Fathers." Pages 109-22 in *The Oxford Handbook on the Trinity*. Edited by Gilles Emery and Matthew Levering. Oxford: Oxford University Press, 2012.

Smith, Mark S. *The Idea of Nicaea in the Early Church and Councils, AD 431–451*. Oxford Early Christian Studies. Oxford: Oxford University Press, 2018.

Soulen, R. Kendall. *The Divine Name(s) and the Holy Trinity*. 2 vols. Louisville: Westminster John Knox, 2011.

Spellman, Ched. *Toward a Canon-Conscious Reading of the Bible: Exploring the History and Hermeneutics of the Canon.* Sheffield, UK: Sheffield Phoenix Press, 2014.

Starling, David I. *Hermeneutics as Apprenticeship: How the Bible Shapes Our Interpretive Habits and Practices.* Grand Rapids, MI: Baker Academic, 2016.

Steinmetz, David C. "The Superiority of Pre-Critical Exegesis." *Theology Today* 37, no. 1 (1980): 27-38.

Stewart, Alexander E. *Soteriology as Motivation in the Apocalypse of John.* Gorgias Biblical Studies 61. Piscataway, NJ: Gorgias, 2015.

Striet, Magnes. "Konkreter Monotheismus als trinitarische Fortbestimmung des Gottes Israels." Pages 155-98 in *Monotheismus Israels und christlicher Trinitätsglaube.* Edited by Magnus Striet. Freiburg: Herder, 2004.

Stuckenbruck, Loren T. *Angel Veneration and Christology: A Study in Early Judaism and in the Christology of the Apocalypse of John.* Wissenschaftliche Untersuchungen zum Neuen Testament 2, no. 70. Tübingen: Mohr Siebeck, 1995.

Suetonius. *The Twelve Caesars.* Translated by Robert Graves. London: Penguin, 1957.

Swain, Scott R. "'To Him Who Sits on the Throne and to the Lamb': Hymning God's Triune Name in Revelation 4-5." *Reformed Faith & Practice* 4, no. 2 (2019): 4-22.

———. *The Trinity and the Bible: On Theological Interpretation.* Bellingham, WA: Lexham, 2021.

———. *Trinity, Reading, and Revelation: A Theological Introduction to the Bible and Its Interpretation.* London: T&T Clark, 2011.

Swartz, Michael D. *Mystical Prayer in Ancient Judaism: An Analysis of Maʿaseh Merkabah.* Texts and Studies in Ancient Judaism 28. Tübingen: Mohr Siebeck, 1992.

Sweet, John. *Revelation.* London: SCM Press, 1979.

Tabb, Brian J. *All Things New: Revelation as Canonical Capstone.* Downers Grove, IL: IVP Academic, 2019.

Ter Ern Loke, Andrew. *The Origin of Divine Christology.* Cambridge: Cambridge University Press, 2017.

Thomas, Heath A. "The Telos (Goal) of Theological Interpretation." Pages 197-217 in *A Manifesto for Theological Interpretation.* Edited by Craig G. Bartholomew and Heath A. Thomas. Grand Rapids, MI: Baker Academic, 2016.

Thomas, John Christopher. "Revelation." Pages 257-66 in *A Biblical Theology of the Holy Spirit.* Edited by Trevor J. Burke and Keith Warrington. Eugene, OR: Cascade, 2014.

Thomas, John Christopher, and Frank D. Macchia. *Revelation*. The Two Horizons New Testament Commentary. Grand Rapids, MI: Eerdmans, 2016.
Tilling, Chris. *Paul's Divine Christology*. Grand Rapids, MI: Eerdmans, 2015.
Treier, Daniel J. "Biblical Theology and/or Theological Interpretation of Scripture?: Defining the Relationship." *Scottish Journal of Theology* 61, no. 1 (2008): 16-31.
——. *Introducing Theological Interpretation of Scripture: Recovering a Christian Practice*. Grand Rapids, MI: Baker Academic, 2008.
——, and Uche Anizor. "Theological Interpretation of Scripture and Evangelical Systematic Theology: Iron Sharpening Iron?" *The Southern Baptist Journal of Theology* 14, no. 2 (2010): 4-17.
Vanhoozer, Kevin J. *The Drama of Doctrine: A Canonical-Linguistic Approach to Christian Doctrine*. Louisville, KY: Westminster John Knox, 2005.
——. "Introduction: What is Theological Interpretation of the Bible?" Pages 19-25 in *Dictionary for Theological Interpretation of the Bible*. Edited by Kevin J. Vanhoozer. Grand Rapids, MI: Baker Academic, 2005.
Vidu, Adonis. *The Same God Who Works All Things: Inseparable Operations in Trinitarian Theology*. Grand Rapids, MI: Eerdmans, 2021.
Voss, Hank. "From 'Grammatical-historical Exegesis' to 'Theological Exegesis': Five Essential Practices." *Evangelical Review of Theology* 37, no. 2 (2013): 140-52.
Wagner, J. Ross. *Reading the Sealed Book: Reading Old Greek Isaiah and the Problem of Septuagint Hermeneutics*. Waco, TX: Baylor University Press, 2013.
Watson, Francis. "Authors, Readers, Hermeneutics." Pages 119-24 in *Reading Scripture with the Church: Toward a Hermeneutic for Theological Interpretation*. Edited by A. K. M. Adam et al. Grand Rapids, MI: Baker Academic, 2006.
——. *Text and Truth: Redefining Biblical Theology*. Grand Rapids, MI: Eerdmans, 1997.
Webster, John. *The Culture of Theology*. Edited by Ivor J. Davidson and Alden C. McCray. Grand Rapids, MI: Baker Academic, 2019.
——. *Holy Scripture: A Dogmatic Sketch*. Current Issues in Theology. Cambridge: Cambridge University Press, 2003.
Wellum, Stephen J. *God the Son Incarnate: The Doctrine of Christ*. Foundations of Evangelical Theology. Wheaton, IL: Crossway, 2016.
Whitaker, Robyn J. *Ekphrasis, Vision, and Persuasion in the Book of Revelation*. Wissenschaftliche Untersuchungen Zum Neuen Testament 2, no. 410. Tübingen: Mohr Siebeck, 2015.

Whitfield, Keith S., ed. *Trinitarian Theology: Theological Models and Doctrinal Application*. Nashville: B&H Academic, 2018.

Widdicombe, Peter. *The Fatherhood of God from Origen to Athanasius*. Rev. ed. Oxford: Oxford University Press, 2000.

Williams, Rowan. *Arius: Heresy and Tradition*. Grand Rapids, MI: Eerdmans, 2001.

———. "R. P. C. Hanson's Search for the Christian Doctrine of God." *Scottish Journal of Theology* 45 (1992): 101-12.

Williamson, Peter S. *Revelation*. Catholic Commentary on Sacred Scripture. Grand Rapids, MI: Baker Academic, 2015.

Witherington, Ben, III. *Revelation*. Cambridge: Cambridge University Press, 2003.

Wright, N. T. *Paul and the Faithfulness of God*. 2 vols. Minneapolis: Fortress, 2013.

———. *Revelation for Everyone*. Louisville: Westminster John Knox, 2011.

Yarnell, Malcolm B., III. *God the Trinity*. Nashville: B&H Academic, 2016.

Yeago, David S. "The New Testament and the Nicene Dogma: A Contribution to the Recovery of Theological Exegesis." *Pro Ecclesia* 3, no. 2 (1994): 152-64.

Young, Frances. "The Trinity and the New Testament." Pages 286-305 in *The Nature of New Testament Theology*. Edited by Christopher Rowland and Christopher Tuckett. Oxford: Blackwell, 2006.

Zachhuber, Johannes. "Nochmals: Der 38. Brief des Basilius von Caesarea als Werk des Gregor von Nyssa." *Zeitschrift für Antikes Christentum* 7, no. 1 (2003): 73-90.

———. "The Soul as *Dynamis* in Gregory of Nyssa's *On the Soul and Resurrection*." Pages 142-59 in *Exploring Gregory of Nyssa: Philosophical, Theological, and Historical Studies*. Edited by Anna Marmodoro and Neil. B. McLynn. Oxford: Oxford University Press, 2018.

Zanker, Paul. *The Power of Divine Images in the Age of Augustus*. Translated by Alan Shapiro. Ann Arbor, MI: University of Michigan Press, 1988.

Zehnder, Markus. "Why the Danielic 'Son of Man' Is a Divine Being." *Bulletin for Biblical Research* 24, no. 3 (2014): 331-47.

Name Index

Aetius of Antioch, 45, 145-46
Alexander of Alexandria, 40, 43, 46-47, 82, 86
Allen, Garrick V., 30
Anatolios, Khaled, 17, 40, 44-45, 47, 83, 87, 90, 99, 146, 149
Andrew of Caesarea, 160-61, 172
Anizor, Uche, 12
Arius of Alexandria, 40, 44-47, 81-83, 85, 87, 98, 142
Athanasius of Alexandria, 43, 45-46, 48, 81-85, 89-91, 93, 98-99, 142-44, 149-50, 161-62, 172, 175, 185
Augustine of Hippo, 191
Aune, David E., 49, 56-60, 71, 103-04, 116, 125, 127, 130-31, 134
Ayres, Lewis, 16, 18, 20, 35, 39-41, 43-45, 78-79, 83-84, 86-90, 111, 139, 141, 144-46, 148-50
Bandy, Alan S., 105
Barnes, Michel René, 40, 44, 82, 86, 91, 140-41
Bartholomew, Craig G., 191-92
Basil of Ancyra, 143
Basil of Caesarea, 38, 43, 88, 91, 143-46, 148, 151, 162
Bates, Matthew W., 26, 36
Bauckham, Richard, 9-10, 53, 55, 61, 66, 71, 74-76, 94, 114, 152, 155, 164, 178-79, 181, 190
Bawulski, Shawn, 145
Beal, Timothy, 7
Beale, G. K., 30, 50, 52-53, 58, 64, 99, 106, 109, 113, 116, 128, 135, 156
Beckwith, Isbon T., 50
Bede the Venerable, 136
Beeley, Christopher A., 4, 144-45
Behr, John, 16, 18, 41, 84
Benham, Priscilla, 119, 159

Billings, J. Todd, 191-92
Bird, Michael F., 22, 31-32, 48, 72, 73, 104
Boring, M. Eugene, 10, 65, 167
Bousset, Wilhelm, 71-76
Boyarin, Daniel, 104
Breed, Brennan W., 101
Briggman, Anthony, 109
Briggs, Robert A., 58
Brütsch, Charles, 119
Bucur, Bogdan G., 81, 97, 136, 153, 157-58, 160-61, 182-83
Bultmann, Rudolf, 25, 73-74
Burr, David E., 157
Callahan, Allen Dwight, 51, 53
Carey, Greg, 72
Carrell, Peter R., 120, 121, 133
Carroll, John T., 168, 171
Carter, Craig A., 78
Casey, Maurice, 120
Charles, R. H., 24, 50, 154-55, 171
Chester, Andrew, 8
Childs, Brevard S., 13-14, 23, 35, 36, 183
Clement of Alexandria, 98, 136
Clement of Rome, 33
Cohen, Shaye J. D., 158
Cole, Graham A., 140, 142
Collett, Don C., 23, 29
Collins, Adela Yarbro, 8-9, 26, 75, 95, 96-97, 99, 103-4, 106, 124
Crawford, Matthew R., 44, 169
Crouzel, Henri, 42
Cullman, Oscar, 4, 134
Cyril of Alexandria, 44, 169, 171
Cyril of Jerusalem, 143
DelCogliano, Mark, 86, 88, 144

Daley, Brian E., 132
deSilva, David A., 57
Dionysius of Alexandria, 43, 89
Dionysius of Rome, 89
Dixon, Sarah Underwood, 99
Duby, Stephen J., 77
Dunn, James D. G., 10, 75, 116-18, 124
Ehrman, Bart D., 74-75
Emerson, Matthew Y., 26, 192
Emery, Gilles, 1, 20, 146
Erickson, Millard J., 34
Eunomius of Cyzicus, 45, 91
Eusebius of Caesarea, 142, 144
Eusebius of Nicomedia, 46, 82, 83, 91
Evans, Craig A., 115
Fairbairn, Donald, 45
Fee, Gordon D., 35
Fekkes, Jan, 35
Fletcher-Louis, Crispin, 76
Ford, J. Massyngberde, 63
Foster, Paul, 99
Foulkes, Ricardo, 59
Fowl, Stephen E., 24
Friesen, Steven J., 113, 118, 167
Gallusz, Laszlo, 59, 113, 121, 122
Gieschen, Charles A., 9, 81
Gignilliat, Mark S., 26
Gilbertson, Michael, 27, 156
Gilhooly, John R., 63, 162
Goldsworthy, Graeme, 105
Gorman, Michael J., 58, 60, 122
Gradl, Hans-Georg, 170
Grant, Robert M., 62
Gregory of Nazianzus, 1, 44, 87, 90, 144, 145, 146-47
Gregory of Nyssa, 91, 92, 110, 144, 148, 165, 186
Gundry, Robert H., 101
Hall, Christopher A., 63, 146
Hanson, R. P. C., 16, 88-89, 140, 141, 142, 143, 144, 145
Harrington, Wilfred J., 57, 58, 60
Harrower, Scott, 22, 34
Hays, Richard B., 36, 94, 129
Heine, Ronald E., 42
Hengel. Martin, 8-9, 71, 73-74, 190
Hieke, Thomas, 95
Hildebrand, Stephen M., 44, 144, 162
Hill, Kevin Douglas, 149
Hill, Wesley, 15, 19, 20, 179, 180
Holmes, Michael W., 32
Holmes, Stephen R., 40, 77, 80, 81, 98, 145
Holtz, Traugott, 64

Horton, Michael, 146
Hübner, Reinhard, 148
Hughes, Kyle R., 140, 141
Hultberg, Alan David, 103, 115, 122, 125
Hurtado, Larry W., 4, 9-11, 32, 34, 71, 73, 74-76, 118, 178, 179, 182-83, 190
Ignatius of Antioch, 32, 33, 55
Ip, Pui Him, 77
Irenaeus of Lyons, 18, 52, 62-63, 78-79, 88, 109-10, 130, 132-33, 140, 141, 161
Jamieson, R. B., 2
Johnson, Dennis E., 102, 168
Josephus, 71, 169
Jowett, Benjamin, 23
Justin Martyr, 72, 77
Kannengiesser, Charles, 148, 149
Keener, Craig S., 49, 50, 58, 59, 62, 124, 125
Kimble, Jeremy M., 12
Knight, Jonathan, 153, 165-67
Koester, Craig R., 109, 114, 115, 169
Kovacs, Judith, 65-66, 117
Krautheimer, Richard, 40, 44
Ladd, George Eldon, 50
Lafont, Ghislain, 20
Lang, Bernhard, 71
Leithart, Peter J., 31, 33, 50, 53, 61-62, 93, 99, 100, 102, 103, 128-29, 168
Levering, Matthew, 26, 146
Levison, Jack, 168
Litwa, David M., 76
Lyman, J. Rebecca, 81
Macchia, Frank D., 49, 58, 108, 111, 152, 158
MacDonald, Nathan, 71
Macedonius I of Constantinople, 143, 149
Mangina, Joseph L., 109
Marcellus of Ancyra, 90, 91
Marcion of Sinope, 78
Marsh, William M., 23
Marshall, I. Howard, 164
Mateo-Seco, Lucas Francisco, 91
Matera, Frank J., 3
Mauser, Ulrich, 26
Maximus the Confessor, 1-2, 60
Mayordomo, Moisés, 61
Mburu, Elizabeth, 2
McCall, Thomas H., 34
McDonough, Sean M., 50, 53, 59, 100, 105, 109, 156
McGrath, James F., 8-10, 109, 116-18, 122, 124, 126-27
Metzger, Bruce, 107-8, 109
Morris, Leon, 110

Name Index

Morton, Russell S., 112, 115
Müller, Ulrich B., 112
Muse, Robert L., 111
Newman, John Henry, 17
Newsom, Carol A., 101
Ngundu, Onesimus, 128
Oehler, Klaus, 60
Origen of Alexandria, 18, 21, 40-43, 45, 46, 77, 79-82, 88, 89, 95, 97, 98, 111, 132, 133, 139, 140, 141-42, 163-64, 172, 175
Osborn, Eric, 18, 136
Osborne, Grant R., 53, 54
Parvis, Sarah, 90
Paul, Ian, 9, 10, 22
Paulien, Jon, 30
Peppard, Michael, 76
Pierce, Madison N., 26, 34
Presley, Stephen O., 79
Prestige, G. L., 88, 89
Prigent, Pierre, 58, 98
Putman, Rhyne R., 27
Radde-Gallwitz, Andrew, 146
Radner, Ephraim, 26
Reeves, Ryan M., 45
Resseguie, James L., 53, 57, 63, 64, 67, 94, 157
Reynolds, Benjamin E., 96
Rowe, J. Nigel, 40
Rowe, Kavin C., 13-14, 35, 183
Rutherford, Janet E., 141
Sanders, Fred, 19, 79, 146
Sarisky, Darren, 26
Schnelle, Udo, 10
Schrage, Wolfgang, 73
Schüssler Fiorenza, Elisabeth, 60
Scott, J. Julius Jr., 31
Seitz, Christopher R., 27-29
Shepherd, Massey H. Jr., 58
Shepherd, Michael B., 51, 97
Sheridan, Mark, 39
Silvas, Anna M., 148
Skaggs, Rebecca, 119, 159
Slater, Thomas B., 94
Smalley, Stephen S., 51, 58, 59, 63, 64, 131, 134, 135
Smith, Brandon D., 7

Smith, J. Warren, 146
Smith, Mark S., 18, 45, 144
Soulen, R. Kendall, 50-53, 94, 155
Spellman, Ched, 12, 24-25, 26
Stamps, R. Lucas, 192
Starling, David I., 115
Steinmetz, David C., 24
Stewart, Alexander E., 111
Striet, Magnes, 119
Stuckenbruck, Loren T., 9, 101
Suetonius, 71-72
Swain, Scott R., 26, 55-56, 79
Swartz, Michael D., 56
Sweet, John, 167
Tabb, Brian J., 104, 113
Ter Ern Loke, Andrew, 22
Tertullian of Carthage, 18, 81, 88, 95, 140
Thomas Aquinas, 20, 24
Thomas, Heath A., 191
Thomas, John Christopher, 49, 58, 108, 111, 152, 158, 159, 170
Tilling, Chris, 22
Treier, Daniel J., 11, 12, 26, 35
Vanhoozer, Kevin J., 24, 26
Vidu, Adonis, 20, 39, 148, 178
Voss, Hank, 12
Wagner, J. Ross, 97
Watson, Francis, 26, 191
Webster, John, 5, 22, 26
Whitaker, Robyn J., 52, 57, 58, 95, 101, 115-16, 154
Widdicombe, Peter 42, 43, 46
Williams, Rowan, 40, 41, 81, 82, 142
Williamson, Peter S., 105, 156
Witherington, Ben, 52, 62, 65, 66, 95, 100, 136, 152, 153
Wittman, Tyler R., 2
Wright, N. T., 33, 61, 74
Yarnell, Malcolm B., 10, 158
Yeago, David S., 12, 13, 35, 183
Young, Frances, 173-74
Zachhuber, Johannes, 91, 148
Zanker, Paul, 72
Zehnder, Markus, 97

Subject Index

Christology
  angel/angelomorphic, 9, 52, 56, 63, 11, 74-75, 81, 95-99, 101, 103, 107, 116, 119, 121-22, 125, 131, 133, 137, 138, 179, 183, 185
  Arian, 44-46, 82-83, 87
  divine identity, 74-76, 178-81
  in early Christian worship, 11, 73, 118, 178, 182-83, 190
  eternal generation of the Son, 19, 39, 65, 79, 84-88
  high/low, 7-11, 70-137, 177-86
  hypostatic union, 44, 79-80, 102, 136, 182, 185, 188
  Logos, 18, 81, 133
  Son of Man, 96-106, 107, 116
  Subordinationist, 40-44, 122, 142-43
Church councils
  Alexandria (362), 89, 143
  Ancyra (358), 143
  Chalcedon (451), 18, 182
  Constantinople (360), 143
  Constantinople (381), 16, 18, 139, 142-43, 160, 182
  Ephesus (431), 182
  Nicaea (325), 16, 18, 82-83, 86-87, 89-90, 140, 142-44, 182
Creator-creature distinction, 9, 39-40, 44, 75, 83, 85, 158
Exegesis
  biblical pressures, 11-14, 55, 133, 169, 171, 176, 183
  historical-critical method, 13, 23-24, 178
  historical-grammatical method, 23-24, 27, 178
  intertextuality, 27-29, 79, 107, 174
  partitive, 44, 106, 136, 184-85
  premodern, 24, 178, 183
  sensus literalis, 23, 27
  sensus plenior, 23-26
  theological-canonical approach, 26-29, 35-36
  theological interpretation, 11-15, 19-36, 191
Father
  enthronement of, 37, 39, 59-61, 67
  as source of divine life, 4, 39, 42, 46, 49, 64, 67
God
  analogical language for, 39-40, 45, 52, 65
  binitarian conceptions of, 7, 11, 34, 140, 160, 177-84
  monotheism, 8-9, 11, 29, 32, 67, 69-71, 73-75, 112, 116, 127, 129
  providence, 15, 21, 24, 28-29, 30, 32, 107, 133, 177, 178, 183
  throne, 4, 9, 37, 47-48, 54, 55-64, 65, 66, 67, 67-68, 69, 74, 75, 90-91, 92, 100-101, 104, 105, 112-24, 126, 127, 137, 138, 153-58, 159, 161, 162, 166-68, 169, 172, 175, 176, 183-85, 186-187, 188
Pneumatology
  angel/angelomorphic, 139, 150, 152, 153, 156, 157-59, 161-62, 171-72
  divine titles, 31, 146-51
  illumination, 14, 23, 186, 188-89
  pneumatomachianism, 143, 147, 149, 150, 162, 172, 182
  spiration and procession, 34, 38-39, 46-47, 77, 139, 146-47, 155, 168, 185
  Spirit as speaker, 137, 138, 160, 169-71, 183

Trinity
    eternal relations of origin, 20, 139, 147, 176, 184
    inseparable operations, 20, 33, 68, 108, 124, 139, 145, 148, 150, 168, 169, 170, 172, 176, 178, 180, 184, 188, 189, 190
    non-Nicene, 40-42, 65, 80-81, 84
    order/*taxis*, 20, 33, 34, 38, 39, 46, 47, 48, 49, 65, 68, 77, 139, 184
    person/*hypostasis*, 18, 20, 21, 33-34, 38, 40, 41, 44, 48, 55, 70, 77, 79-80, 89, 90, 102, 109, 113-14, 121, 127, 137, 138, 147, 148, 155, 161, 164, 172, 180-82, 184, 185, 190
    pro-Nicene, x, 18-19, 33-34, 38-48, 76-93, 139-51
    as a reading strategy, 4, 15, 16-26, 44, 177-78
    redoublement, 20, 22, 48, 93, 106, 108, 109, 110, 124, 137, 148, 171, 176, 180, 184
    same nature/*homoousios*, 12, 41, 43, 45, 46, 48, 68, 82-84, 89-90, 145, 150, 183, 185
    simplicity, 45-46, 65, 77, 83, 87, 98, 109
    theology and economy, 18, 21-22, 39, 41, 47, 80, 107
    will, 20, 21, 38-39, 42-43, 45, 46, 47, 68, 77, 83, 114-15, 137, 139, 165, 172, 177, 180

Scripture Index

Old Testament

Genesis
1, *105, 111*
1:16, *103*
2:7, *160*
32:29, *131*
41:39, *169*
49:9, *112, 155*

Exodus
3:13-14, *98*
3:14, *42, 50, 51, 52, 53*
7:14, *24*
19:6, *134*
19:16, *99*
19:20, *59*
19:24, *59*
20:1, *99*
24:9-11, *57*
24:10-12, *59*
31:1-5, *169*
32:31-33, *108*
33:20, *133*
35:31, *169*

Leviticus
4:16-17, *163*

Numbers
27:18, *169*

Deuteronomy
5:26, *103*
6:4, *47*

7:11, *99*
10:17, *128*
32:35, *117*

Judges
3:10, *160*
13:17, *131*

1 Samuel
10:10, *169*
16:12-13, *169*
16:14, *160*
17:26, *103*

1 Chronicles
24:4, *62*

2 Chronicles
1, *57*

Ezra
7:12, *129*

Nehemiah
9:6, *160*

Psalms
1, *60*
2:1-2, *125*
2:2, *64, 66*
2:6, *125*
50:12-14, *145*
51:11, *160*
75:7, *117*
89, *110*

90:2, *125*
110, *103*
110:1, *116*
136:3, *128*

Proverbs
15:3, *154*

Isaiah
1, *131*
2:19, *124*
6, *58, 112, 165, 187*
6–7, *154*
6:1-4, *57*
6:3, *60, 63*
6:5, *37*
9:5, *131*
9:6, *109*
11, *155*
11:1-6, *130*
11:2-3, *156*
11:4, *105, 130*
12:3, *86*
18, *104*
19:1, *104*
22, *109*
22:22, *109*
24:23, *125*
33:22, *117*
40, *135*
41–52, *94*
41:4, *53*
43, *94*
43:10, *110*
43:10-12, *110*

44:4, *53*
44:6, *53, 103*
45, *109*
49:2, *105*
52:9-10, *188*
53:7, *188*
60:14, *125*
61:6, *134*
63:9-10, *158*
65:1, *49*
65:16, *110, 111*

Jeremiah
1:5, *24*
9:23, *33*
10:10, *103*
11:20, *117, 130*
17:10, *107*
28:33 (LXX), *104*
30:2, *24, 100*
32:30, *104*
42:5, *110*

Ezekiel
1, *57, 58, 59, 62*
1–2, *112*
1:1, *58*
1:24, *101*
2:9-10, *114*
3:12, *168*
9:2, *101*
10, *62*
11:1, *165*
11:19-20, *159*
33:27, *106*
33:29, *106*
37, *154, 169*
37:13-14, *159*

Daniel
2, *61*
2:47, *128*
4:8-18, *169*
4:37, *128*
5:11-12, *169*
6:3, *169*
6:27, *103*
7, *58, 95, 96, 97, 102, 115*
7:9, *101*
7:9-14, *101, 115*
7:11, *99*
7:13, *51, 96, 97, 101, 103*

7:13-14, *116*
7:14, *97*
7:21, *128*
10, *100, 106*
10:5, *101*
10:5-6, *101*
10:6, *101*
10:9, *102*
10:16, *96*
12:4, *100*
12:4-9, *115*

Joel
2:11, *124*
2:31, *124*
4:10 (LXX), *104*

Obadiah
21, *125*

Micah
4:3, *104*
4:7, *125*

Nahum
1:6, *124*

Zephaniah
1:14, *124*

Zechariah
4, *157*
4:1-14, *155*
4:6, *155, 156*
4:10, *155*
12:10, *93*

Malachi
3:2, *124*
3:6, *47*

Apocrypha

4 Ezra
3:9-11, *130*
10:60–12:35, *112*
15:20, *125*

Tobit
1, *153*
12:15, *153*

Wisdom of Solomon
1, *105*
1–2, *154, 169*
7–8, *154, 169*
15–16, *154, 169*

2 Baruch
21:6, *56*

2 Maccabees
13:4, *128*

3 Maccabees
5:1, *128*
5:35, *128*

New Testament

Matthew
2, *65, 156, 166*
11:27, *32*
12:2, *145*
12:31-33, *160*
26:27-28, *93*

Mark
1:10, *165, 166*
8:27–16:20, *115*
9:37, *32*
12, *103*
14:62, *101, 112*

Luke
2:26, *64*
10:16, *32*
10:22, *32*
11:26, *163*
24:36-49, *14*

John
1, *100, 105, 132*
1:1, *46, 63, 86, 88, 132, 144*
1:1-1, *130*
1:1-3, *77, 86, 111*
1:1-14, *32*
1:3, *47*
1:3-4, *160*
1:5, *81*
1:29-36, *187*
3:16, *39, 46, 65, 77*
4:10-24, *160*
4:34, *32*

5:17, *65*
6:3, *65*
6:39-44, *32*
6:63, *159*
7:2, *77*
7:3, *160*
7:37-38, *86*
8:58, *94*
10:33, *83*
12:28, *145*
14, *39, 44*
14:6, *160*
14:15-26, *189*
14:16, *145*
14:26, *14, 33, 156, 160, 171, 188*
15, *138, 147*
15:26, *77, 108, 145*
16:13, *33, 160*
16:13-14, *170, 171*
16:14, *145*
17:4, *145*
17:5, *119*
17:11, *192*
20:22, *33, 155*

Acts
1, *33*
1:2, *171*
2:33, *155*
4:25-26, *125*
4:26-28, *64*
5:1-9, *39*
7:55, *165, 166, 187*
7:55-56, *103, 116*
9, *187*
20:2, *93*

Romans
1:7, *54*
2:5, *93*
3:25, *93*

1 Corinthians
1, *92*
1:3, *54*
1:24, *86*
2, *14, 188*
2:10-16, *189*
2:13, *33, 160*
3:16, *188*
5-6, *117*
6:19, *33*

11, *34*
12:3, *162*
15:24-28, *65*

2 Corinthians
1:2, *54*
1:20, *110*
3:4-6, *159*

Galatians
1:3, *54*
1:5, *163*
4:4, *32*
4:6, *171*

Ephesians
1:2, *54*
1:7, *93*
1:20, *103, 116*
3:3, *93*

Philippians
2:5-11, *77*
2:6-11, *12*

Colossians
1:15, *88*
1:15-17, *111*
3:1, *103, 116*

2 Thessalonians
2, *105*

1 Timothy
1:15, *32*
6:15, *128*

2 Timothy
3:16-17, *24*
4, *130*

Titus
2:13, *123*

Hebrews
1:2, *32*
1:3, *39, 43, 86, 88, 103, 116*
1:5-14, *99*
1:6, *99*
1:10-12, *77*
1:14, *153*
5, *118*
9:12-14, *93*

1 Peter
1:2, *93, 160*
2:5, *134*
2:23, *130*
4:11, *163*

2 Peter
1, *169*
1:20-21, *160*
1:21, *24, 29, 168, 169*
2, *54*
3:15-16, *24*
3:16, *29, 33*

1 John
1:5, *81*
4:10, *32*

Revelation
1, *48, 53, 97, 100, 130, 136, 192*
1–5, *49, 58, 59*
1–11, *31, 50, 62, 93, 99, 100, 102, 103, 168*
1:1, *32, 37, 67, 84*
1:1-8, *49, 93*
1:1-20, *96*
1:4, *50, 51, 52, 94, 98, 155, 157, 163*
1:4-5, *51, 151*
1:4-6, *24, 163*
1:5-6, *67*
1:6, *121, 163*
1:9-19, *67*
1:9-20, *96*
1:10, *33*
1:10-11, *165, 166*
1:11, *24*
1:12, *132*
1:15, *132*
1:17, *94, 133*
1:17-18, *81, 82*
1:19, *37*
1:20, *157*
2–3, *33, 111, 169, 170, 188*
2:1, *32, 121*
2:7, *33*
2:11, *33*
2:18, *106*
2:23, *106*
3, *161*
3:1, *157*
3:1-6, *107*

3:7, *108, 110*
3:12, *156*
3:14, *101, 110*
3:21, *111, 112, 113*
4, *158*
4–5, *10, 56, 58, 59, 60, 63, 67, 74, 100, 101, 105, 112, 116, 117, 153*
4:1-11, *55, 57*
4:2-3, *58*
4:5, *157*
4:5-6, *161*
4:7, *62, 63*
4:11, *50*
5, *64, 115, 116, 118, 122, 155*
5:1-14, *112*
5:3-4, *114*
5:5, *123*
5:5-6, *114*
5:6, *132*
5:12, *67*
5:13, *163*
6, *63, 67*
6–16, *104, 125*

6:2, *130*
6:10, *108*
6:15-17, *124*
7, *117*
7:9-17, *112*
7:12, *163*
7:17, *67*
11, *65, 66*
11:1, *156*
11:15-19, *64, 67*
12, *123*
12–14, *66*
12–22, *33, 53, 129, 136*
12:5, *105, 123*
12:10, *121*
13, *108*
13:1, *131*
14:1-5, *125*
14:6, *164*
14:14, *104*
17, *52*
17–18, *131*
17–22, *128, 130, 131, 134*
17:3-5, *131*

17:14, *128, 129*
19, *132*
19–22, *134*
19:10, *95, 116*
19:11, *132*
19:11-16, *130*
19:12, *131*
19:13, *105*
19:16, *128*
19:19, *128*
20:6, *123, 134*
21, *59*
21–22, *125, 192*
21:22–22:1, *112*
21:23, *122*
22, *154*
22:1, *160*
22:4, *191*
22:6-21, *99*
22:9, *95, 99, 116, 162*
22:12-13, *135*
22:13, *116*
22:17, *153*
22:21, *24*

Also in the SCDS series

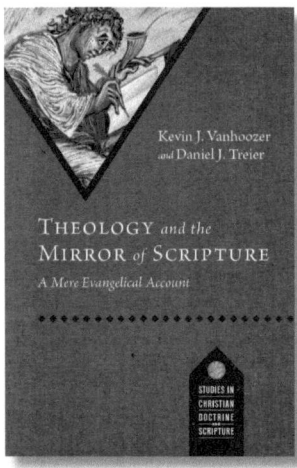

Theology and the Mirror of Scripture
978-0-8308-4076-2

Political Church
978-0-8308-4880-5

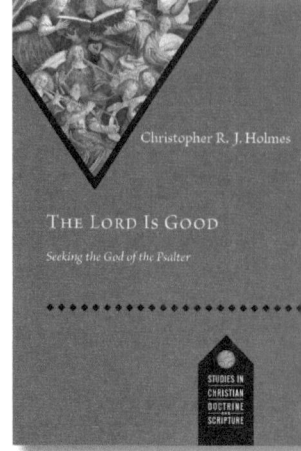

The Lord is Good
978-0-8308-4883-6

Seeing by the Light
978-0-8308-4885-0

God in Himself
978-0-8308-4884-3

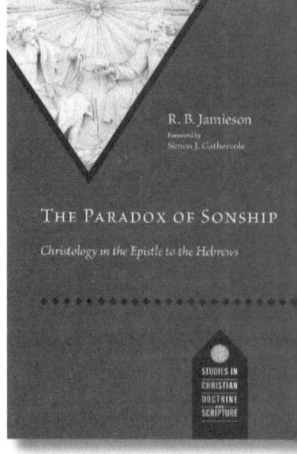

The Paradox of Sonship
978-0-8308-4886-7